Curriculum Integration
K–12

Theory and Practice

Edited by
James S. Etim

UNIVERSITY PRESS OF AMERICA,® INC.
Lanham • Boulder • New York • Toronto • Oxford

Copyright © 2005 by
University Press of America,® Inc.
4501 Forbes Boulevard
Suite 200
Lanham, Maryland 20706
UPA Acquisitions Department (301) 459-3366

PO Box 317
Oxford
OX2 9RU, UK

Library of Congress Control Number: 2004111055
ISBN 0-7618-2898-2 (paperback : alk. ppr.)

Dedicated to Alice, David,
my late mother, Arit, and my father, Sunday Etim

Contents

List of Tables

List of Figures

Acknowledgements

I begin by thanking all the contributors who made this volume possible. Without their hard work, dedication and adherence to deadlines, this book would not have been produced. I wish also to thank the reviewers including, Dr. Vincent Snipes, Dr. H. Gopalan and Professor Edwin Bell all at Winston Salem State University for their help in the review and production process.

I am also indebted to my former students and colleagues at Chewning Middle School who cooperated as we planned and implemented many portions of the units on Freedom and Intelligence discussed in this book. I am also forever grateful to my current students at Winston Salem State University (especially Lateral Entry teachers) who have been involved in curriculum integration as part of their class in Methods of Integrative Teaching.

I want to thank my Chair in the Department of Education, Dr. Manuel Vargas, for all the help he gave me.

Dr. Susan Drake would like to thank Gail Higenell for allowing her to use the curriculum unit found in Chapter 3.

Finally, I thank my wife, Alice Etim, who read many parts of the book and made useful suggestions.

Section One

THEORETICAL FRAMEWORK

Chapter One

Curriculum Integration: The Why and How

James S. Etim

There have been various definitions for the term curriculum integration (Beane, 1993, 1997; Fogarty, 1991; Jacobs, 1989; Post, Ellis, Humphreys and Buggey, 1997; Roberts and Kellough, 2004). These definitions have ranged from interdisciplinary teaching to a complete integration where subject boundaries are lost. For me, curriculum integration involves helping students see and make connections between and among subjects. It is a pedagogical approach that is student-centered and focuses on a theme organized around real life issues and problems drawn from several subject areas For example, if a teacher or a group of teachers were to teach on the theme, "The Future," concepts could be drawn from History, Science, Technology, Language Arts and Health Education in such a way that in the study, subject boundaries are lost. During the study of the theme, concepts such as democracy, cooperation and cultural diversity are encouraged and practiced.

According to Julie Lemond in "Curriculum Integration Models" (online), curriculum integration adheres to the following models:

1. constructing content that is grounded in state and national standards, but transcends subject-specific isolated facts,
2. focusing on processes that enhance thinking critically and creatively,
3. connecting learning to real-life experiences, and
4. serving and respecting all students and their needs, learning styles, interests, etc.

Beane (1996, p. 6) sees four parts of curriculum integration

1. the curriculum is organized around problems and issues that are of personal and social significance.

2. learning experiences related to the theme are selected without regard to subject boundaries.
3. knowledge is developed and used to address the organizing center instead of to prepare for tests or to accumulate specific facts.
4. emphasis is placed on projects and activities that lend themselves to the real application of knowledge.

Curriculum integration is not a recent phenomenon. According to Vars (2001 p. 8), curriculum integration has been advocated for more than a century. In the 1930s, the Progressive movement advocated a problem centered curriculum (Beane, 1993), which has semblance to the present day curriculum integration. John Dewey (1956) in his writings called for the balancing of these three curricular sources: needs of learner, demands of society living in a democratic society and the subject content, all parts of our current understanding of curriculum integration. John Goodlad in *A Place Called School* (1989) reported on the unconnectedness between what happens in school and the reality beyond school and advocated for using knowledge for problem solving. Boyer (1986) criticized the fragmentary nature of the presentation of school subjects and called for an integrated curriculum that allowed students to see relationships of school to real life. Recently, James Beane, Gordon Vars and J. Lounsbury have been the strongest advocates. In *Curriculum Integration: Designing the Core of Democratic Education* (1997). Beane discusses the concept, history and process of curriculum integration. Advocates point out several advantages for curriculum integration:

1. Developmentally appropriate and responsive to the needs of young children and emerging adolescents. Those who hold to this view believe that traditional subjects have been largely fragmented and not responsive to student needs. (Beane, 1997, Jacobs, 1989, Paterson, 2003, p. 11, Vars, 2001, pp. 7–16, Vars and Beane, 2000). Integration, it is believed, would cater to these personal and developmental needs.
2. Students' learning and achievement is greatly enhanced (Jackson and Davis, 2000, Lewis and Shaha, 2003, Nesin and Lounsbury, 1999, Vars and Beane, 2000). Lewis and Shaha declared:

   . . . results from these studies clearly establish that integrated curricula produce superior learning and attitudinal results versus traditional curricula. . . . Integrated curricula consistently outperformed all other approaches, regardless of content area addressed.

3. Students become actively involved in their learning (Springer, 2003 p. 15). They are highly motivated because they take part in the selection of the

theme and learning objectives and due to the fact that some of the work is project centered also helps to increase interest.

4. Students become the focus of learning. The teacher is the facilitator of student learning instead of being the center. This type of learning makes for long-term retention by students.
5. Helps students make connections between their school activities and their personal life experiences.
6. Students have the opportunity to choose what they want to learn.
7. Encourages teaming among teachers and cooperative learning among students. For teachers, this teaming may help broaden their knowledge of other disciplines and provide other skills to teachers of lesser abilities.
8. Students are better prepared for life today since curriculum integration addresses current social problems (Vars, 2001 p. 9).

One major critic of curriculum integration is Paul George (1996a, 1996b). In the article "The Integrated Curriculum: A Reality Check," he goes on to discredit some of the claims made on integrated curriculum by concluding the following:

1. there is no evidence IC provides more opportunity for student involvement in planning the curriculum.
2. there is no evidence IC allows teachers more opportunity to be "facilitators."
3. there is no evidence IC encourages more transfer or retention of what is learned.

In George and Alexander (2003, pp. 109–111), they add that one major concern of integrated curriculum is that it abandons special subject areas that teachers have come to identify and have been trained in. Moreover, teachers may "feel threatened by a curriculum with which they have no familiarity and uncomfortable when they are asked to teach what they themselves do not already know," p. 109.

THE PROCESS OF CURRICULUM INTEGRATION

The process will involve the following steps:

1. Brainstorm possible themes with students and teachers in the team.
2. Teacher(s) selects a theme.
3. Decide on Essential Questions with student input.

4. Decide on time frame for the unit.
5. Write Objectives and Desired Skills for the unit.
6. Implement the unit using integration.
7. Culminating event.
8. Evaluate/Assess.

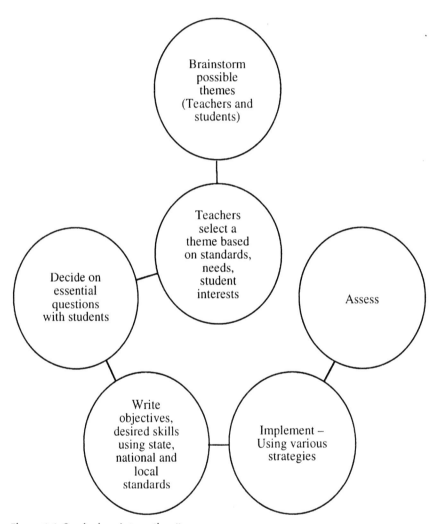

Figure 1.1 Curriculum Integration Process

Step 1

In planning an effective integrated unit, it is always good to begin by brainstorming possible themes with students. All teachers in the team who will be part of the integrated unit should be involved with the brainstorming. This is to encourage student participation and make the unit relevant to students by dealing with the issues and problems confronting them. In class discussions, ask them what interests them, what they want to learn about the world and what current issues and topics they would like to have a more detailed investigation on.

Step 2

Select the theme. Tomlinson (1998) suggests that for integration, concepts instead of topics should be encouraged and used. Although the theme selected should be derived from student interests, it should also have some relationship to national and state goals and district curriculum guides in the face of the standard based movement so that parent support will be maximized. Beane (1993, 1997) suggests that the theme selected should involve questions and concerns that are widely shared by young adolescents, engage a wide range of knowledge, skills and resources and pose opportunities for in-depth and extended work. In a document published by the North Carolina Department of Public Instruction (1987), it was pointed out that the criteria for theme selection must include "potential for direct linkage to goals in the *Standard Course of Study*, the richness and possibilities for classroom activities, and the overall relevance and excitement to students" (p. 19) Beane (1993 p. 61; Muir, 1998 pp. 13–14, Tomlinson, 1998, pp. 3–8 and Van Til,1976, p.197) give a list of selected themes which could form the basis of the integrated curriculum unit.

Step 3

The next step is to decide on the Essential Questions for the unit. According to Brough (2003, p. 27) these are the essential questions to be considered: "What are the essential leanings? What key standards, concepts and skills need to be addressed? How are students actively involved? How are their interests and special needs accommodated?"

Step 4

The next step is to decide on the time frame for the unit. As a teacher in the middle school, I have been engaged in units that lasted three weeks and some that lasted up to a term of nine weeks. As a teacher educator, I have talked with teachers who told me they had themes that lasted from three weeks to five weeks. I am aware of a middle school in Winston Salem, North Carolina that had a year-long theme. So the time frame would be dependent on the complexity of the theme, how much time teachers think students will need in order for learning to occur and how much time teachers in the team want to use in exploring the theme.

Step 5

Following the determination of the time frame, the teacher(s) should write objectives and desired skills for the thematic unit. Reference should always be made to national, state and district standards. In writing these objectives, the use of Bloom's taxonomy would be most useful so that assessment can also be easily done. At this stage in the process, teachers will also inform students about the broad and specific goals and objectives, including answers to some of the essential questions drawn up earlier with the students about the unit. Teachers will also discuss with students and decide on the assessment strategies for the unit. The assessment must be varied, continuous and used to further instruction and support student learning.

Step 6

Then teachers in the team begin the implementation of the thematic unit. Activities are developed for each objective of the unit. Activities may require the integration of technology (use of internet, CD-ROMs and other relevant software for information and research), field trips and guest speakers. For example, in a unit on pollution, students may visit a waste disposal system, receive a guest speaker who will talk on recycling and visit a water treatment plant. They may also attend a city council meeting and interview complainants to city government of individual or industrial activities in the area of pollution. Finally, they may have a nurse/dietician visit and talk about the human body, bacteria and pollution. Teachers in the team will have to include student interests in planning the activities and be willing to change as they see fit. As in all other curriculum designs and teaching methods, flexibility, adequate planning and monitoring of student needs are the keys to effective implementation. Implementation should also encourage group work and problem-solving skills.

Step 7

The culminating event involves student presentation of some project which was carried out by the student individually or in teams. Presentation could take various forms:

1. Power Point
2. Video
3. Poster
4. Create a classroom newspaper on the theme
5. Make a travel guide
6. Create vocabulary word games or puzzles using Puzzlemaker
7. Research reports
8. Portfolio

Step 8

The final step is the evaluation of not only the work of the students but also all the teachers evaluating themselves—what went right and how they can improve some of their teaching strategies. Evaluation must be based on objectives set at the beginning of the unit. As indicated earlier, evaluation must be varied and continuous and used to advance student learning.

PROBLEMS

While implementing an integrated curriculum unit, there could be some problems. I describe below some problems and reflections by teachers engaged in a four week unit on Changes: Africa. This was a seventh grade unit implemented by two teachers and two pre-student teaching interns involved in a course "Methods of Integrative Teaching." The two teachers had four years of teaching experience and were completing their courses for certification in middle grades education. The other two were students in the final part of their preparation for certification in middle grades education. They all had to take the course as part of their certification requirements.

Teacher 1: I think that the planning part of this unit was the hardest. It was hardest aligning activities that were challenging for students while still following the standard course of study in all of the areas. Intertwining these activities so that they flowed together and created a meaningful learning experience for students was a task easier said than done.

Teacher 2: I had to spend more time to find different resources to try and support the new theme for this new approach to teaching.

Student teacher 1: I had to sift out what was not needed or beneficial and yet still create something meaningful and interesting for the students.

However, these same teachers spoke of the joys and successes they had in implementing the unit.

Teacher 1: I think that curriculum integration is a neat way to teach . . . it is one of the best methods of teaching students so that they can remember once easily forgotten subject matter. . . . When done well, curriculum integration should be easier on teachers as they are sharing the load in teaching.

Teacher 2: Some students are more interested.

Student teacher 1: Curriculum integration is an excellent way for students to make connections and relate them to real world situations. When they have done this, they automatically develop in their learning process.

Student teacher 2: Curriculum integration is a way to apply real world situations to the learner, which makes the learner feel more involved and more interested in learning.

THE FUTURE

We have had some form of curriculum integration for more than half a century. Currently, this approach is under siege given the issues of high stakes testing and accountability. The future of integration will depend on teacher commitment, their ability to marry standards into curriculum integration and the kinds of support they receive from administrators, parents and other stake holders as they plan and execute integration.

BIBLIOGRAPHY

Beane, James A. *Curriculum Integration: Designing the Core of Democratic Education.* New York Teachers College, Columbia U.P., 1997.

———. "On the Shoulder of Giants: The Case for Curriculum Integration" *Middle School Journal* 28, no. 1 (September 1996): 6–11.

———. (1993) *The Middle School Curriculum: From Rhetoric to Reality,* Columbus, OH.: National Middle School Association.

Boyer, Ernest. "The Future" Address at Superintendents Summer Leadership Conference, Asheville, NC, July 1986.

Brough, Judith. "Designing Effective and Meaningful Integrated units" *Middle Ground* 7, no. 1 (August 2003): 27–28.

Fogarty, R.A. *The Mindful School: How to Integrate the Curricula.* Palatine, IL: IRI/Skylight, 1991.

George, Paul. "The Integrated Curriculum: A Reality Check" *Middle School Journal.* 28 no. 1 (September 1996a): 12–19.

———. "Arguing Integrated Curriculum" *Education Digest* 62, no. 3 (1996b): 16–22.

George, Paul and William M. Alexander. *The Exemplary Middle School*. Belmont, CA: Wadsworth/Thomson Learning, 2003.

Jackson, A.W. and G.A. Davies. *Turning Points 2000: Educating Adolescents in the 21st Century*. New York: Teachers College Press, 2000.

Jacobs, Heidi. "The interdisciplinary concept model: A step-by-step approach for developing integrated units of study." In H.H. Jacobs ed. *Interdisciplinary curriculum: Design and Implementation*. Alexandria, VA: ASCD pp. 53–65, 1989.

Lemond, Julie. " Curriculum Integration Models" Online <*http://www.misd.net/Curriculum/models.html*> October 23, 2003.

Lewis, Valerie K. and Stephen H. Shaha. (2003) "Maximizing learning and attitudinal gains through integrated curricula" *Education* 123, no. 3 (2003): 537.

Muir, Mike. "Planning Integrative Curricula with Skeptical Students" *Middle School Journal*. 30, no. 2 (November 1998): 9–17.

North Carolina Department of Public Instruction "Integrated Learning: What, Why, How" Raleigh, NC: Instructional Services, North Carolina Department of Public Instruction, 1987.

Nesin, Gert and John Lounsbury. *Curriculum Integration: Twenty One Questions- With Answers*. Atlanta, GA: Georgia Middle School Association, 1999.

Paterson, Jim. "Curriculum Integration in a Standards-Based World" *Middle Ground* 7, no. 1 (August 2003):10–12.

Post, T.R., Ellis, A.K., Humphreys, A.H and Buggey, L.J. *Interdisciplinary Approaches to Curriculum: Themes for Teaching*. Upper Saddler River, NJ: Prentice-Hall, 1997.

Roberts, Patricia and Richard D. Kellough. *A Guide for Developing Interdisciplinary Thematic Units,* Columbus, OH: Merrill Prentice- Hall, 2004.

Springer, Mark "A View from the top: Scaling the Heights of Curriculum Integration" *Middle Ground* 7, no. 1 (August 2003): 14–18.

Tomlinson, Carol A. "For Integration and Differentiation Choose Concepts over Topics" *Middle School Journal* 30, no. 2 (November 1998): 3–8.

Van Til, W. "What should be taught and learned through secondary education?" In W. Van Til ed. *Issues in Secondary Education* 75th Yearbook of the National Society for the Study of Education. Part 1 Chicago: University of Chicago Press, 1976.

Vars, G. F. "Effects of integrative curriculum and instruction" In J.E. Irvin ed. *What Current Research Says to the Middle Level Practitioner* pp. 179–186 Columbus, OH: National Middle School Association, 1997.

———. "Can Curriculum Integration Survive in an Era of High-Stakes Testing" *Middle School Journal* 33, no. 2 (November 2001): 7–17.

Vars, Gordon and Beane, J.A. (2000) "Integrative Curriculum in a Standards-based World" ERIC Document ED 441618. <http://www.nmsa.org/research/res articles_integrated.htm> (July 2, 2003).

Chapter Two

Are Middle School Educators Ready for Curriculum Integration?

Ann L. Barefield

INTRODUCTION

For decades, educational literature has made references to curriculum integration. Many different names have been used for the subject. However, until recently very little formal research has been done on the topic, and most educators do not fully embrace the concept. Why is this true? In order to answer this question, several other questions will be discussed in this chapter. The questions will serve as the subheadings and they are: (a) What is curriculum integration? (b) Why should curriculum integration be considered? (c) Who are the proponents of curriculum integration? (d) Where can one find information about implementing curriculum integration? (e) How can one implement curriculum integration successfully? (f) Why do teachers and principals find it difficult to implement curriculum integration?

What Is Curriculum Integration?

The literature on curriculum integration can be found under numerous keywords. Integrated curriculum, interdisciplinary curriculum, student centered curriculum and core curriculum are among the most prevalent names that are used. However, it is difficult to find much research about curriculum integration in the most recent journals even though the concept has remained viable for several decades. According to Vars and Beane:

> "Curriculum integration has long been proposed as a way of organizing the "common learnings" or life skills considered essential for all citizens in a democracy. Curriculum is organized around real-life problems and issues signifi-

cant to both young people and adults, applying pertinent content and skills from many subject areas or disciplines." (Vars and Beane 2000, para.1).

According to Drake (1993), curriculum integration is an idea with an intellectual history, and Fogarty and Stoehr (1991) describe 10 models of curriculum design that proceed from a fragmented to a networked curriculum. Beane states that:

> "An authentic middle school curriculum ought to be based on a view of general education that combines the *common and shared* concerns of the early adolescent and the larger world. Clearly these are found not in the narrow interpretations of academic, 'special,' and pseudo-vocational subjects, but rather in the developmental issues of early adolescence and social issues that do and will face them as participants in the larger world." (Beane, 1993, 80).

Beane, Vars and other middle grades researchers indicate that teachers must involve the students in planning *and* implementing the curriculum. In a 1995 article on curriculum integration and disciplines of knowledge, Beane states that the disciplines of knowledge are important but they must be appropriately brought into the lives of young people (Beane 1995). Gordon Vars defines what he calls a core curriculum as follows:

> "In brief, core curriculum as I interpret and teach it, is a curriculum design in which teachers and students jointly plan, carry out and evaluate learning experiences focused on problems or issues of genuine significance both to learners and to society, and also consonant with the purposes of education in a democratic society." (Vars, 2000, 78)

Although Vars calls the concept core curriculum rather than integrated or interdisciplinary curriculum, his message is much the same. The students need to be involved and the issues need to be from the real world. Richard and Noreen Kellough say much the same thing in the following quote:

> "The term integrated curriculum . . . refers to both a way of teaching and a way of planning and organizing the instructional program so the discrete disciplines of subject matter are related to one another in a design that (1) matches the developmental needs of the learners, and (2) helps to connect their learning in ways that are meaningful to their current and past experiences. In that respect, IC is the antithesis of traditional disparate subject matter oriented teaching and curriculum designations." (Kellough and Kellough, 1999, 193).

The Kelloughs' statement implies that integrative education provides a holistic approach to learning that allows students to think creatively, question, interact with their peers and teachers and in general operate in an enriched environment. References to teaching holistically rather than teaching isolated subjects and facts can be found in the works of Piaget (1970), Dewey (1907), Vars (2002) and Caine and Caine (1991).

In this writer's experience, curriculum integration has been a way to involve students in their own learning from the elementary grades through college. It has also been a means to get students excited about learning and to encourage them to use critical thinking and decision making skills. The writer has actually been involved in the development of numerous models for integrating curriculum while serving as a public school administrator, classroom teacher in elementary and middle schools and a college professor.

There are a variety of ways to integrate curriculum. The following practices are several in which this writer has been personally involved. The faculty and students can choose a school-wide theme around which all core subjects and/or curriculum standards are studied. This can be a valuable learning experience for everyone in the school. This practice requires collaboration with colleagues and students. Teachers also have to give up some control to students and other teachers with whom they are collaborating.

Two or more teachers can work together with their students, special teachers and parents to choose a theme into which they integrate their subjects and/or school district curriculum standards. In addition to collaboration and a willingness to give up some control, teachers need planning time and flexibility in scheduling classes.

Teachers of an entire grade level can choose a theme around which they teach the curriculum standards and/or special and core subjects. This requires advance planning, and students have an opportunity to choose how they will develop the various components of the theme.

A professor of middle grades education at a university can team with a team of teachers and students at a middle school to allow pre-service teachers to participate in the development and implementation of integrated units. This requires collaboration not only among teachers in a middle school but also among university professors, pre-service teachers, middle schools, students and public school administrators. It requires flexibility in scheduling at the university and the middle school and a great deal of trust.

This author has observed teachers and student teachers implementing integrated units by planning together with one another and their students. The students indicated interest in topics such as endangered species, the Titanic and the Olympics. As the middle grade teachers, preservice teachers and their students worked together to plan and implement these units, the author watched all of them learn and develop together. As the group presented a workshop for middle level teachers, one of the veteran teachers involved in this experience said, "This was the most rewarding teaching and learning experience I have had in my 25 years of teaching."

Why Should Curriculum Integration Be Considered?

According to George, Lawrence and Bushnell:

> ". . . if critics are correct, the traditional curriculum has less and less vitality and relevance in the schools of the last years of the twentieth century and the first years of the twenty-first. . . . Little wonder, then, that today's middle school educators are more interested and enthusiastic about parallel, interdisciplinary and integrated curriculum models." (George, Lawrence and Bushnell. 1998, 342).

If this is true, it behooves educators to find ways to include the vitality and relevance in their teaching. Curriculum integration, appropriately implemented, can help teachers involve the students and make the lessons relevant to their needs and interests.

According to John Dewey:

> "There is very little place in the traditional schoolroom for the child to work. The workshop, the laboratory, the materials, the tools with which the child may construct, create and actively inquire and even the requisite space, have been for the most part lacking. The things that have to do with these processes have not even had a definitely recognized place in education. They are what the educational authorities who write editorials in the daily paper generally term 'fads' and 'frills.'" (Dewey 1907, 48–49).

This appears, in many cases, to still be true today. The straight rows and the lack of student involvement in the planning and implementation of the curriculum are too often the norm in the classrooms. Even though 96 years have passed since this statement was written, educators continue to emphasize the need for student involvement, inquiry methods, hand-on activities and critical thinking that are all part of an integrated curriculum. According to Caine and Caine, "Integration of the curriculum is an excellent way to increase richness and contribute to meaningfulness." (Caine and Caine 1991, 119).

Caine and Caine also stated that the reasons interdisciplinary teaching is important are as follows:

1. The brain searches for common patterns and connections.
2. Every experience actually contains within it the seeds of many and possibly all disciplines.
3. One of the keys to understanding is what is technically called redundancy. (Caine and Caine 1991, 119–20).

Thus, as the teachers and students work together to develop the integrated learning activities, they must search for the patterns and connections. As they look for those patterns and connections, they find them in all the disciplines. As they find the patterns and connections, the redundancy occurs.

The following quote from a case study of interdisciplinary teaching describes what occurred when teachers planned and worked together for the benefit of their students:

> "Perhaps the most important theme contained in the data was the sense of community that teaming encouraged. As a result of their close working relationship, the teachers came to trust and respect each other even more than they had initially. Even though they had chosen one another, they did not expect to derive as much personal and professional satisfaction from the relationship as they did. . . . A feeling of trust and enhancement also resulted in the lessening of feelings of isolation." (Murata. 2002, 72).

Who Are The Proponents of Curriculum Integration?

There are numerous educators who have advocated and written about curriculum integration over the past five decades. Their articles and books can provide a wealth of information for one who is interested in delving deeper into the history of the topic. Some of the middle level educators are listed in this chapter for your consideration. There are many others who have not been mentioned due to space. However, if you go to the National Middle School Association (NMSA) Website at www.nmsa.org, you will find a wealth of information about the educators who are intricately involved in middle level education.

James Beane is a professor in the College of Education at National-Louis University in Madison, Wisconsin. He is well known for his works on curriculum and self-esteem. Dr. Beane is a Lounsbury Award winner, which is the highest recognition awarded by the National Middle School Association. His books include *A Middle School Curriculum: From Rhetoric to Reality* and *Curriculum Integration: Designing the Core of Democratic Education*.

Robin Fogarty is a leading advocate of curriculum integration. She received her doctorate from Loyola University in Chicago. She has taught at every level from kindergarten to college, served as an administrator, and consulted with state departments and ministries of education. Dr. Fogarty has authored numerous publications in the field including *The Mindful School: How to Integrate the Curricula* and *Integrating Curricula with Multiple Intelligences: Teams, Themes and Threads*.

Heidi Hayes Jacobs is well known for her books titled *Interdisciplinary Curriculum: Design and Implementation* and *Mapping the Big Picture: Integrating Curriculum and Assessment K–12*. Both books are published by the Association for Supervisions and Curriculum Development. Dr. Jacobs has served as adjunct associate professor in the Department of Curriculum and Teaching at Teachers College of Columbia University in New York City since 1981.

John H. Lounsbury is the Senior Editor of Professional Publications for the National Middle School Association. He is a Professor and Dean Emeritus of the John H. Lounsbury School of Education at Georgia College and State University in Milledgeville, Georgia. Dr. Lounsbury was the first recipient of the Lounsbury Award, an award which is the highest recognition awarded by the National Middle School Association. He is one of the educators responsible for the middle school movement in the United States. His books, *Perspective: Middle School Education* and *Middle School Education: As I See It* are available from the National Middle School Association.

C. Kenneth McEwin is a professor of education at Appalachian State University, Boone, North Carolina. He is an author of the National Middle School Association Standards for Middle Level Teacher Preparation. Dr. McEwin also serves on the National Forum to Accelerate Middle Grades Reform. He received the Lounsbury Award from the National Middle School Association in 1989. He is co-author with Thomas S. Dickinson and Doris M. Jenkins of *America's Middle Schools: Practices and Progress: A 25 Year Perspective.*

Sandra L. Schurr is the Director of the National Resource Center for Middle Grades/High School Education located at the University of South Florida in Tampa where she is a tenured faculty member in the Secondary Education Department. She has authored several books with Imogene Forte, including *The Definitive Middle School Guide: A Handbook for Success.* She is also a consultant in the areas of authentic assessment and restructuring of middle and high schools.

Chris Stevenson has been a writer, presenter, consultant and a professor of education at the University of Vermont, Burlington. He has been a teacher, coach, teaching principal, parent, professor, researcher and author. He is the author of *Teaching Ten to Fourteen Year Olds.* Dr. Stevenson was the fifteenth recipient of the Lounsbury Award from the National Middle School Association in 2002.

Gordon Vars has been a teacher of middle school teachers and preadolescents for approximately 49 years. He was the founder of the National Middle School Association and its first president. He was also the Executive Director of the National Association for Core Curriculum. He is Professor Emeritus of Teaching, Leadership and Curriculum Studies at Kent State University in Kent, Ohio. Dr. Vars is also a winner of the Lounsbury Award. He is the author of *Interdisciplinary Teaching Why and How.*

Where can one find information about implementing curriculum integration successfully? There are numerous resources available to those who wish to learn more about curriculum integration. One source is the National Middle School Association site at www.nmsa.org. One can go to the online bookstore to find many books on the topic. Also, *Middle Ground* is the magazine of middle level education published by NMSA. The August 2003 issue contains excellent articles on curriculum integration.

The Association for Supervision and Curriculum Development has a long list of video tapes, books and kits on curriculum integration. Heidi Jacob's book *Mapping the Big Picture: Integrating Curriculum and Assessment K–12* is also available at the site. The address is www.ascd.org.

For those who wish to integrate technology into their activities, the WebQuest site at http://webquest.sdsu.edu is an outstanding source of information about an inquiry oriented activity that is excellent to use with an integrated curriculum.

In addition to the books listed in the references, Chris Stevenson and Judy F. Carr edited an excellent book in 1993 titled *Integrated Studies in the Middle Grades: Dancing Through Walls.* It is published by Teachers College Press. One can find many examples of integrated units and lessons prepared by middle level teachers in this book.

How Can One Implement Curriculum Integration Successfully?

Students' academic success appears to be significantly related to how well their interests are integrated into the curriculum that is taught (Cummins, 1989). Therefore, it is important for teachers to ensure that each lesson they teach is directly related to the interests of their students. Curriculum integration can help the teachers plan their lessons around the interests of their students. However, in these days of standards-based education, teachers must also plan their lesson around the state and district requirements. According to George, Lawrence and Bushnell (1998):

> ". . . because even teachers of integrated curriculum work in real world public schools, planning must acknowledge and include the subject matter from curriculum guides and other sources. It may be more realistic to envision the integrated curriculum as the intersection of three sets, drawing perhaps equally from (1) the concerns students have about their own lives, (2) the social problems of the larger world, and (3) the subject matter that has been designed and mandated for the curriculum from more traditional sources" (George, Lawrence and Bushnell, 1998, 241–42).

Therefore, the job of those who wish to implement an integrated curriculum seems to be threefold. They must first look to their students for input about their interests, then identify the current social problems, and lastly correlate both the students' interest and the social problems with the state and local mandated standards.

According to Caine and Caine:

> "What the brain principles collectively describe is that to some extent all meaningful learning is experiential. They also point out the multifaceted nature of experience. Our task is to ensure that anything that we wish to teach or to have children learn needs to be embedded in multiple, rich, interactive experiences where most of what is to be learned is left open ended, ready for discovery by and consolidation within the learner." (Caine and Caine, 1997, 119).

Once the students' interests and social problems have been identified and correlated with the state and local standards, it is important to plan the lessons in such a way that the students are actively involved in discovering new meaning form the lessons. Curriculum integration is ideal for this because the process of relating the learning across disciplines is by nature open ended and allows for discovery.

In *Teaching in the Middle School*, Manning and Bucher (2001) indicate that:

> "In an integrated curriculum, the student needs to be involved; learners are no longer passive and waiting for knowledge to be conveyed. They are expected to assume at least some responsibility for their learning. Whether involved in the planning of the integrated curriculum, offering input on learning methods to use, selecting materials and resources that complement the curricular content or choosing the most effective means of evaluating outcomes, young adolescents begin to take an integral role in the learning process." (Manning and Bucher, 2001, 85).

As the learners assist the teacher in the implementation of the integrated lesson plans, they become active learners, and there is an excitement that is not prevalent in the traditional classroom. This writer has watched students who have seldom participated in the classroom lessons become so involved that they not only participate in the small groups and share their discoveries with their classmates, they involve their parents also.

Integrating the curriculum begins with collaboration. First, the teachers must be open to the suggestions of the students. Second, teachers cannot go into their rooms and close the door. Subject area specialists must share their knowledge with the whole team so that they all become generalists. However, it is important not to lose the knowledge of the disciplines or there is a danger that there will be nothing to integrate. Third, sharing and integrating take time. Therefore, the team members need a common planning time that will allow them to work together to incorporate their knowledge, the needs and interests of the students and the real world happenings.

Once the sharing and planning have taken place, it is time to begin the implementation. This is the hard part for some teachers and some students. The teachers have a hard time letting go and allowing the students the freedom to search and discover on their own. Some students have difficulty dealing with the freedom. It takes time for the teachers to practice letting go and for the students to learn to deal with the freedom. It also takes time for some teachers to learn to work with their teammates.

Trust is the key word in this process. Teachers need to trust the students, students need to trust the teachers and teachers need to trust their teammates. When teachers have confidence in one another and their students, little errors and slips do not get blown out of proportion. The colleagues and students feel accepted and are able to take the risks that are necessary when new procedures are being implemented. Learning from ones mistakes rather than being chastised for them becomes the norm. Thus, it is important to spend time developing a trusting relationship from the very first day of school. By an open and honest sharing of ideas, teacher and students can begin to search, inquire, discover and learn together. Planning and implementing an integrated curriculum can lead to deeper levels of critical thinking and problem solving that will assist the students throughout their lives.

As indicated throughout this chapter, the planning process involves the teachers and the students. As they discuss the topics that are of interest to them, they begin to know one another more intimately and trust begins to develop. The inquiry that takes place during this interaction can lead them to use many resources such as technology, library books, parents, business partners and experts in a field that goes far beyond what a textbook can offer. This kind of teaching and learning allows the educators to bring the real world into the classroom.

Why Do Teachers and Administrators Find It Difficult To Implement Curriculum Integration?

There are many reasons that teachers and administrators avoid the use of curriculum integration. For example, many teachers were not exposed to curriculum integration during their elementary or high school experiences. Since teachers tend to teach as they were taught, it is difficult for some to use a concept they have not experienced. Many teachers have been taught to use the teacher's manual for each textbook as their cookbook for the course. This does not require the teachers to design curriculum, teach across curriculum or involve the students in the planning.

Another reason middle schools have difficulty implementing curriculum integration is aptly stated in the following James Beane (1993) quote. He states that:

"The problem of curriculum reform in the middle schools is compounded by the fact that they, like other schools, are subject to many pressures: external curriculum mandates, expectations of parents and the society, the structure of tradition, the interests of subject area specialists, theories and concerns about middle school reform concerns and interests of local educators and the expectations of local adolescents. Difficult as curriculum reform may be under any circumstances, the fact that these pressures present competing and conflicting interests makes the matter of rethinking the middle school curriculum thoroughly problematic." (Beane, 1993, 24).

In our current standards driven environment, teachers and administrators are hesitant to try new avenues of teaching and learning.

Administrators are pressured to ensure high student test scores and an orderly environment. One can read news and journal articles on a regular basis about principals being removed from their positions because of the students' low test scores. This stymies their willingness to try anything other than strategies that teach to the test, of which there is an abundance. However, there are just as many news and journal articles that deplore the teaching to the test mentality that has recently taken over education. However, the standards and tests that are currently demanded by state departments of education across the country are causing teachers and administrators to avoid innovative practices. According to Vars:

"Integrative curriculum can thrive within standards-based education. It cannot thrive within the confines of standardized education_that means that everyone does exactly the same thing. And that's what scares people about the standards movement. In an effort to get all students to come up to higher standards, they're forgetting that kids are different and they can't all do it the same way." (Vars, 2002, 4).

According to Caine and Caine:

"Integration of the curriculum is an excellent way to increase richness and contribute to meaningfulness" (Caine and Caine, 1991, 119).

In an age when we are reading so much about the need to make the curriculum meaningful for the students, it seems important to take seriously the possibility that curriculum integration could be an answer to many problems that face educators. However, change is difficult and educators resist change for a variety of reasons. Also, Gatlin and Margonis (1995) postulated that change does not work because many reformers are not working within the culture of the schools. This tends to increase the educators' resistance. Often, the teachers and administrators are so busy implementing mandated standards that they do not have time to study their environment and make the changes necessary from within.

According to Kant (1996), it is important for teachers to have time to investigate the concept and implications of curriculum integration. However, there is often not enough time for teachers to truly research, investigate and implement new strategies. In many schools, there is no time scheduled for teachers to investigate new ways of teaching. Therefore, they continue teaching as they were taught regardless of whether they are getting the desired results or not.

According to George, Lawrence and Bushnell:

> "The traditional discipline-based curriculum provides a familiarity comforting to almost all adults who have completed a traditional college major in one of those disciplines." (George, Lawrence and Bushnell. 1998, 342).

Many teachers do not receive the support necessary to try new ways of teaching. Therefore, they continue to use the traditional disciplined-based curriculum with which they are familiar. In order to help teachers change, it is important for the administration to provide the support and staff development necessary for the teachers to feel confident with and to eventually adopt new strategies. "Realistically speaking, many middle school teachers have mixed feelings about using integrated, cross-curricular themes. Often these educators perceive a conflict between the disciplines and the integrated curriculum." (Manning and Bucher. 2001, 82). Teachers and administrators who have been trained in a particular discipline often find it difficult to work with other disciplines. Becoming a generalist requires that teachers have an openness to new ideas and a willingness to compromise with peers who have expertise in other disciplines. This means they must develop a tolerance for ambiguity which is difficult for many adults.

Working collaboratively is difficult for many teachers. Generally, teachers have been able to close the door to their classroom and teach as they wish. However, teaching an integrated curriculum requires them to not only collaborate with their peers but with their students. Some teachers have not yet developed the skills or level of trust necessary for this kind of teaching.

Planning and implementing an integrated curriculum is hard work. It takes time and energy to involve colleagues and students in the planning, and there is no cookbook type guide available to help with the process. However, the outcomes can be very rewarding for the teachers and the students. The author has heard many students and teachers say that the teaching and learning experiences they have had in an integrated curriculum setting are the best they have ever had.

Providing time for curriculum integration must involve the whole school. Scheduling so that the mathematics, science, social studies, language arts, music and art teachers can plan together and their classes can often meet together can be difficult. However, it is not impossible, particularly if the teachers work in teams.

ARE MIDDLE SCHOOL EDUCATORS READY FOR CURRICULUM INTEGRATION?

It is now time to answer the question asked in the title of this chapter. Educators are probably as ready as they will ever be unless more schools of education at colleges and universities model and teach about curriculum integration. Schools are made up of human beings and human beings have varied ideas about how schools should be run and how curriculum should be taught. Human beings like other animals, stake out their territory and protect it. The social studies teachers protect the social studies curriculum, the mathematics teachers protect the mathematics curriculum, and so on. Only when educators go beyond protecting territory to collaboration will they be able to develop an integrated curriculum that will help their students better understand themselves and the world in which they live. Also, in order to prepare students to work in teams and use critical and creative thinking, teachers must be able to model these skills in their daily actions in the school. This can and does happen daily in schools, colleges and universities across the nation. However, it does not happen as often as it could if more teachers and professors collaborated to provide real world experiences for their students.

Some educators are not ready because they do not have the leadership and support necessary to help them implement an integrated curriculum. It must be understood that administrators are not the only ones who can provide leadership. Teachers or a team of teachers who are willing to take risks can also provide the leadership. This means that they must, at times, go against the system in order to do what is in the best interests of their students. The leaders must be willing to ask for the staff development necessary to appropriately implement system or school-wide change. They must also be willing to work hard to develop and implement an integrated curriculum. However, it has been this author's experience that the hard work pays great dividends for professors, teachers and students in improved teaching, learning, caring and sharing.

There are educators who are not ready because they are hesitant to give up the security of the prescribed curriculum in the teacher's guides and state and local standards manuals. Until they are willing to use the guides and manuals as a starting point and go beyond them to use the interests and needs of their students as their focus, they will not be ready for curriculum integration. Gordon Vars and James Beane addressed this concern in the following quote:

> "Integrative curriculum in the new millennium will have to deal with societal expectations, as spelled out in standards and state tests, while still giving primary emphasis to student needs, problems, and concerns." (Vars and Beane. 2000, para. 13).

The pressures of accountability and standards-based curriculum have made educators leery of trying anything new. Therefore, many educators are not ready to try curriculum integration for fear of losing their jobs. It is difficult to trust a strategy one has not experienced or used successfully. More reading about the topic might be a good beginning for developing the necessary trust.

Many educators are not ready to implement an integrated curriculum because they are wedded to a disciplined-based curriculum. They have been taught that way, and they have taught that way and they have come to believe it is the only way to teach. However, the research on curriculum integration indicates that there is another way that might be more meaningful to many of their students. This author has witnessed the excitement the students experience when they discover the connections among the subjects and when they have an opportunity to be involved in planning their curriculum. She has seen students who have not been attending school or have been causing problems in the classroom participate everyday because they are involved in the learning. Also, she has heard mainstream special education students express a desire to stay in the regular classroom because they do not want to miss anything. This is what needs to happen for all our students. Whether it happens with curriculum integration or another strategy, it needs to happen for every student.

SUMMARY

The readers of this chapter have had an opportunity to gain a brief overview of curriculum. It is the author's desire that this was enough information to entice them to delve more deeply into the possibilities of the integrated curriculum by reading the books and articles listed in the document and in the references. Perhaps you too will find that involving students and colleagues in the development and implementation of an integrated curriculum can be a very rewarding experience.

In closing, the author would like to share a favorite quote from *The Aims of Education* written by Alfred North Whitehead in 1929.

Let us ask how in our system of education we are to guard against this mental dryrot. We enunciate two educational commandments, "Do not teach too many subjects," and again, "What you teach, teach thoroughly.

"The result of teaching small parts of a large number of subjects is the passive reception of disconnected ideas, not illumined with any spark of vitality. Let the main ideas which are introduced into the child's education be few and important, and let them be thrown into every combination possible. The child should make them his own, and should understand their application here and now in the circumstances of his actual life. From the very beginning of his education, the child should experience the joy of discovery. The discovery which he has to make is that general ideas give an understanding of that stream of events which pours through his life, which is his life. By understanding, I mean more than a logical analysis, though that is included. I mean 'understanding' in the sense in which it is used in the French proverb, 'To understand all, is to forgive all.' Pedants sneer at an education that is useful. But if education is not useful, what is it? Is it a talent, to be hidden away in a napkin? Of course, education should be useful, whatever your aim in life. It was useful to St. Augustine and it was useful to Napoleon. It is useful, because understanding is useful." (Whitehead. 1929, 2).

BIBLIOGRAPHY

Beane, J. A., *A middle school curriculum: From rhetoric to reality.* Columbus, OH: National Middle School Association, 1993.

———. Curriculum integration and the disciplines of knowledge. *Phi Delta Kappan* 76 (1995) 616–22.

Caine, N., & Caine, G., *Making connections: Teaching and the human brain.* Alexandria, VA: Association for Supervision and Curriculum Development, 1991.

———. *Education on the edge of possibility.* Alexandria, VA: Association for Supervision and Curriculum Development, 1997.

Cummins, J., *Empowering minority students.* Sacramento, CA: California Association for Bilingual Education, 1989.

Dewey, J., *The school and society.* Chicago: University of Chicago Press, 1907.

Drake, S. M., *Planning integrated curriculum: The call to Adventure.* Alexandria, VA: Association for Supervision and Curriculum Development, 1993.

Forgarty, R. Ten ways to Integrate Curriculum. *Educational Leadership*, 49 (1991): 61–65.

Fogarty, R., and Stoehr, J. *Integrating curricula with multiple intelligences: Teams, themes and threads.* Palatine, IL: Skylight Publishing, Inc., 1991.

Gatlin, A., & Margonis, F., (1995). The political aspect of reform: Teacher resistance as good sense. *American Journal of Education*, 103 (1995): 377–405.

George, P., Lawrence, G., & Bushnell, D. *Handbook for middle school teaching*. New York: Longman, 1998.

Kant, D., Recipes or dialogue? A middle school team conceptualizes curricular integration. *Journal of Curriculum and Supervision,* 11 (1996) 163–87.

Kellough, R. D., & Kellough, N. G., *Middle school teaching: A guide to methods and resources*. Upper Saddle River, NJ: Prentice Hall, 1999.

Manning, M.L., & Bucher, K.T. *Teaching in the middle school*. Columbus, OH: Merrill Prentice Hall, 2001.

Murata, R., What does team teaching mean? A case study of interdisciplinary teaming? *The Journal of Educational Research 96* (2002): 67–77.

Piaget, J., *The Science of Education and the Psychology of the Child*. NY: Grossman,1970.

Vars, G. F., Viewpoint with Gordon F. Vars. *Curriculum Technology Quarterly, 11(2002)*: 1–8.

——. *Interdisciplinary teaching: Why and how*. Columbus, OH: National Middle School Association,1993.

Vars, G.F. & Beane, J.A., (2000). Integrative curriculum in a standards-based world. *ERIC Digest*. <http://www.nmsa.org/research/res_articles_integrated.htm> (June 29, 2003).

Whitehead, A. N., *The Aim of Education*. New York: The Free Press, 1929.

Chapter Three

Meeting Standards Through Curriculum Integration: A Bridge To The Mainstream

Susan M. Drake

This chapter explores interdisciplinary curriculum as a viable approach to educational reform. In an age of accountability, relevance of the curriculum for students has often taken a back seat in the need to cover disciplinary standards and prepare for standardized tests. Descriptions of successful standards-based integrated programs are offered with supporting data for academic achievement and other positive student outcomes. A "scan and cluster" approach for rethinking standards is offered with a sample attached. It is suggested that standards themselves can be a vehicle to move the integrated curriculum into the mainstream now that a supporting body of research is being developed through the standards.

I really need to find a way to motivate my students. Integrated curriculum? Oh, I can't do that. I have so many standards in different disciplines that I need to cover. Teacher

Integrated curriculum? There is no way that is coming back. Integrated curriculum is DEAD! Teacher educator

These are two typical comments that I heard recently in my teaching environment. These types of responses are not limited to Ontario, Canada. Indeed, since the latest wave of educational reform and the advent of standards and accountability mandates, interdisciplinary issues have more or less disappeared from the educational landscape. Many educators, in fact, believe that standards and interdisciplinary work are an impossible fit and that never the twain shall meet. (Vars & Beane, 2000).

But . . .

Now that I understand the standards, I realize that the only way I can cover them is to do interdisciplinary work. Teacher

I used to be swamped with so much assessment with this standards-based approach. Now that I do interdisciplinary work, I can assess more than one subject at a time. Teacher

*I love working with other teachers to create interdisciplinary curriculum.
It keeps me energized and has forced me to be more reflective about what I
am teaching. Teacher*

These are the voices of educators who have learned how to create and implement interdisciplinary programs using standards-based curriculum. There
is a dramatic shift from the impossibility of marrying standards and interdisciplinarity to believing that this is the only way to approach curriculum in an
age of accountability.

The purpose of this chapter is to demonstrate that integrated approaches are
far from impossible in today's climate of reform. Indeed, there is sound evidence that such approaches can flourish. One of the largest obstacles to implementation of integrated approaches has been the lack of quantitative evidence to support such programs. Wineburg and Grossman (2000), for
example, state that there is not a body of research to attest to better learning
with integrated approaches as compared to traditional ones. Indeed much of
the research reported in the late '80s and early '90s was anecdotal in nature.
(An important exception was the longitudinal quantitative eight-year study
reported on by Aikin in 1942.) The general response to anecdotal research
was to dismiss interdisciplinary work as untested, and therefore, unfounded.

Practitioners of integrated approaches were frustrated by the lack of acceptance of their work without quantitative measures. Personal experience
told them that this was an effective way to teach. I often heard advocates
claim that they could not apply quantitative measures to their classroom
work. For them, comparing traditional classrooms to integrated ones was like
comparing apples and oranges; they claimed serious flaws in accepting
quantitative work in looking for new directions (Drake, 1998). For better or
worse, with the advent of accountability measures there will continue to be a
need for quantitative research. With standards and standardized testing, we do
now have ways to compare apples with apples. Ironically, it is the standards
that are allowing us to create a bridge to the mainstream for interdisciplinary
programs.

THE NEED FOR RELEVANCE

Historically, integrated curriculum has been a response to a need for a more
motivating curriculum for students. During the 30s, the interdisciplinary approach was popular with the rise of the progressive movement in education.
The progressive movement heralded constructivism and was heavily influenced by John Dewey (1969) and his belief in experiential learning. The
Eight Year Study, a longitudinal study, effectively showed that progressive

schools with an interdisciplinary program had a positive impact on success in higher education (Aikin, 1942).

In the late '80s and '90s school reforms focused on the relevance of curriculum for students—particularly middle school students. By the mid-nineties, this focus was replaced by standards-based reform in most jurisdictions. In Ontario, for example, an integrated curriculum was mandated in *The Common Curriculum: Grades 1–9* (Ontario Ministry of Education, 1993, 1995). These efforts were largely forgotten when a new government was ushered in, and they set about introducing a new curriculum that focused on accountability: expectations (standards) and testing.

Today, there is perhaps an even greater need for relevance. The focus on standards and testing means some teachers "teach to the test." Others put their heads down and "cover the standards." This approach is hardly motivating for students who learn simply to pass a test. Yet, the higher the stakes of the test, the more likely this kind of practice happens. In the United States, there is a heavy emphasis on high stakes testing. This had led to practices such as extra pay for teachers if their students do well.

Integrated Curriculum as Effective Educational Reform

It seems that standards are here to stay, and we need to make standards-based reform a success for the long term (Gandal & Vranek, 2001). Yet, there is a general consensus that student achievement has not reached acceptable levels even with the new accountability measures. Arguably students will do better on standardized measures when the learning is meaningful to them. Research supports this view. Recent overviews of research from the field reveal an interesting conclusion. Students in integrated programs do as well academically as, or better than, students in traditional programs (Vars, 2000; Hartzler, 2000; Drake & Burns, in press). Also, students in these programs do better in many other dimensions. For example, students across various interdisciplinary Expeditionary Bound programs showed:

1. significant academic improvement on standardized tests and portfolio measures
2. positive changes in instructional strategies
3. improved attendance and parent participation
4. less need for discipline (Expeditionary Outward Bound, 2001).

One of the contradictions of school reform is the unintended consequence of deskilling teachers and the collusion of teachers and students to create lowered educational expectations to pass standardized tests (McNeil, 2000). In fact, Hargreaves (2001) suggests one of the reasons that teachers are leaving the profession in unprecedented droves is that in fulfilling their accountability mandates they abandon their creativity. For him, developing interdisciplinary curriculum allows teachers to set curriculum in a context of relevance for students, provides opportunities for collaboration, and opens the door for creativity and personal renewal. A positive outcome for educators working collaboratively to design standards-based curriculum is experiencing a high level of professional development (Allen, 2002). As well, teachers emerge from the process, more reflective and acting as teacher leaders (Attenborough & Drake, 2001; Drake, Upton, Phillips & Rubocki, 2002).

Given these positive outcomes, it seems that interdisciplinary approaches are a good fit for reform movements fueled by accountability mandates.

CREATING RELEVANCE IN A STANDARDS-BASED CURRICULUM

How can educators make a standards-based curriculum relevant? It requires a delicate balance between covering standards and creating curriculum that fits the needs and interests of students. Here two programs are explored that demonstrate that it is very possible to teach with an integrated perspective and cover standards in a meaningful way.

PROJECT-BASED LEARNING

Project-based learning is interdisciplinary curriculum that has great potential to balance accountability and relevance. Typically, project-based learning is set in a real life context—presumably making the curriculum more relevant to students when they see that they are learning something connected to their lives. Project-based learning results in students:

1. going far beyond minimum effort
2. applying learning to real life problems
3. being absent less and incurring fewer discipline problems (Curtis, 2002).

For an ongoing account of project-based learning and exemplary schooling one need only look at the newsletter disseminated by the George Lucas Educational Foundation—GLEF Newsletter (www.glef.org).

Project-based learning has three phases according to Sylvia Chard (2001).

1. A topic of study for the project is selected on the basis of student interests, resources and curriculum standards.
2. Students investigate the problem with fieldwork and talking to experts.
3. Students demonstrate their learning in a culminating activity. For example, in a project students might explore the history of the community or design a school of the future (Curtis, 2002).

A good example of the effectiveness of Chard's problem-based learning is Newsome Park Elementary School—K to 5 (http://npes.nn.k12.va.us). After introducing the project approach in 1998, students made dramatic gains in student test scores on the Virginia Standards of Learning Test (Drake & Burns, in press). Principal Peter Bender attributed this gain to the fact that project-based learning begins with the students' questions. Interestingly the school had previously tried an integrated approach but it was not until they moved to the projects that test scores improved. Bender suggested that it is not the integration itself that motivated students but rather the student owner-ship of curriculum.

The two major groups in the school are white and African American. From 1999 to 2002, African American third graders who received passing grades increased by 45 percentage points in English, 30 in math, 51 in science and 34 in history. Passing rates for white students increased by 17 percentage points in English, 8 in math and 12 in history. Although not as dramatic, there are similar results for fifth-grade students. Significant in an era of "No Child Left Behind" legislation, the gap between African American and white stu-dents narrowed.

STUDENTS AS STANDARDS-BASED CURRICULUM DESIGNERS

The Alpha program is a "school" within the Shelburne Community School, Shelburne, Vermont. The program takes student questions one step further (Drake & Burns, in press). Alpha is an alternative integrated program for 70 students in sixth to eighth grade. It is based on the work of James Beane (see, for example, Beane, 1993) who believes that all curricula should be derived from student concerns that can be categorized as personal or social. For Beane and the three Alpha teachers, young people can and do ask good questions.

Students in this program begin with their own questions. The teachers fa-cilitate the process while students design the curriculum—content, activities and assessment. They do this by aligning the curriculum with the state stan-dards. The curriculum does not distinguish between subject areas (except for math), but rather relies on themes that emerge from student questions. Examples of past themes are:

1. We the People (government)
2. Culture
3. Nutrition
4. Conflict resolution
5. Natural resources

The curriculum at Alpha is relevant and covers standards—the students make sure of this. It is also heavy on assessment tasks such as goal setting, conferencing and portfolios. Although students take required tests, they do not explicitly prepare for them. They do as well as, or better than the students in traditional programs on the required achievement tests. For example, from 1998 to 2000 Alpha students consistently produced results at or above those of the rest of the school, the district and the state on both the mandated standards-based math and literature tests. Also, they do as well as, or better than, their counterparts on standardized tests such as Stanford Achievement Test. In 2000, the Alpha seventh-graders lapsed slightly behind in only one of 13 measures—spelling. In 2003 the National Middle School Association awarded Alpha with one of the two national "Teams that Make a Difference" awards for Academic Excellence.

RETHINKING THE CURRICULUM FOR INTEGRATION

How do teachers approach integrating the curriculum when they must cover the standards and prepare students for required testing? The first step is to approach the curriculum in a different way. Educators often look at curriculum as a "bunch of seemingly disparate standards" in different and disconnected subject areas. Indeed, this is the way that most documents are presented. Yet, teachers do notice that there is duplication and/or things missing in the documents. Rethinking the curriculum for integration means seeing the standards in related clusters rather than as separate entities.

THE KNOW/DO/BE FRAMEWORK

The "KDB" framework acts as a 'bridge' that connects subject areas in substantive ways (Drake & Burns, in press). Curriculum planners begin by asking: What is most important to know? To do? To be? The answers determine the "KDB" Bridge. Planners need to scan the standards from involved subject areas both horizontally and vertically to determine the similarities across and through the curriculum. For the "Know," they look for interdisciplinary concepts such as patterns cause and effect, systems, cycles, model, interaction, interdependence or order. It also includes "enduring understandings" (Wiggins & McTighe, 1998)—the things that teachers want students to remember years later. Enduring understandings are generalisations that are interdependent variables in a relationship that are broad, abstract and universal (Erickson, 2001). In practice, Drake finds that enduring understandings are often science-based. Some recent examples developed by local curriculum builders are: "Weather has an effect on ecosystems," "All living things are interdependent" and "Human actions have either positive or negative effects on living things."

The "Do" from the "KDB" Bridge involves interdisciplinary complex performance skills such as communication, problem solving, research, construction and design and interpersonal skills. This allows for the direct teaching of process skills such as in language and math at the same time as one can teach the procedures for the scientific method. These generic skills remain the same from K to 12 but increase in complexity as the students develop. The skills can be found in curriculum documents—although often this requires planners to chunk together standards that represent the various parts of the complex performance.

The "Be" acts as an umbrella for the "Know" and the "Do." Admittedly, the "Be" goes beyond most standards documents that generally avoid any commitment to values. Yet, this framework requires planners to consider how they want students to Be when they are doing whatever they Do with the knowledge they are learning. This moves into the action realm of learning. For example, if students are learning how to be good citizens, then they should demonstrate these behaviors in class (and hopefully outside of class). Typically, planners choose characteristics such as: cooperative, responsible, creative, respectful and being a good citizen. Interestingly, curriculum planners often add environmental stewardship. Although the Be may elude objective assessment, the framework allows planners to move into areas that focus on strategies to act in socially responsible ways.

These clusters revolve around interdisciplinary concepts and skills. The concepts need to be ones that transfer across the disciplines. Examples of such concepts are change, interdependence, conflict, patterns, cause/effect and systems. Similarly, interdisciplinary skills are found in more than one discipline and are complex performances that involve a subset of skills. Examples are research, information management, communication, data management and systems thinking.

SCAN AND CLUSTER

With a KDB framework in hand, curriculum planners can begin the scan and cluster process. This involves a horizontal and vertical scan of the curriculum in order to cluster the standards in meaningful chunks. The horizontal scan involves looking over the standards across the subjects in the grade level being taught. The vertical scan means looking back two or three years and forward one year to see what the students are expected to learn.

Melissa Rubocki (2003) of District School Board of Niagara, Ontario describes the experience as she begins the vertical scan with a grade two and grade three language arts document.

Initially the curriculum seemed daunting. There were numerous standards (learning expectations in Ontario) per grade and subject area. I knew there was no way I could cover every standard. In making vertical curriculum connections I had to start with looking at the overall standards and what was most important to learn.

When starting to plan I chose Language, as it seemed the easiest subject area for me to plan. Language is divided into three areas set out by the Ministry of Education: reading, writing and oral and visual communication. I began by examining the overall standards in both grade two and three in the Ministry documents. As I read through the various standards I realized that many of the skills were similar while the wording was different. As a result, in both grades students were expected to:

1. *read a variety of materials*
2. *read aloud, read independently using reading strategies*
3. *express clear responses to written materials, select material from different sources*
4. *understand the vocabulary and language structures and use conventions of written materials*

In writing, I again started with overall standards that were quite similar for both grades. For example, both grades required students to:

1. *communicate ideas for specific purposes*
2. *organize information*
3. *produce pieces of writing*
4. *spell correctly grade level vocabulary, and use conventions correctly*

In the oral and visual communication strand once again there were commonalities. Students in both grades were expected to:

1. *communicate messages and follow instructions*
2. *listen to discussions and ask questions*
3. *retell stories, talk about characters and situations in stories*
4. *apply the rules for working with others*
5. *create and learn about media works, and use the conventions of oral language*

Although the specific standards varied in each strand in each grade, each grade built on the skills of the grade preceding it.

Now that Melissa looks for meaningful clusters of standards, it is much easier to integrate the curriculum. As she completes a horizontal scan she can see that each subject includes standards for communication skills. This means that she can teach and "cover" some of the communication skills while she is, for example, teaching science or social studies. There are other skills that can be chunked together across and through the curriculum—research skills, for example, are evident in every subject. As she begins to think about integrating curriculum to cover standards, she makes new connections such as using math skills for presenting data for research.

Melissa then looks for interdisciplinary or transferable concepts through and across the curriculum. Such concepts may be obvious, or she may need to create a concept that acts as an umbrella for topics mandated by the curriculum. For example, Melissa finds Habitats and Communities under a category called Life Systems in science. In social studies, Urban and Rural Communities is a mandated topic. Focusing on the interdisciplinary concepts of "community" and "systems," she can develop an integrated science/social studies unit on "Relationships between Communities and Natural Environments." A suitable enduring understanding would be "There are relationships between communities and natural environments."

The scan and cluster process does take a lot of time and thoughtfulness the first time around. But once teachers are familiar with the curriculum document from this perspective, this stage of curriculum design is much quicker and becomes second nature.

AN APPLICATION

The building of integrated curriculum using this method employs backward design (Wiggins & McTighe, 1998) and uses the KDB Bridge as its organizing center. Once the Know, Do and Be are decided, planners determine the culminating activity where students can demonstrate the achievement of the KDB. Guiding questions are created to frame the unit. Finally activities are developed that lead toward the demonstration of the KDB in the culminating activity. In the Appendix there is an example that has been created by Gail Higenell of Brock University. It is intended as an example only and hopefully will shed light on how to apply this framework to other educational levels, contexts and subject areas.

Reflections

The intent of this chapter has been to demonstrate that integrated approaches can work in an era of standards-based curriculum and standardized testing. Although this context of accountability would not likely be the first choice of most educators who favor interdisciplinarity, it seems that the standards do have an important role to play. Viewing standards through a lens of connected clusters allows teachers the opportunity to create curriculum that is relevant in individual contexts. Integrated curriculum created with standards has the potential to be rich, substantive and rigorous. Simultaneously, teachers can demonstrate that they are indeed following current mandates and that their students are succeeding in measurable and traditionally recognized ways. Now integrated approaches can be compared with traditional approaches and therefore can be taken seriously by those who previously dismissed them. This may be the silver lining of the accountability movement—a bridge is slowly, but surely, being built to the mainstream of education.

BIBLIOGRAPHY

Allen Rick. "Collaborative curriculum planning." *Education Update*. 43, no. 3, (2000): 1, 4–5, 6.

Attenborough, Debra and Susan Drake. "Integrated curriculum as a vehicle for teacher transformation." Paper presented at American Educational Research Conference, New Orleans, April, 2001.

Beane, James. *A middle school curriculum: From rhetoric to reality.* Columbus, OH: National Middle School Association, 1993.

Chard, Sylvia. "Project approach; Three phases." http://www. project-approach.com/development/phases.htm (2001).

Curtis, Diane. "The power of projects." *Educational Leadership*. 60, no 1, (2002) 50–53.

Dewey, John. *Experience and education.* New York: Macmillan/Free Press, 1969. (Originally published in 1938).

Drake Susan, M. and Sonja Upton, Ellie Phillips and Melissa Rubocki. "Novice teachers search for accountability through integrating the curriculum." Paper presented at Canadian Society for Studies in Education, Toronto, Ont. June 2002.

Drake Susan M. and Rebecca Burns, Rebecca. *Meeting standards through integrated curriculum.* Alexandria, VA: Association for Supervision and Curriculum Development, in press).

Erickson, Lynne. *Stirring the head, heart and soul: Redefining curriculum and instruction,* 2nd edition, Thousand Oaks, CA: Corwin Press, 2001.

Expeditionary Learning Outward Bound. "Evidence of success." http://www.elob.org/evidence/evidence.html (Nov, 12, 2001).

Gandal Matthew and Jennifer Vranek. Standards: Here today, here tomorrow. *Educational leadership,* 59, 1, (2001) 6–13.

Hargreaves, Andy. "Beyond subjects and standards: a critical review of educational reform." *Ontario ASCD,* (2001) 46–51.

Hartzler, Deborah, H. "A meta-analysis of studies conducted on integrated curriculum programs and their effect on student achievement."

Unpublished Ed.D. dissertation. Indiana University, Bloomington, IN. *Dissertation Abstracts International—A,* 61 (03). P. 865 (2000).

McNeil, L. *Contradictions of school reform: Educational costs of standardized testing.* New York: Routledge/ Falmer, 2000.

Ontario Ministry of Education, *The common curriculum: grades 1–9.* Toronto, ON: Ministry of Education and Training, Government of Ontario, 1993, 1995.

Rubocki, Melissa. "How to Survive a Split Grade: A Teacher's Perspective on Life in a Combined-Grade Classroom." Unpublished Masters of Education project housed at Instructional Resource Centre, Brock University. St. Catharines, ON, Canada (2003).

Vars, Gordon F. News of NACC Members, *The core teacher, 50,* (2000) 3.

Vars, Gordon F. and James Beane. "Integrative curriculum in a standards-based world." *ERIC Digest.* ERIC Clearinghouse on Elementary and Early Child Education, EDO-PS-00-6. (June, 2000): 1.

Wineburg Samuel S. and Pamela L. Grossman. *Interdisciplinary curriculum: challenges to implementation.* (New York: Teachers College Press, 2000).

APPENDIX

Interpretative Trails

An Interdisciplinary Standards Based Service Learning Curriculum for Grade 6 (see Figures 3.1 through 3.5 and Table 3.1).

Step 1: Scan and Cluster of Broad-based Standards

Language Arts

Code	Description of Standard
6e1	Communicate ideas and information for a variety of purposes (to inform, to persuade, to explain) and to specific audiences.
6e3	Organize information to convey a central idea, using well-linked paragraphs.
6e23	Read a variety of fiction and non-fiction materials (eg. Novels, short stories, poetry, myths, articles) for different purposes.
6e50	Express and respond to a range of ideas and opinions concisely, clearly and appropriately.
6e61	Use constructive strategies in small-group discussions (eg. Invite other group members to contribute; ask questions to clarify a point; negotiate to find a basis for agreement).
6e62	Follow up on others' ideas, and recognize the validity of different points of view in group discussions or problem-solving activities.

Math

6m1	Represent, and explore the relationships between, decimals, percents, rates and ratios using concrete materials and drawings.
6m42	Demonstrate an understanding of and ability to apply appropriate metric prefixes in measurement and estimation activities.
6m56	Relate dimensions of rectangles and area to factors and products.

Health

6p16	Perform movement skills in the kind of combinations that are required in a variety of modified games, gymnastics, dance and outdoor pursuits: locomotion/traveling, manipulation and stability.
6P26	Participate on a regular basis in physical activities that maintain or improve physical fitness.

Visual Arts

6a25	Produce two and three-dimensional works of art that communicate a range of ideas for specific purposes and to specific audiences, using a variety of familiar art tools, materials and techniques.

Science

6s1	Demonstrate an understanding of ways in which classification systems are used to understand the diversity of living things and the interrelationships among living things.
6s12	Formulate questions and identify the needs of different types of animals and explore possible answers to these questions and ways of meeting these needs.
6s16	Communicate the procedures and results of investigations for specific purposes and to specific audiences, using media works, oral presentations, written notes and descriptions, charts, graphs and drawings.

Figure 3.1.

Step 2: Web to Identify Potential Clusters of Standards/Content

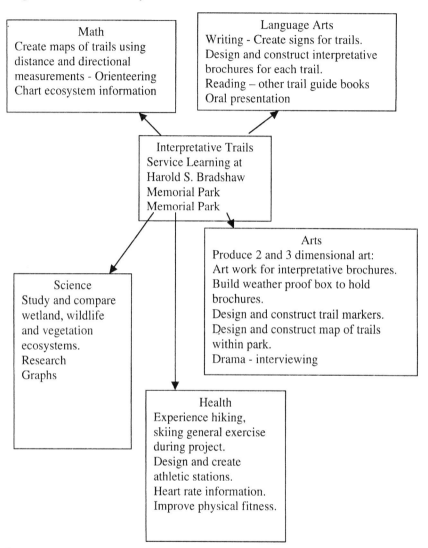

Math
Create maps of trails using distance and directional measurements - Orienteering
Chart ecosystem information

Language Arts
Writing - Create signs for trails.
Design and construct interpretative brochures for each trail.
Reading – other trail guide books
Oral presentation

Interpretative Trails
Service Learning at
Harold S. Bradshaw
Memorial Park
Memorial Park

Arts
Produce 2 and 3 dimensional art:
Art work for interpretative brochures.
Build weather proof box to hold brochures.
Design and construct trail markers.
Design and construct map of trails within park.
Drama - interviewing

Science
Study and compare wetland, wildlife and vegetation ecosystems.
Research
Graphs

Health
Experience hiking, skiing general exercise during project.
Design and create athletic stations.
Heart rate information.
Improve physical fitness.

Figure 3.2.

Step 3: This Step is Optional and Particular to a Service Curriculum

Web of the four cornerstones of Harold S. Bradshaw Memorial Park Project

Preparation		Service
• Contact park Stewardship Committee. • Parents, students and teacher visit site. • Contact Brock University ecology, art and physical education students. • Specific activity preparation. • Involvement in search for funding for implementation of design and transportation.		• Research, design and construct three interpretative trails for park; a hiking nature trail, an athletic trail and a cross country skiing trail.
	Service Learning at Harold S. Bradshaw Memorial Park	
Reflection Ongoing assessment tools: ▪ Portfolio creation ▪ Journal writing ▪ Extensive written critique with revision ▪ Research skills ▪ Small group discussion ▪ Oral presentation techniques ▪ Individual conferencing with students, teacher and parents		**Celebration** Culminating Activity: ➢ Opening of trails ➢ Student presentations ➢ Community and media participation

Figure 3.3.

Step 4: Construct a KNOW/DO/BE Bridge

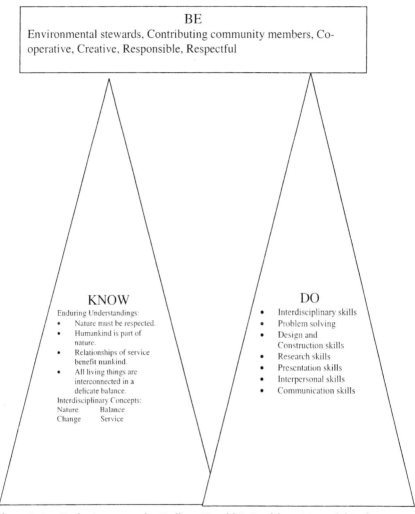

BE
Environmental stewards, Contributing community members, Co-operative, Creative, Responsible, Respectful

KNOW
Enduring Understandings:
- Nature must be respected.
- Humankind is part of nature.
- Relationships of service benefit mankind.
- All living things are interconnected in a delicate balance.

Interdisciplinary Concepts:
Nature   Balance
Change   Service

DO
- Interdisciplinary skills
- Problem solving
- Design and Construction skills
- Research skills
- Presentation skills
- Interpersonal skills
- Communication skills

Figure 3.4.   Topic: Interpretative Trails at Harold S. Bradshaw Memorial Park
Conceptual Themes: Change, Balance, Relationships, Service

Step 5: Culminating Assessment

You agree with community members that Harold S. Bradshaw Memorial Park would provide a greater range of recreational and informative activities with the development of interpretative trails. You are responsible for creating three interpretative trails. Working in small groups over the year you will spend one day a week at the park and be responsible for: (See Table 3.1)

Table 3.1.

Teaching/Learning Experience	Standards	Assessment
Students write an ongoing journal throughout the year that reflects on their experiences in each mini-unit	6e1, 6e50	Ongoing teacher dialogue and assessment
Interactive presentation by St. John's Ambulance covering: a) exercise safety b) safety issues associated with project c) exercise and heart rate	6p10, 6p11, 6p16, 6p17, 6p18, 6p19, 6p23, 6p25, 6p26, 6p31, 6p32, 6p33, 6p34	Holistic teacher observation Self-assessment in journal
Individually practice taking heart rate while standing still and then again after jumping for three minutes. As a group record heart rates in a chart. Monitor your fitness by repeating this exercise on site at the park as a baseline and repeat each month throughout the year and record in a personal journal.		Teacher assessment of journal
In groups research and practice healthy stretching exercises.	6p16, 6p17, 6e23, 6e32 6e50, 6e61, 6e62	Teacher assessment of research Teacher and peer assessment of healthy stretches
In groups research different fitness activities. Perform a variety of these activities and create your own fitness station suitable for training. Create a drawing of station with written instructions. Design a symbol or drawing as a trail marker for the station and explain your work to the class. Present your finished station to the class. As a group pool information into a brochure for athletic training trail.	6p23, 6p24, 6p25, 6a25, 6a26, 6a28, 6a32, 6a33, 6a37, 6a38, 6a39, 6361, 6e62	Self assessment Peer assessment Teacher assessment • diagrams • research (written) • symbols • oral presentation
As a class, create a map of the course of stations. In groups estimate and then measure the distance between each station and record on map. Add directions to the map. Create distance and direction markers for the trail.	6m1, 6m2, 6m3,6m10, 6m42, 6m56, 6m60	Teacher assessment • map • accuracy of distance markers

Working together, develop a brochure for the trail. It should include: a map of the stations showing the distance between each station, a picture of the station and a description of the athletic activity involved and the symbol or marker for the station. Also include a fitness chart for visitors to use. Revise upon assessment. Be prepared to answer questions about the trail at the culminating activity.	6e1, 6e2, 6e3, 6e4, 6e7, 6e8, 6e9, 6e10, 6e11, 6e12, 6e13, 6e14, 6e21, 6e22, 6e49, 6e50, 6e51, 6e52, 6e55	Peer assessment Teacher assessment • brochure • revisions
Each group of students will be given a red plastic squeaky heart. Whenever a student witnesses an outstanding act of service the heart will be given to that student in recognition, for them to pass on as they see fit.	6p34, 6e61, 6362	Peer evaluation

Mini unit: Athletic Training Trail

1. Hiking/nature trail: In a small group, research, study and write about the ecosystem you selected on the trail. Within that ecosystem design and construct directional, distance and points of interest markers. Dialogue with university ecology students regarding your project. Pool the group work to produce a hiking/nature interpretative trail. Create a brochure to describe the trail.
2. Athletic training trail: Your small group is responsible for creating an athletic training station that will allow visitors to perform one activity. Design plans for the construction of the station and write an instructional piece for the activity. Dialogue with university physical education students regarding your project. All of the group work will be pooled to produce an athletic training trail. Create a brochure to describe the trail.
3. Cross-county skiing trail: Your group researches and develops a map of a selected section of a cross-country skiing trail. Determine the difficulty level of your section. Design and construct directional, distance and level of difficulty markers. Pool group work to produce a cross-country skiing trail. Test out the trail by skiing it in the wintertime. Create a brochure to describe the trail.

In June, there will be an official opening of the three trails. Community members and the media will be invited to participate. You will lead tours, present your work and answer questions. There will be an exhibition of the work you have done to complete the trails. A panel of community members (including the family who has donated the land) will assess your work and the quality of the trails.

Step 6: Create guiding questions:

1. How can we learn from nature?
2. How can we be of active service to the community?
3. Why is physical activity important in life?
4. Why is recreation important in life?
5. How are the different ecosystems different from one another? How are they the same?

Step 7: Reclustering of standards to develop mini-units

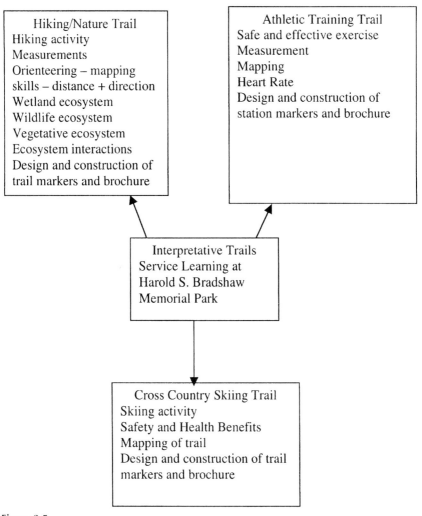

Figure 3.5.

Section Two

IMPLEMENTATION FRAMEWORK

Chapter Four

Reading Across the Curriculum: Supporting The Marginalized Reader

Kathy B. Grant

Reading across content areas, as an integrative approach, deserves special attention. Consciously embedding specific higher level reading skills such as making inferences, identifying key concepts, evaluating author's purpose/ intent and even critical reading across content area classes should be a priority for all teachers. This chapter's focus on marginalized middle school and high school readers, a huge population of students at serious risk of literacy failure, acknowledges the major challenges of creating successful reading experiences for this group. The International Reading Association's Position Statement on Adolescent Literacy (Moore, Bean and Birdyshaw, 1999) strongly recognizes the commitment to active engagement of marginalized readers that must be made by content area teachers.

Clearly, exemplary elementary teachers infuse a love of literacy into their daily teaching repertoires. Pappas, Kiefer and Levstik (1999) describe reading activities and experiences that occur in the integrated elementary language classroom. A sample of these might include reading aloud to students through the use of big books and quality children's literature, storytelling, sustained silent reading, buddy reading, book talks, literature response groups, reading conferences and use of cloze passages (278–284). Although elementary students' struggles with reading are well documented, reading skills development is generally addressed daily in the elementary classroom. However, Unrau (2004) stresses the magnitude of the reading struggles many middle school and high school students experience labeling it a "serious literacy problem."

Some students arrive in middle school and high school unable to read grade-level text fluently or comprehend its meaning. Although most students grasp literal meanings, they have significant difficulties with more complex reading tasks. Teachers work in content area classrooms with students who are reading many grade levels below their age-equivalent classmates. The incidence of struggling readers varies—but they comprise approximately 25% of all middle school and high school students. (311)

The Carnegie Task Force on the Education of Young Adolescents (1989) employed the term "volatile mismatch" to describe the gap existing between the intellectual and affective needs of struggling students and present academic programs (in Ferree 2001). Students perceive they have no stake in the immediate literacy task, they are not shareholders in the overall classroom reading agenda, and they see no value in the information they are expected to consume.

Again compounding the issues of infusing reading into subject areas is the immediacy and priorities of standardized testing in the form of end-of-course evaluations. Yet, is it ethical to ignore the "marginalized reader" (Moje, Young, Readance, Moore 2000, 405) in lieu of the demands of misconstrued accountability? Tatum (2000) found that lower reading achievement is associated with high stakes testing; in fact, a basic skills orientation to obtain minimal reading skills can hinder the reading growth of African American adolescents.

The marginalized reader, according-to Moje et al., (2000) are those students not connected to classroom literacy, who value alternative means of communication such as electronic discourse and may be outside the dominant group based on their race, class, gender or sexual orientation. Frequently language activities in traditional classrooms have no bearing on the real world challenges of the marginalized student. (Knobel, 2001). Because of this marginalization from mainstream traditional classroom literacy or that which is valued by the school district, these students often become struggling readers of classroom materials. Hence, frustrated students and teachers, each valuing literacy from personal perspectives—electronic versus traditional—resist meeting on "neutral communicative grounds."

Stanovich (2000) reiterates that "print is a uniquely rich source of content—providing opportunities for acquiring broad and deep knowledge of the world." (306–7). Electronic informational resources, such as television, radio and the internet lack depth and can be slanted towards majority culture perspectives. Personal experiences can be misleading, and provide only narrow knowledge of the world. (Stanovich 2000, 306–7). Alas, text sources, although essential, can prove immensely frustrating to the marginalized reader. "Written texts have a disembedded quality—readers and writers are frequently unknown to each other—therefore students need to constantly strive to validate the author's message." (Pappas, Kiefer & Levstik 1999, 21). By supplementing difficult textbook materials with lower level readability trade books, students have the opportunity to develop schemas supportive of the reading material. "Adolescents deserve access to a variety of reading material that they can and want to read." (Moore, Bean and Birdyshaw 1999, 4). Resistance to reading lessens when students feel connected to the text source chosen by the teacher.

Furthermore, using culturally relevant reading material aids students in developing a sense of belongingness in the classroom or a feeling of cultural competence. (Ladson-Billings 1995b). To substantiate the disenfranchisement many minority students perceive, a preservice teacher candidate wrote reflectively about her public school experience of "never learning about people like me—having teachers [who] never showed much interest in my culture. Often minority students lack confidence in school because they are intimidated and because they feel their culture is not important." (Littlejohn 2003, 1–2). Clearly, when textual information connects to what students value, a purpose for reading is established.

STUDENT-TEXT INTERACTIONS

For many struggling marginalized students the sheer size of the content area textbook is the first sign of trouble. Students who have traditionally had little reading success view the text with a sense of foreboding and dread. The textbook is not viewed by the marginalized reader as a student-friendly vehicle to enhance learning, a view probably contrary to that held by the teacher. Focusing on the readability of content textbooks is many times an adventure in futility, for students have already come to the decision that the text is overwhelming. Singer (1992) reports that some high school content textbooks may contain over 400 terms in their glossaries. We know the readability alone as a general indicator of a text's difficulty can often hit high school level for selected subject areas and may well reach the college reading level.

How to make the interaction with the text palatable for the reader, or is this possible? In my work with middle school students, I found many struggling readers unable to handle much more than three-quarters of a page of conceptually dense text without reverting back to the beginning of the page searching for meaning. Many savvy middle/high school teachers have come to the harsh realization that the text designated by their school district for utilization in their content area is virtually unusable for the majority of students. Textbook usage remains a necessary evil. However, Nelson-Herber (1978) provides several sound pieces of advice when utilizing content area textbooks.

1. Whenever possible, provide materials containing the essential facts, concepts and values of the subject at varying levels of readability within the reading range of your students.
2. Subject area textbooks are not designed for *independent reading*. To enhance reading comprehension in your subject area, provide instruction which prepares students for the assignment, guides them in their reading and reinforces new ideas through rereading and discussion. (624–625).

The marginalized reader would benefit from instruction in effectively using text patterns to "break down" the reading content into mentally manageable sections. In chunking reading material, discriminating patterns in text, such as cause/effect, comparison/contrast, sequence, listing or description help scaffold student cognition. Students should be taught to recognize and annotate patterns to support sentence and paragraph comprehension. The ability to paraphrase the material in small chunks ensures comprehension. In addition, advance organizers developed by the teacher aid students in making predictions about the content of a chapter, thereby establishing a mindset for learning through this prereading strategy.

Cooperative Learning Groups, as envisioned by Johnson and Johnson (1993) and Smith (1993), are based upon the premise of structuring group goals and activities from consensus of group rules. Utilizing this classroom approach supports the comprehension of the marginalized reader. Difficult reading terminology, concepts and text patterns can be explained student-to-student. Group discussion strengthens the knowledge base of the struggling reader. Smith (1993) compares the benefits of Cooperative Learning Groups over those of traditional learning groups:

1. High positive interdependence—members are responsible for their own and each other's learning
2. Both group and individual accountability—members hold self and other accountable for high quality work
3. Members promote each other's success—doing real work together, helping and supporting other's efforts to learn
4. Teamwork skills are emphasized—leadership shared by all members
5. Group processes quality of work and how effectively members are working together (17).

To alleviate student anxiety and sense of frustration in dealing with textbooks the "Jigsaw" technique (Aronson 1978) has remained a tried and true strategy to develop "students as experts" in their assigned area of the text reading. Vacca & Vacca (1999) describe the Jigsaw strategy as follows:

Jigsaw teaching requires students to specialize in a content area literacy task that contributes to an overall group objective. Jigsaw groups are composed of students divided heterogeneously into three-to six-member teams. Each student becomes an expert on a subtopic of a theme or topic that the class is reading about. Not only is the student accountable for teaching the other members of the group about his or her subtopic, but he or she is also responsible for learning the information other group members provide during jigsaw discussions (226).

The Jigsaw technique is valuable across curricular areas as a group mechanism to increase student acquisition of knowledge.

READING STRATEGIES FOR THE MARGINALIZED READER

Text sources addressing the needs of marginalized readers should, at a minimum, emphasize the following components:

1. The reading selection is of reasonable length for a struggling reader.
2. Readability is at the instructional level; interest level of material is high and engaging for students.

Furthermore, reading strategies across the curriculum should not be limited to only prereading activities, but should encompass the whole instructional framework, including during and postreading activities. The learning structure for across the curriculum reading strategies should provide opportunities for productive cooperative group work.

Making textbook reading palatable by supplementing strategies with related trade books would meet the instructional interests of the marginalized reader. The infusion of trade books across the content area curriculum can not only add to student enjoyment of the subject, but can also enhance schema development. I have found some "gems" in the arena of both fiction and nonfiction trade books and poetry resources which I would highly recommend, some from main line presses, others from regional presses. These valuable text resources with readability levels kind to struggling middle school/high school readers offer alternative sources for students to garner the information necessary for concept attainment, vocabulary development and comprehension. Both narrative and expository selections complementing a technically dense textbook alleviate students' anxieties about "dealing" with a tough textbook.

Critical to success for marginalized readers, different learner response modalities, such as drawing, oral expression, written reaction and drama should be incorporated. The strategies appeal to marginalized readers as bridge-building techniques to understanding difficult content in a safe, risk-free classroom environment. Motivating reluctant readers through high interest trade books or reading selections often opens the door to success for these students.

INTRA-ACT

According to Hoffman (1979), when students engage in the process of valuing as they reflect about what they have read, critical reading becomes imbued with thoughts and feelings. The small group Intra-Act strategy requires students to reflect and react to value statements based on a reading selection from a content textbook, newspaper article, historical document, or short story with a controversial theme (Vacca and Vacca 1999). There are four components to the intra-act strategy:

1. comprehension or understanding the topic under discussion through a sustained discussion of the selection
2. relating or seeking students' personal reactions, impressions and opinions to the material
3. evaluation or either agreeing or disagreeing with declarative statements and in addition, predicting how other group members would respond to the statements
4. reflection with each member revealing how they responded by agreeing or disagreeing with the statements along with revealing their predictions about others' responses

A game sheet for Intra-Act was developed for high schools students based on the Jonathan Kozol excerpt "The Human Cost of an Illiterate Society" (from "Illiterate America," 1985 in Axelrod and Cooper 1993, 310–15). Students determine whether they agree (A) or disagree (D) with the statement presented; in addition, they predict how their teammates will feel about the same statements based on the previous discussion of the selection. They indicate the accuracy of their predictions on the short line below A/D by notating + for correct or − for incorrect as they move into the reflection stage of Intra-Act (seeTable 4.1).

As both a prereading and postreading activity, Intra-Act promotes active debate, enhancing students' ability to anticipate others' reactions to text in a risk-free classroom setting. I have found students joyfully anticipate their involvement with Intra-act, for their opinions are respected yet sometimes contested.

Name _____

Date_____

Total Score_____

Percentage of correct predictions_____

Table 4.1.   Intra-Act

	Jo	Lisa	Rod	Tim
1. Illiteracy in the United States is a nationwide problem, not just an individual one.	A D	A D	A D	A D
2. Aliteracy, or lack of desire to read, can be as big a problem as illiteracy.	A D	A D	A D	A D
3. By providing a solid reading program throughout the school years, illiteracy can be eliminated.	A D	A D	A D	A D

+ : Jo's predictions were correct.
− : Jo's predictions were incorrect.

SUMMARIZATIONS

Friend (2000) describes explicit instruction through summarizing to boost comprehension and retention of new material from a lengthy textbook chapter. Although highlighting and rereading of a text chapter is an inefficient way for most students to process and retain information, it has proven to be the strategy of choice for students. Summarization, according to Friend (2000), has four important components: it is concise, it tells what is critical to the author, it is written in the student's own words and lastly, information is strictly on a "need to know basis" (320). Providing guidelines for students to discover repeated references and fine-tuning generalizations, this strategy can aid in subject area test preparation, writing skills and also enhance confidence that a 20–30 plus page text chapter is approachable. To support struggling readers, summarizations can be completed in a cooperative group setting, with each student contributing one or more sentences to the total summary.

TALKING DRAWINGS

McConnell's (1992/3) Talking Drawings proves a strong strategy for the marginalized reader especially in science. Wood (2001) describes the benefits of this multi-sensory strategy relying strongly on visualization techniques. Students develop mental images at the prereading stage on a selected science topic; next they sketch out their impressions and then discuss and analyze the illustrations with a partner. After reading, the partners redraw the existing picture in correspondence with recently read text information. An optional step includes written response explaining the revisions made to the illustration.

Science terminology can prove dense to struggling readers above and beyond the technical nature of the terms; students often feel overwhelmed by the sheer number of new words presented each class session. For that reason, I recommend *Owls: Whoo are They?* authored by Kila Jarvis and Denver Holt in cooperation with the Owl Research Institute of Missoula Montana (1996) as a great source to use in conjunction with Talking Drawings. This up-to-date and comprehensive book connects concise one page text with pictures or graphics of the magnificent predators. The glossary—Words for the Wise about Owls—compliments the highlighted terminology included throughout the text. The approximate readability range encompasses third to fifth grade, with a high interest level. *Owls: Whoo are They?* is a valuable non-fiction resource for students who are overwhelmed by traditional science textbook terminology concerning owls.

TAB (TALKING ABOUT BOOKS)

The TAB book club approach (Talking about Books in the Content Areas) is a method to integrate reading across the content areas (Wood 2000). By sourcing out trade books that may be at a lower readability level for those struggling readers, and by choosing those that appeal to interests of the marginalized reader, the literacy practitioner may cover several content areas through book discussions. An excellent trade book to employ, *Witness* (2001), by Karen Hesse explores through free verse the induction of the Klux Klux Klan into a small Vermont town in 1924. Hesse unflinchingly unveils the voices of eleven townspeople chronicling their various reactions to racial bigotry and hate. The steps to the TAB book club approach include teacher book selection based on unit of study, explanation of the TAB process, modeling a "think aloud' in response to reading and then assigning students to heterogeneous book club groups. Following teacher guidelines, the students chart the information on specific topics of interest, respond individually in their journals, and then discuss their responses. Lastly, their reaction statements are transferred to the larger TAB chart (see example).

A TAB chart could be used effectively to expose students to pertinent issues and to gauge their reactions to those issues.

Group Reaction Statement: The Klan did not survive or thrive in their promotion of hatred and bigotry in the small Vermont town in the 1920s. The cit-

Table 4.2. TAB Chart

What the author is telling us about the Klux Klux Klan in 1924 in a small town in Vermont.	Our reaction to the organization of the Klux Klux Klan moving into a small town in Vermont.
Political clout	Although the Klan appears powerful and pro-American, in reality the townspeople understand the Klan's real mission—one of promoting hate and discrimination.
Bigotry	*Witness* mentions the Klan as anti-Black, anti-Jewish, and anti-Catholic. They target Leanora Sutter, a young African American girl, for their racial hatred.
Revenge	Johnny Reeves, clergyman, is attracted by the brotherhood of the Klan and ends his life jumping off the arch bridge, citing fear of the Klan.
Safety	Attempted poisoning and shooting by people recruited by the Klan.

izens came to their senses and realized the danger of this organization and realized the lies told to achieve their goals.

Literary Report Cards could well be utilized as a strategy in a response-
centered curriculum (Galda and Cullinan 2002). Students are afforded the opportunity to "feel secure in their responses to literature" (Galda and Cullinan
2002, 316).

LITERATURE CIRCLES

Literature Circles (Daniels 1994), workable from kindergarten through college, promotes student self-selection of trade books. Flexible, dynamic
groups of students share the same interest in a trade book highlighted by the
teacher. The strength of this approach for the marginalized reader is the au-
tonomy to choose a trade book based on interest and hopefully reading com-
patibility. Daniels (1994) describes his version of literature circles:

Literature circles are small, temporary discussion groups who have chosen to read the same story, poem, article or book. While reading each
group-determined portion of the text (either in or outside of class), each
member prepares to take specific responsibility in the upcoming discussion, and everyone comes to the group with notes needed to perform that
job. The circles have regular meetings, with discussion roles rotating each
session. (13).

Students are responsible for preparing for their assigned discussion roles: discussion director, literary luminary, illustrator, connector, summarizer, vocabulary enricher, travel tracer or investigator. Possibilities to expose students to nonfiction selections with ensuing expository-based roles can be added.

The study of historical conflicts can often prove thorny in the secondary history classroom. In addition, the National Council for the Social Studies' delineates time, continuity and change as central themes of study. How everyday people, especially the young have contributed, even in a small way, to the historical mosaic, often proves interesting to reluctant readers.

A notable children's trade book in the field of social studies, *Sky: A True Story of Resistance during World War II*, by Hanneke Ippisch (1996), provides an insider's view of the Dutch resistance movement. The book is greatly aided by historical artifacts—documents, photographs, verses, and newspaper clippings—scaffolding the reader's journey into Holland of the 1940s. Historical empathy developed through memoirs can promote and sustain interest for students, especially knowing Ippisch was only a teenager herself when jailed by the Germans. This inspiring book maintains a reasonable readability throughout, while building suspense about the fate of the Dutch resistance fighters. *Sky: A True Story of Resistance during World War II* would generate awareness about the horrors of war for students while engaged in their designated roles in Literature Circles.

Humor and Exaggeration

Humor and the use of exaggeration in texts can act as motivational devices to claim the attention of even the most reluctant reader. I highly recommend a delightful book of math poems, *Marvelous Math: A Book of Poems* (Hopkins 2001), as a fun source for thought-provoking short poems on math concepts. Humorous poems cover math operations—fractions, math machines—calculators or math anxiety. Utilizing these poems as inspiration for student discussions about upcoming math units or creatively reading these poems focusing on affective response, they provide a safe zone for those students who may struggle with more complex math materials. Reading and reciting short humorous poems can be an excellent prereading strategy for those of us who are "math anxious."

In the arena of word study, *The Weighty Word Book* (Levitt, Burger & Guralnick 1985), takes a humorous twist by using puns to "serve as memory hooks" for comprehending challenging multi-syllabic words. For example, the mnemonic tale for the word "*abasement*" involves a defeated Benjamin Van der Bellows, a worker at a steamship company, who through his own incompetence, is incrementally lowered in office rank from the 40th floor to finally an office in "*a basement*." Humans depicted as anthropomorphized culturally diverse animals add to the charm and interest of this trade book. Utilizing humor to promote vocabulary development can be a potent medium for developing an increased awareness of the English language. Words that marginalized readers would probably skim over in their assigned readings are now linked to memorable moral tales.

LITERARY REPORT CARDS

Pictures, 1918, by Jeanette Ingold, features Asia, an independent young woman who has a fascination with the "new fangled" art of photography. Set in a small Texas town in 1918, Asia struggles with changing family dynamics and a budding maturity. Personal and occupational advancement for women in the early 1990s are themes running through the book that could be integrated into a unit in social studies.

A variation of the Literary Report Card (Johnson and Lewis in Yopp & Yopp 2001) is a postreading strategy for either narrative or expository text exemplifying a strong main character with personal motives and challenges. In the original strategy developed for elementary reading, students were allowed the opportunity to assign grades to characters from the trade book. Personality traits (see Table 4.3), such as courage, patience or persistence could be graded or commented upon by students. Thus students could identify with a character's actions and rate their responses to such actions.

To promote the dramatic, students could then precede to role play character's actions with commentary from the audience on how they might change the characters' reactions to pivotal events. As a collaborative group strategy Literary Report Card encourages students' interpretations of character intentions and ensuing events.

Table 4.3.   Literary Report Card

Character's Actions/Motives: Asia	Grade	Student Comments
Asia accuses Boy Blackwell of setting fire to her rabbit hutch.	A–	Bravery: Asia is brave to do this; Boy Blackwell has a bad temper. She is forthright and courageous because she knows he set the fire that killed her rabbit, Little Bit.
Asia informs Mr. Riley, the owner of the portrait studio, that she will be his apprentice.	B+	Determination: Women at that time in the early 1900s did not work outside the home; besides Asia was only a teenager. Asia was determined to learn photography. She might have been too pushy.

CLOSING CONCERNS FOR MARGINALIZED READERS

In my literacy consulting work with teachers of marginalized middle school/high school readers, a growing sense of their desperation is evident, especially in states with high-stakes testing accountability. Teachers reason that text selections should be at a grade-level readability to prepare students for end-of-year testing and graduation requirements. They are deeply concerned that many students cannot grasp the reading material presented and feel they are losing their attention in classrooms. Secondary teachers search, often in vain, for appropriate content area reading level selections—as low as third or fourth grade—to support marginalized readers. Yet, teachers remain unacquainted with the cadre of reading strategies and trade books to revitalize reading in their content classrooms.

However, the advice I continue to give reinforces the gradual scaffolding of reading material to meet the literacy needs of the marginalized reader, coupled with a strong effort to develop content knowledge. Implementing reading strategies across all curricular areas—science, math, social studies, and the language arts—ensures the greatest chance of success for the marginalized reader. Support across the instructional framework—prereading, during reading and post- reading activities—for the struggling reader is essential. Teachers networking to locate high interest, low readability trade books and then designing appropriate literacy strategies to accompany the book should be an integral part of every content classroom.

BIBLIOGRAPHY

Aaronson, Elliot. *The Jigsaw Classroom.* Thousand Oaks, CA: Sage, 1978.

Axelrod, Rise B. and Cooper, Charles R. *Reading Critically, Writing Well: A Reader and Guide (third edition).* New York: St. Martin's Press, 1993.

Daniels, Harvey. *Literature Circles: Voice and Choice in the Student-Centered Classroom.* York, ME: Stenhouse Publishers, 1994.

Ferree, Angela. "Soaps and Suspicious Activity: Dramatic Experiences in British Classrooms." *Journal of Adolescent and Adult Literacy,* 45, (2002):16–23.

Galda, Lee and Cullinan, Bernice E. *Literature and the Child.* Belmont, CA: Wadsworth/Thompson Learning, 2002.

Hesse, Karen. *Witness.* New York: Scholastic, Inc. 2001.

Hoffman, James V. "The Intra-Act Procedure for Critical Thinking." *Journal of Reading,* 22, (1979): 605–8.

Hopkins, Lee Bennett. *Marvelous Math: A Book of Poems.* New York: Aladdin Paperbacks, 2001.

Ingold, Jeanette. *Pictures, 1918.* New York: Puffin Books, 1998.

Ippisch, Hanneke. *Sky: A True Story of Resistance during World War II.* New York: Simon and Schuster Publishing, 1996.

Jarvis, Kila and Holt, Denver. *Owls: Whoo are They?* Missoula, MT: Mountain Press Publishing Co., 1996.

Knobel, Michele. "'I'm Not a Pencil Man.' How One Student Challenges our Notions of 'Literacy' Failure in School." *Journal of Adolescent and Adult Literacy, 44*, (2001): 404–14.

Kozol, Jonathan. "The Human Cost of an Illiterate Society." from *Illiterate America.* New York: Bantam Doubleday Dell Publishing Group, Inc., 1985.

Ladson-Billings, Gloria. "Towards a Theory of Culturally Relevant Pedagogy." *American Educational Research Journal, 32*, (1995b): 465–91.

Levitt, Paul M., Burger, Douglas A., and Guralnick, Elissa S. *The Weighty Word Book.* Boulder, CO: Manuscripts Ltd., 1985.

Littlejohn, Tandice. *Preservice Teacher Reflection on Teaching Social Studies.* Winston-Salem State University School of Education, 2003.

Moje, Elizabeth Birr, Young, Jospehine Peyton, Readance, John E., and Moore, David W. "Reinventing Adolescent Literacy for New Times: Perennial and Millennial Issues." *Journal of Adolescent and Adult Literacy, 43*, (2000): 400–10.

Moore, David W., Bean, Thomas W., Birdyshaw, Deanna, and Rycik, James A. *Adolescent Literacy: A Position Statement.* Newark, DE: International Reading Association. (1999).

National Council for the Social Studies. *http://www.ncss.org.* (5 Nov. 2003).

Nelson-Herber, Joan. "Readability: Some Cautions for the Content Area Teacher." *Journal of Reading, 21.* (1978): 620–25.

Pappas, Christine C., Kiefer, Barbara Z., & Levstik, Linda S. *An Integrated Language Perspective in the Elementary School.* New York: Longman, 1999.

Smith, Karl A., Johnson, David W., & Johnson, Roger T. "Cooperation in the College Classroom," from *Active Learning: Cooperation in the College Classroom.* Edina: MN: Interaction Book Co, 1991.

Stanovich, Keith E. *Progress in Understanding Reading: Scientific Foundations and New Frontiers.* New York: The Guilford Press, 2000.

Unrau, Norman. *Content Area Reading and Writing: Fostering Literacies in Middle and High School Cultures.* Upper Saddle River, NJ: Pearson Merrill Prentice Hall, 2004.

Vacca Richard T. and Vacca, JoAnne L. *Content Area Reading: Literacy and Learning Across the Curriculum.* New York: Longman, 1999.

Wood, Karen D. *Literacy Strategies Across the Subject Areas.* Boston: Allyn and Bacon, 2001.

Wood, Karen D. and Harmon, Janis. *Strategies for Integrating Reading and Writing in Middle and High School Classrooms.* Westerville, OH: National Middle School Association, 2001.

Yopp, Ruth H., and Yopp, Hallie K. *Literature-Based Reading Activities.* Boston; Allyn and Bacon, 2001.

Chapter Five

Integrating Technology And The Internet In Middle School Classrooms

Alice S. Etim

INTRODUCTION

Technology has become an integral part of most of our every day living. Every industry today depends on computer technology to run their affairs. Schools and educators need access to computers and the Internet to effectively integrate technology into instruction. An integrative approach to delivering instruction is gaining ground and acceptance in schools since it allows student-centered learning. The National Educational Technology Standards for Teachers (2002) explains that teaching in all settings should encompass student-centered approaches to learning. Technology therefore, should not be used only as a tool for demonstration, such as an electronic overhead projector but should be integrated into the learning process.

Integrating computer technology into the middle level classrooms started in the last decade and with the Internet boom, it is gaining momentum in recent times. However, not every school or teacher is having a full awareness and exposure to technology integration in the classroom. The National Middle School Association Research #19 [Online] gives this summary on technology impact to our schools and indicates the need to reflect and consider research on technology impact to middle level student achievement.

> The potential impact of new technologies in our schools is beyond measure. The last decade began with minimal integration of technology in classrooms and ended with entire curricular units taking place online. No one could have predicted the emergence of the Internet as such a powerful tool for education and society as a whole. With the technology revolution taking place, now is an opportune time to reflect and consider research on what impact technology has on middle level students' success and achievement.

The objective of this chapter is to review and discuss the following:

1. Reasons to integrate technology and the Internet in middle school classrooms.
2. The Internet resources available to help teachers in technology integration.
3. How a technology tool can be integrated into instruction that effectively allows the coverage in Science, Mathematics, Language Arts, Social Studies and Health/Physical Education through a unit in Nutrition.

Reasons To Integrate Technology And The Internet In Middle School Classrooms

Milken Exchange on Educational Technology (1998) states that: Technology

i. Accelerates, enriches and deepens basic skills
2. Motivates and engages children in learning
3. Helps relate academics to the practices of today's workforce
4. Strengthens teaching
5. Contributes to change in schools
6. Connects schools to the world
7. Increases economic viability of tomorrow's workers

The workplace is computerized and almost all industries today use the computer and Internet technology to carry out their daily operations. Contents, standards and curriculum resources in use for educating middle school students need to have technology integration so that the students are adequately prepared for the next level of their education and transition into the workplace.

Technology integration in instruction brings about a positive effect on student achievement and performance. Studies by Kulik (1994) and Mann et al (1999) support the interrelationship between technology use and non-cognitive but empowering effects. Technology application has also been found to support higher order thinking (Means, Blando, Olson, Middleton, Morocco, Remz and Zorfass, 1993) and Gahala points out that technology use promotes engaged learning (2001). There is also abundant research supporting a positive relationship between technology and student achievement at the middle level of education (Follansbee et al, 1997; Wenglinsky, 1998; Middleton & Murray, 1999). Cradler and Bridgforth (1996) in a comparable research on technology and learning maintained that technology is related to an increase in student performance when interactivity and other significant aspects of instructional design are applied to its use including a planned integration of technology in education.

However, while some communities are moving quickly to help their schools integrate technology in their classrooms, some are lagging behind. Less affluent communities and their schools are facing a huge gap in technology integration and a "digital divide." Teachers in these schools have a limited exposure to technology and often lack the skills or resources to implement technology or to integrate it in their instruction.

The National Center for Education Statistics (2000) found that teachers use of the computer or the Internet "for instructional purposes was related to their training and preparation and their work environments." Teachers used the computer or the Internet to create instructional materials, gather information for their lesson planning and communicate with colleagues. Teachers also frequently assigned students to use the computer and the Internet for research and solving problems and analyzing data. However, teachers used these technologies "less frequently for such tasks as accessing research, best practices and model lesson plans."

The U.S. Department of Commerce report (1998) showed that although more Americans now own computers, certain groups are still less likely to have computers or online access. Lack of such access to technology and the Internet affects the ability of children from such households to enhance their learning process with educational software. Adults are less likely to tap into valuable technology skills, and families are less likely to benefit from online connections and resources including access to important health, civic and school information.

A similar study by the U.S. Department of Education highlights a "digital divide" in our nation's schools, with children attending high poverty schools less likely to have access to computers, the Internet or high quality educational technology programs. Teachers in high poverty schools have fewer advanced degrees, lack certification and core skills including technology integration skills (Barth, 2000; Darling Hammond, 2000; Knapp & Shields, 1995). Students' performance and achievement in standardized tests in the high poverty schools can therefore be linked to their teacher quality. The Digital Divide Network revealed the following statistics in computer use in the U.S. as of 2000: (www.digitalnetwork.org/content/stories/index.cfm?key=168).

1. The United States of America had more computers than the rest of the world.
2. 51% of all U.S. homes had computers.
3. 86.3% of households earning $75,000 and above per year had Internet access compared to 12.7% of households earning less than $15,000 per year.

4. White (46.1%) and Asian American and pacific Islander (56.8%) households continued to have Internet access at levels more than double those
   of Black (23.5%) and Hispanic (23.6%) households.

According to Larry Irving, the digital divide "is now one of America's
leading economic and civic rights issues, and we have to take concrete steps
to redress the gap between the information haves and haves not." *Digital Divide Network Falling Through the Net, a Report on the Reason for Concern
and Optimism.* www.digitalnetwork.org/content/stories/index.cfm?key=168.

The integration of computer and Internet technology in instruction will be
a vital tool to achieving the objectives of the *No Child Left Behind* Act of
2002. President George W. Bush on January 8, 2002 signed the *No Child Left
Behind* act which gives schools ground breaking educational reform. One of
the key ideals of this Act is stronger accountability for results:

> *No Child Left Behind* is designed to change the culture of America's schools by
> closing the achievement gap, offering more flexibility, giving parents more op-
> tions, and teaching students based on what works.

Under the act's accountability provisions, states must describe how they
will close the achievement gap and make sure all students, including those
who are disadvantaged, achieve academic proficiency. They must produce
annual state and school district report cards that inform parents and communities about state and school progress. Schools that do not make progress
must provide supplemental services, such as free tutoring or after-school as-
sistance; take corrective actions; and, if still not making adequate yearly
progress after five years, make dramatic changes to the way the school is run.
[Online] Available: http://www.ed.gov/nclb/accountability/index.html?src=ov.

This proposition can effectively be implemented by first reviewing the dis-
parities in computer and the Internet usage among the rich and the poor.
Schools serving predominantly low-income children tend to have some computers that may be connected to the Internet. However, such computing facilities are few, old and less functional. The Future of Children [Online] agree
with this position by stating that schools that serve low income children have
few computers in each classroom and offer fewer experiences using computers to create presentations and analyze information compared with schools
serving higher income children.

Computer technology and the Internet are essential for learning. Computers are powerful tools for teaching, research and learning. The use of computer technology and Internet tools will continue to impact learning in positive ways and help to make learning more engaging, address the needs of the

individual learner, provide access to a wealth of information and encourage students to explore and create. For computers to be fully integrated into instruction and learning, the following important factors need to be addressed:

1. Professional development of teachers beginning with simple classes such as Introduction to computers and the Internet, Web Design and Development courses that will allow teachers to develop their Web pages, integrate such Web pages into teaching and place home work/classroom assignments for students.
2. A technology plan in place in the School's Curriculum including guidelines for implementing such a plan.
3. Schools should have technology centers or computers in their classrooms that provide access to computer training and the use of the Internet for integrated teaching.
4. Positive attention and reinforcements for teachers who embrace technology integration in their classrooms.

The last point, positive attention for teachers who embrace technology integration in their classrooms needs to be expanded and substantiated. Byrom et al (2001) provides some examples on how to provide positive reinforcements for teachers who embrace technology. One such example is that school districts award credit to teachers who complete technology and Internet workshops and hand in their lesson plans integrating the new teaching strategy or application for their classrooms.

THE INTERNET RESOURCES AVAILABLE TO HELP TEACHERS IN TECHNOLOGY INTEGRATION ASYNCHRONOUS AND SYNCHRONOUS COMMUNICATION TOOLS

There are two forms of communication that are possible using the Internet—Asynchronous and Synchronous Communication. An example of asynchronous communication is e-mail. Teachers can write one e-mail and mass mail it to the class. For example, a class assignment or a project's detail instructions may be sent to the students at the end of the teacher's work day. The teacher uses the class roll to create a group list. When sending the e-mail, the teacher addresses it to the group list and includes the relevant subject heading and attachment (if applicable). The students will each access their mail box during their next class period and review the e-mail, send responses or start planning their work before the lesson starts. The teacher can allot the first ten minutes or twenty minutes (if block schedule) for students to access the assignments the teacher sent to them by e-mail. This could be a useful time of preparation for the task of the day.

· The teacher can use e-mail as a good tool of exchanging information among learners and fellow educators. E-mail is a very convenient tool because it uses asynchronous communication or person-to-person written communication. The message is written at a person's convenience and sent out. The recipients get the message when they access their mail box and act on the message at their convenience. In addition to using e-mail to communicate with learners, the Heartland Technology Team [Online] lists the things teachers can use e-mail for:

1. Communicate with colleagues and family members who have e-mail
2. Collaborate with groups of people with similar interests
3. Subscribe to other electronic services
4. Get answers to technical questions
5. Send files to anyone with e-mail
6. Participate in on-line projects
7. Conduct pen-pal (key-pal) mail exchanges with remote classrooms

Synchronous communication on the other hand is real-time written text or video communication. Examples of synchronous communication tools currently available today are chat room and video conferencing. Synchronous communication tools can be used by teachers if their school systems have set up such facilities for them.

Web Sites with useful resources on technology integration in classrooms

1. Best Practices of Technology Integration in Michigan: http://www.remc11 .k12.mi.us/bstpract/. This site has sample lesson plans in all subject areas written by teachers actively practicing technology integration in their classrooms.
2. Technology Integration: http://www.lburkhart.com/. This site provides information about using the Internet in the classroom. The site also has a wealth of information on search tools for students, Web Quests, references, directions and handout preparations.
3. Integrating Technology: http://www.awesomelibrary.org/Classroom/Technology/Integrating_Technology/Integrating_Technology.html. This site has integrating the Internet in classrooms, Math lessons and creative writing in a "world" classroom.
4. Integrating Technology in the Classroom: http://www.wtvi.com/teks/. Reference this site for articles on current technologies applicable to the classroom, handouts and materials.

5. classrooms@work/tools@hand: http://www.netc.org/classrooms@work/ references/howto.html. Use this site to review virtual classrooms. It has classroom models of technology integration for teacher professional development.
6. Technology Integration: http://www.education-world.com/a_tech/. This site has articles for the teacher needing to learn about technology integration, tutorials, distance learning and projects and granting opportunities.

Lesson plan examples: Integrating technology with other school subjects on the theme of Nutrition

Lesson Topic: Nutrition
Grade Range: 7 and 8

For an integrated theme on nutrition, lesson objectives will include:
1. Discussion on healthy living
2. Using the food pyramid to list types of healthy foods
3. Graph weight loss for subjects participating in a cardiovascular study
4. List and discuss diseases caused by non-healthy living
5. Using the Internet to research and produce a paper on a disease afflicting a group of people

A Sample Lesson Plan #1

Topic: Food Pyramid
Integration: Science, Technology and Language Arts
Resources: Internet Reference—The Food Guide Pyramid
http://www.pueblo.gsa.gov/cic_text/food/food-pyramid/main.htm
Text References: *Foods Power* by Sid Kirchheimer, AARP Magazine, September/October 2003, pp. 60–64.
Health Media of America (1986), *Children, Adolescents, and Nutrition*, pp. 21–38.

Focus And Review

Students will write on the prompt: "Write about the five things you and your family members can do to live healthily."
    Students write in their journals for five minutes and a brief discussion follows.

Table 5.1.

Activity	Description	Materials/Supplies	Time
1. Focus and Review	(Journal) Discussion on healthy living		8 minutes 3 minutes
2. Objectives	Students will use the Food Pyramid to list and discuss healthy foods	LCD Projector, Teacher Notes	
3. Teacher Input	Power Point presentation on Food Pyramid	Computer, LCD Projector, Web Page, Handouts	17 minutes
4. Guided practice	Food Pyramid handouts to list food types for each food group	Worksheets	10 minutes
5. Independence Practice	Students read short article on Foods and place each in a Food Pyramid	Worksheets	12 minutes
6. Closure	Review Food Pyramid		3 minutes

OBJECTIVE

Students use the Food Pyramid to list, discuss and place different types of foods in their respective food groups.

TEACHER INPUT

The teacher gives a Power Point presentation on Food Pyramid incorporating into the discussion the Web Page contents and the text materials. The trend of the discussion is reviewed briefly in the following paragraph:

1. One of the ways to help adolescents stay healthy is to feed them with nutritive foods that are high in fiber, vitamins and minerals.
2. Fruits such as apples, bananas, grapes, oranges, grapefruits, melon, avocado, pears and other forms of pear fruits.
3. Vegetables such as tomatoes, broccoli, cauliflower, carrots, string beans and spinach.
4. Beans such as black beans, lima beans, pinto beans
5. Nuts and nut spreads—peanut butter, peanuts, cashew nuts, pecans and almonds

These foods are high in fiber. Research shows that foods with high fiber content provide health benefits such as reducing bad cholesterol and improving glucose levels in the blood. This is good prevention for health risks and diseases such as obesity, high blood pressure and diabetes. Schools should incorporate these foods into the school menus and finds ways for the FDA to require restaurants to put nutrition information on menus. (Kirchheimer, 2003 and *The Journal of the American Medical Association,* November 2002).

GUIDED PRACTICE

Provide students with Food Pyramid handouts to list food types for each food group.

Independent Practice

Students read short article on Foods and place each in a Food Pyramid.

CLOSURE

The teacher provides a quick review on the Food Pyramid and uses "Exit Slips" to finish the lesson and dismiss the students.

Integration

The lesson has integrated Science concepts (nutrition) with Language Arts (reading of short articles and using of cognitive skills). The lesson also integrated technology and the Internet through the teacher use of Web Page on Food Pyramid and Power Point presentation.

A Sample Lesson Plan #2

Topic: Graph calories dispensed for subjects participating in cardiovascular study/activities.

Integration: Science, Technology, Language Arts, Mathematics and Health/Physical Education

Resources: Internet Reference — http://www.truestarhealth.com/tour/ rp_exercise.asp; http://www.truestarhealth.com/MembersKids/index.asp? Code=google.

Table 5.2.

Activity	Description	Materials/Supplies	Time
1. Focus and Review	Students list the foods they ate earlier in the day and their position in the Food Pyramid	Food Pyramid handouts, students notebooks	6 minutes
2. Objectives	Students will draw graphs of calories dispensed using data obtained from cardiovascular study/activities.	LCD Projector, Teacher notes	3 minutes
3. Teacher Input	Review exercises and activities that help dispense calories, types of graphs, present students with data to use for graphs	Computer, LCD Projector, Web Page, CALObrator	19 minutes
4. Guided practice	Students are helped to graph data given	Worksheets	10 minutes
5. Independent Practice	Students go to URL presented to generate data using cycling at different pace in groups; then they graph data generated	Web Page (Resource URL),students notebooks	12 minutes
6. Closure	Activities that result in high calories dispensed and why?	Student notebooks	3 minutes

FOCUS AND REVIEW

Students list the foods they ate earlier in the day and attempt to place such in the Food Pyramid. Students gain understanding on balanced diet through this exercise.

Objectives

Students will draw graphs of calories dispensed using data obtained from cardiovascular study/activity. Students learn the importance of limiting "empty calories" intake (Ortiz, 2004, junk foods and soft drinks have what many nutritionists call "empty calories"). A CALObrator (Energy Expenditure Analyzer) is used to determine the calories dispended by subjects in a cardiovascular activity such as walking, jogging and cycling.

TEACHER INPUT

The teacher reviews with the students exercises such as walking, jogging, cycling and sports. Each activity helps to dispense calories which may lead to weight loss and fitness. The teacher also reviews types of graphs and presents students with data to use for graphs. A sample data shown below is used. Students plot Type of Exercise against Calories Dispensed.

GUIDED PRACTICE

The teacher works with the students to help them graph the data presented to them using a bar graph.

INDEPENDENT PRACTICE

Students use the resource URL to generate data using a cycling exercise done at different pace. Activity is done in groups of threes and students graph the data generated independently.

Closure

The teacher provides closure using a question prompt to relate energy level involved in an activity and the calories dispensed.

Table 5.3.

Age/Sex/Weight	Type of Exercise	Calories Dispensed	Time (Duration of Activity)
25yrs/Male/160 lb	Walking, 2.0 mph, level, slow pace	200 Calories	30 minutes
25yrs/Male/160 lb	Walking, 3.0 mph, level, moderate pace, firm surface	280 Calories	30 minutes
25yrs/Male/160 lb	Walking, 3.5 mph, level, brisk	320 Calories	30 minutes
25yrs/Male/160 lb	Jog/walk combination (jogging component of less than 10 minutes)	480 Calories	30 minutes
25yrs/Male/160 lb	Running, 10 mph (6 min/mile)	1280 Calories	30 minutes

CONCLUSION

For technology to make a lasting impact, educators must use a variety of teaching and learning approaches and integrate technology with other subjects in their classroom instruction. Teachers need to be given the resources to participate and learn in using technology and the Internet in teaching their specific subjects. Technology implementation should start at the core of curriculum planning and professional development opportunities be made available weekly to teachers on using technology and the Internet in their classroom.

BIBLIOGRAPHY

Awesome Library. "Integrating Technology" <http://www.awesomelibrary.org/Classroom/Technology/Integrating Technology/Integrating_Technology.html> (18 January 2004).

Becker, Henry. "Internet Use by Teachers" http://www.crito.uci.edu/TLC/FINDINGS/internet-use/startpage.htm (15 January 2004).

Berrien County Intermediate School District "Best Practices of Technology Integration" <http://www.remc11.k12.mi.us/bstpract/> (January 15, 2004).

Burkhart, Linda J. "Technology Integration" <http://www.lburkhart.com/> (12 January 2004).

Byrom, Elizabeth, Margaret Bingham (2001). Factors Influencing the Effective Use of Technology for Teaching and Learning: Lessons Learned from the SEIR.TEC Intensive Site Schools. SERVE in association with UNC, Greensboro, NC. 9–13.

Education World "Technology Integration" <http://www.educationworld.com/a_tech/> (15 January 2004).

Follansbee, S., Hughes, R., Pisha, B. & Stahl, S. Can online communications improve student performance? Results of a controlled study. *ERS Spectrum*, 15 (1), 15–26, 1997.

Fryer, Wesley A. "Integrating Technology in the classroom" <http://www.wtvi.com/teks/> (19 January 2004).

Gahala, Jan. "Critical Issues: Promoting Technology Use in Schools" http://www.ncrel.org/sdrs/areas/issues/methods/technlgy/te200.htm (19 January 2004).

Honey, M., & Henriquez, A. Union city interactive multimedia education trial: 1993–1995 summary report. CCT reports, Issue No. 3, New York, NY: Center for Children and Technology, 1996.

Kulik, J. Meta, Analytic studies of findings on computer-based instruction. In E.B. Baker and H. F. O'Neil Jr. (Eds.). *Technology assessment in education and training*. Hillsdale, NJ: Lawrence Eribaum. 1994.

Means, B., Blando, J., Olson, K., Middleton, T., Morocco, C., Remz, A. & Zorfass, J. (1993). *Using technology to support education reform*. Washington, DC: U.S. Department of Education. http://www.ed.gov/pubs/EdReformStudies/TechReforms (December 15, 2003).

Mann, D., Shkeshaft, C., Becker, J. & Kottkamp, R. *West Virginia's basic skills/computer education program: An analysis of student achievement.* Santa Monica, CA: Milken Family Foundation, 1999.

Milken Exchange on Educational Technology (1998). *Technology in Schools: Seven Dimensions for Gauging Progress.* [Online]. Available: http://www.milkenexchange .org/policy/sevendimensions.pdf (January 7, 2004).

National Center for Education Statistics (NCES). (2002). *Teachers' Tools for the 21st Century: A Report on Teachers' Use of Technology.* [Online]. Available: http://nces .ed.gov/pubsearch/pubsinfo.asp?pubid=2000102 (January 5, 2004).

National Educational Technology Standards for Teachers (2002). *Preparing Teachers to Use Technology,* PBS.org/TeacherLine, 22.

NMSA Research Summary #19: *What impact does the use of technology have on middle level education, specifically student achievement?* [Online]. Available: http://www.nmsa.org/research/ressum19.htm (December 17, 2003).

Northwest Educational Technology Consortium "classrooms@work tools@hand" <http://www.netc.org/classrooms@work/> (18 January 2004).

Ortiz, Deborah "Food Fight: Should Schools Keep Kids From Eating Junk?" *Smart Money* Vol. XIII, No. II (February 2004): 56.

Sivin-Kachala, J. (1998). *Report of the effectiveness of technology in schools, 1990–1997.* Washington, DC: Software Publisher's Association.

The Future of Children (Online). *Children and Computer Technology.* Available: http://www.futureofchildren.org/usr_doc/vol10n2ES%2E.pdf.

U.S. Department of Commerce report (1998). *Falling through the Net II: New Data on the Digital Divide.* [Online]. Available: http://www.ed.gov/Technology/digdiv .html.

Wenglinsky, H. (1998). Does it compute? The relationship between educational technology and student achievement in mathematics. Princeton, NJ: ETS Policy Information Center-Research Division.

Chapter Six

Thinking Strategically About Technology In The Middle School Classroom

Julie Edmunds and Nita Matzen

Computers are more common in schools now than ever before. Along with an increased presence of technology comes an increased expectation that teachers will use the technology in their classroom to support student learning. In this chapter, we share some of the recent literature about using technology to enhance student learning. We then give teachers a way to think about how to use technology to maximum effect in the classroom and provide a sample unit plan that incorporates technology appropriately and effectively.

Researchers suggest that students can use technology in the classroom in two main ways: to "learn *from*" and to "learn *with*". Learning *from* technology means that it is the technology itself that provides the content. Many teachers begin using technology this way, with Integrated Learning Systems, learning games or drill and practice type software. Although there is a role for this type of technology use, research suggests that learning with technology is potentially much more powerful. Learning *with* technology means that the use of technology is tied to the curriculum goals teachers have for their students. Technology is used in open-ended and productive ways and is one tool among many. How can teachers help their students learn with technology?

In our work helping teachers integrate technology effectively in the classroom, we have found that the key to learning with technology is to have teachers think strategically about its use. Learning with technology requires that the technology use must be tied to teachers' learning goals. Thus, to incorporate technology effectively, teachers must start with their learning goals. Then, they identify the activities and strategies to meet those goals and the resources they will use. Since learning with technology also means that technology is one resource to use, teachers must be able to identify the places where technology can effectively and appropriately support teachers' learning goals. To help teachers think strategically about the best ways to use technology, we recommend a three-step process: first, identify learning goals; second, determine the activities and practices that achieve these learning goals; and, third, determine how technology can help achieve those learning goals. We consider each of these steps in the strategic use of technology and then describe the thought process in which a teacher would engage as she plans a unit using these three steps.

Step 1: Identify Learning Goals

Virtually all research on lesson planning says that the first step must revolve around establishing learning goals and objectives for the students. In many cases, these goals and objectives are established by state or district curriculum standards. Research also suggests that students do better when they are allowed input into the goal setting process. Whatever the origin of the goals and objectives, a teacher cannot plan a lesson or unit without first considering them.

Step 2: Determine Activities And Practices To Help Achieve The Learning Goals

Once the learning goals are in place, a teacher needs to consider the activities in which her students engage to meet those learning goals. There should be a variety of activities that permit students to actively engage in and work with the concepts and skills to be learned. Effective teachers use different approaches that are appropriate for meeting the learning goals.

In these first two steps, which are described only briefly here but which both have an extensive research base, we have not yet mentioned technology. This does not mean that teachers are not thinking about using technology in their classroom; they may, in fact, have ideas in the back of their mind. To truly incorporate technology effectively, however, teachers need to make some key instructional decisions before they are able to make a strategic decision about the most appropriate use of technology in their classroom. In the past, teachers often started with the technology itself and tried to fit it into the instructional process. The result of starting with technology meant that it was often an isolated activity—"computer time." By flipping this decision process upside down and considering the technology after making other instructional decisions, we place technology in its correct place: as one resource, albeit an incredibly powerful resource, among many to help students learn. If teachers already know their learning goals and the overall activities they want to use, they can then decide the best role for technology.

Step 3: Determine How Technology Can Help Achieve Those Learning Goals

We have one additional consideration before being able to implement Step 3: the possible role that technology can play in instruction. Research suggests that the best roles for technology in instruction revolve around open-ended, productive uses, including data analysis and presentation, communication and research. (Roschelle et al. 2000) This is consistent with how people use technology in the real world. For example, if you ask colleagues and friends how they use technology, you may get answers similar to ones we did:

- "I used the Internet to find out if the reindeer in the poem 'The Night Before Christmas' is really Donner or Donder since I've seen it both ways." (It's Donder.)
- "I use e-mail to cut down on my long-distance phone bill."
- "I use it for everything in my workday, for written communication, documentation, record-keeping, collaboration; virtually every task that is a part of my workday involves technology in some way."
- "I use it for banking, I have to check it everyday. If I don't, I'm in trouble."
- "I use the computer to track financial information for our company."
- "I use the mouse to click on things when I play a game."

We can group these answers in different ways but when we look at the purpose underlying people's use of technology, they tend to fall into certain categories. People use technology:

- to gain access to information, whether it is an account balance or the name of a reindeer in a poem;
- to make sense of information (analyze data, etc). This could be tracking financial information, analyzing survey results, or record keeping.
- to present and share information. People write reports, present information to clients, set up websites to propagate their viewpoints, etc.
- to communicate with others. This is probably one of the most powerful uses in people's personal and work lives through e-mailing family or friends, receiving pictures instantly or facilitating communication across international borders.
- for entertainment. One of the most common uses of technology, this includes playing games, listening to music or watching movies.

Thus, people use technology in a variety of ways because technology helps them accomplish the purposes described above more easily or more effectively. It makes sense, then, that these purposes could create a valid framework for thinking about technology use in the classroom. These "real-world" uses of technology easily convert to broad instructional purposes focused on the processes inherent in working with information. Are there times where students need to gain access to information? To make sense of information? Will they have to present and share information? Will they have to communicate with other people? The answer to these questions is, of course, yes.

The last use of technology mentioned above, for entertainment, might strike some teachers as frivolous. Yet, when we consider the key aspect of motivation in encouraging students to learn, the fact that many students will view using technology as entertaining can help teachers engage their students. Although we do not include motivation in our framework, we do suggest that the motivational value of technology is something that should remain in the back of teachers' minds, even as they consider the instructional purposes of its use.

In Table 6.1, these real-world categories described above form a framework for the instructional purposes behind the use of technology. The table

Table 6.1.   Instructional Purposes behind the Use of Technology

Gain Access to Information		
	Internet	Research on Topics
	Digital microscope	Collecting data
	Handheld computers with probes	Collecting data for science experiments
	Databases	Locating information
	Make sense of information	Graphic Organizer Software
	Brainstorming, organizing, information, planning, writing, categorizing and classifying information in stores or articles	
	Spreadsheets	Analyzing numbers, graphical representation
Present and Share Information		
	Word processing	Reports, stories, class newspapers, literary magazines
	Multimedia presentation	Reports, present results of research, experiments, etc.
	Digital cameras and video	Reports/stories with a visual component
	Web page design	Communicating with a broader audience
Communicate with Others		
	E-mail/Discussion Boards	Communicating with people around the world, experts, other students

also provides examples of the types of hardware and software that can accomplish these purposes and examples of ways in which these would be used in the classroom.

Technology can enhance instruction in the ways described in this framework, providing a true "value-added." When teachers are determining whether and how technology can support their students' learning goals, they should consider the instructional purposes identified in Table 6.1 and whether these purposes overlap with the learning goals or activities they are doing. When there is an overlap, this indicates that using technology there may substantially enhance the lesson or unit.

In the next section of this chapter, we model how the three planning steps combined with the framework would play out in a real life situation. We make a teacher's planning process explicit as she takes us through each of these three steps.

IDENTIFYING THE ROLE OF TECHNOLOGY IN A MODEL THEMATIC UNIT

Laurie, a seventh grade English/Language Arts teacher is planning a unit on literary genres. Here is her thinking process.

Step 1: Identify Learning Goals

Laurie begins the design of her unit by determining its learning goals. For this unit, she wants students to gain an understanding of specific literary genres and some well-known authors of that genre. Narrowing this down to measurable objectives, she specifically wants students to be able to:

1. Determine the characteristics of the specific literary genres of realistic fiction, science fiction, fantasy, historical fiction, and mystery;
2. Analyze how these characteristics influence the meaning of a literary work (book);
3. Locate and relate well-known authors of the specific literary genres;
4. Read a book from a specific literary genre;
5. Synthesize and use information from a variety of sources; and
6. Construct and present a book review that incorporates a discussion of genre specific characteristics as well as listing other well-known authors of that genre.

She also knows that cooperative grouping is valuable for helping students learn. Through working together, each student can use his/her strengths. Based on constructivist theories, group discussion also helps students to gain a deeper understanding—they socially construct meaning. Therefore, she also wants students to:

1. Participate in book discussions
2. Work cooperatively in groups to create a product

Step 2: Determine Activities And Practices To Help Achieve The Learning Goals

With the preceding learning goals in mind, Laurie begins to think about specific activities to accomplish those goals. First, she needs to assess what the students already know about literary genres. What genres do they know? Which characteristics of those genres do they know? Do they know any authors of those genres? This assessment could be done using whole class brainstorming.

Laurie then will let each student select a genre that s/he would like to study in more depth. She'll group students by that genre (grouping by interest). Students will need to use the library media center to do some research on the characteristics of the genre selected and locate authors and books in that genre. Each genre group will then need to select one book to read in that genre.

So that students develop a deeper understanding of their genre, she wants to regroup students to compare two genres. Creating a Venn diagram would be a beneficial visual organizer for students to see the similarities and differences between genres.

As students are reading their books, Laurie thinks she will have the groups participate in book discussions. The discussions will focus on the themes, characters, plot and settings of the book the group is reading. She will have the students discuss within their genre specific group and then regroup the students so that all genres are represented in a group. This will provide further opportunity for comparison of the genres.

Finally, she would like the students to share their learning with a broader audience. Therefore, she wants the genre groups to create a final product that can be used for presentation to the entire class. She also wants to work with the students to design an appropriate assessment for their learning. With a project, a rubric would be an appropriate assessment.

Step 3: Determine How Technology Can Help Achieve Those Learning Goals

Now that she has decided on some of the activities she will use, Laurie goes back and determines if there is any overlap between her learning goals and the goals that technology can support. As she thinks about her goals and activities, she also thinks about the purpose for which technology is used. Would the use of technology help with the learning? If so, how?

To do the group brainstorming, she could list items on the board. But, because her learning goal is making sense of information and she knows that technology allows for easily changing and reorganizing information, the whole class brainstorming might best be done using a graphic organizer such as Inspiration. This would help the class make sense of the information and see how it all fits together. For similar reasons, Venn diagrams comparing two genres could also be created using the computer.

Laurie also wants students to gain access to information for research on their genre and authors. They can use the Internet, electronic databases and other print resources available in the library.

To expand their book discussions to an audience beyond the school, she can locate and have her student participate in online book discussions. This will provide students with the opportunity to communicate with others and move the exchange of ideas and information beyond the scope of the classroom or the school.

Technology provides an excellent tool for creating products to present and share information. Presentation software, such as PowerPoint, could be used for the groups to create their final product. Prior to starting the presentation, Laurie could use an online tool with the whole class to create a rubric to be used to 'grade' the projects. Because the students would know and understand the requirements for the project, the rubric would serve as a guide as the students created their presentations.

To further demonstrate how technology can be used to support instructional goals, two lessons from the unit plan are illustrated below. Although these lesson plans center on the topic of literary genres, the activities and technology could be used in any topic area. In addition, both of these lesson plans assume that Laurie has only one computer with a data projector and Internet access.

Lesson Title: Brainstorming Literary Genres and Authors
Time: One 45-minute class period
Overview

This lesson is used to introduce students to the unit of study. Students tap into prior knowledge, and the teacher is able to assess what students already know about literary genres by using whole class brainstorming with graphic organizer software.
Lesson Objectives

1. To introduce students to the Literary Genre Unit
2. To connect to previous learning/knowledge
3. To graphically organize information to find patterns

Technology Resources Needed

1. Software (such as Inspiration) to create a graphic organizer
2. One computer connected to an LCD projector

Procedures

1. Introduce and briefly explain the Literary Genres and Authors unit of study.
2. Explain that the class will do a whole group brainstorming to see what everyone already knows.
3. Ask students what genres they know.
4. Use one computer projecting on the wall and graphic organizer software. Type in genres provided by students (either the teacher or a student may type this in).
5. Be sure all genres to be studied (realistic fiction, science fiction, fantasy, historical fiction, mystery) are listed. Add any genre to be studied that was not provided by students.
6. Ask for known characteristics of the genres.
7. Have students suggest ways to organize the characteristics of the genres. May have to ask students if they see any similar characteristics among genres. Organize and save each idea.
8. Ask for any known/favorite authors of the genres.
9. Have students suggest ways to organize authors of the genres. Organize and save each idea.
10. Individual students select a favorite genre that s/he would like to study. Group students by genre.
11. Summarize the known genre characteristics and authors.
12. Prepare students for research in the library—they will need to locate and/or confirm the genre characteristics, locate 4 authors of their genre, and select one book to read in that genre.

Lesson Title: Book Discussions
Time: 8 class periods, 45 minutes each
Overview
    Students participate in book discussions, both online and in class, as they read their books. One day is spent in classroom discussions, the following day is spent reading and submitting to the online discussion board.

Lesson Objectives

1. To discuss the setting, characters, plot, and themes of a book
2. To be able to explain how characteristics of the genre influence the preceding elements of story.
3. To communicate to an audience outside of the school.

Technology Resources Needed:

1. Classroom computer connected to the Internet LCD projector
2. Online discussion board

Procedures for Classroom Discussions

1. Use the following questions (one each day) to focus the classroom discussions:
   a. What is the setting for the book?
   b. How does the setting relate to the genre?
   c. Why is the setting important to the meaning of the story?
   d. What is the plot of the book?
   e. Does the plot relate to the genre, i.e., is it possible to use this plot in another genre?
      (i) Who are the major characters in the book?
      (ii) Are the characters believable?
      (iii) What qualities make them believable?
      (iv) Are there any qualities of the characters that relate specifically to the genre?
      (v) What are those qualities?
      (vi) What is the theme of the book?
      (vii) How does the genre used by the author influence the theme?
2. Students discuss one of the questions in their specific genre group. Students should take notes during the discussion.
3. Regroup students so that groups consist of one student representing each genre.
4. These new groups discuss the question and compare/contrast among genres.
5. As a final activity, have a whole class discussion where students explain what they have learned.

Procedures For Online Discussions

1. Use the same questions as listed above
2. Students read their books
3. As students are reading, rotate each genre group through to use the classroom computer to enter the information into the online discussion board.
   a. Demonstrate and model using the discussion board to the whole class
      prior to students' first time use.
   b. Use a chart to manage rotation. The chart should have the genre group
      with time to use the computer.
4. As a final activity, have a whole class discussion where students share
   information about their online discussion board communications.

Both of these lessons could be done with any topic area. For example, a math teacher could do the brainstorming lesson to assess students' knowledge at the beginning of a unit on data analysis and probability. Students in an eighth grade science class could use the online discussion forum for communicating with researchers collecting data on earth's geology.

The process in which Laurie engaged to create her unit represents a strategic use of technology. She has chosen to incorporate technology in ways that naturally connected to and supported her learning goals and activities. She began by identifying her learning goals and sketching out activities to support those learning goals. By considering the purposes behind technology use, she was then able to determine that technology had a role in this unit and what that role should be.

CONCLUSION

In the past, many teachers began with specific technologies and tried to fit those technologies into their curriculum. This resulted in a use that was often tangential at best, distracting at worst, to the regular classroom experience. In this chapter, we have described a much more strategic use of technology. This more strategic use has teachers first identify their learning goals and activities. It then encourages teachers to examine the instructional purposes technology naturally supports, using that information to determine how technology can play a useful role in the middle school classroom.

BIBLIOGRAPHY

Boetel, Martha, and Victoria K. Dimock. *Constructing Knowledge with Technology.* Austin, TX: Southwest Educational Development Laboratory, 1999.

Dwyer, David C., Cathy Ringstaff and Judith H. Sandholz. *Teacher Beliefs and Practices, Part 1: Patterns of Change.* (Apple Classrooms of Tomorrow Research) Cupertino, CA: Apple Computer,Inc.,1990.

Kulik, J.A. "Meta-analytic studies of findings on computer- based instruction" in *Technology Assessment in Education and Training*, edited by E.L. Baker and H.F. O'Neil. Hillsdale, NJ: Lawrence Erlbaum, 1994.

Marzano, Robert J., Debra J. Pickering, and Jane E. Pollock. *Classroom Instruction that Works: Research Based Strategies for Increasing Student Achievement.* Alexandria, VA: Association for Supervision and Curriculum Development, 2001.

Roschelle, Jeremy M., Roy D. Pea, Christopher M. Hoadley, Douglas N. Gordin and Barbara M. Means. "Changing how and what Children learn in school with computer-based technologies" *Children and Computer Technology* 10, no.2 (Fall/Winter 2000) :76–101.

Sandholz, Judith, Cathy Ringstaff, and David C. Dwyer. *Teaching With Technology: Creating Student-centered Classrooms.* New York: Teachers College Press, 1997.

Wenglinsky, Harold. *Does it Compute? The Relationship Between Educational Technology and Student Achievement in Mathematics.* Princeton, NJ: Educational testing Service, 1998.

White, Noel, Cathy Ringstaff and Loretta Kelly. *Getting the Most from Technology in Schools.* San Francisco, CA: WestEd, 2002.

Section Three

IMPLEMENTATION STRATEGIES IN MIDDLE AND HIGH SCHOOL GRADES

Chapter Seven

Freedom Through The Lenses Of Literature And Social Studies

James S. Etim

As part of the Language Arts program for my middle school students, I have devoted at least three weeks yearly to a unit on poetry. Every year, I teach different poems and cover different genres—free verse, lyric, narrative, ballads, haiku, limericks, elergy and odes. I report here on a broader unit that had as a goal this objective—to explore the concept of freedom, independence and justice through poetry, essays, fiction, research and readings in social studies. The unit was built around five ideas

1. it was an integrated unit
2. the theme was centered around freedom, independence and justice
3. skills to be developed included communication, problem solving, inquiry and research and personal construction of meaning
4. it was centered around the national and state standard course of study
5. students had input at various points, and they were to present projects for evaluation

One of the trends in middle school is curriculum integration (Kellough and Kellough, 2003, Tchundi and Lafer, 1997). According to Bragaw and Hartoonian (1995), an integrated curriculum is useful for students because that is how life and knowledge has been organized:

> Life is, and always has been, integrated. And knowledge is culturally and historically determined and interpreted by its seekers. Unless we construct school programs upon these truths, we put our students at risk of misinterpreting, or falsely analyzing, the world around them.

In the same manner, Willis (1992) points out that interdisciplinary teaching provides the potential to motivate students, brings order due to chaos caused by the knowledge explosion and encourages students to learn more, remember more and apply more of what they have learned. In her videotape *Integrating the Curriculum,* Heidi Jacobs (1993) points out that "Curriculum integration can strengthen the importance of the disciplines and bring greater meaning to learning." Furthermore, in a large scale study, Viadero (1996) reported that there was improvement in achievement among middle schoolers as a result of interdisciplinary teaming and teaching.

In envisioning a possible curriculum for middle school, Beane (1991) points out that at "the intersection of concerns from early adolescents and from the larger world, we can begin to imagine powerful themes that connect the two and thus offer a promising possibility. . . ." Such themes include transitions, identities, interdependence, wellness, social structures, independence, conflict resolution, justice, caring, etc. (Beane1993 p. 61). These are some of the themes middle school teachers need to explore to make learning relevant to the developmental needs of 10 to 14-year-old students. In setting up this unit, both the national goals (National Council of Teachers of English, 1999) and state standard objectives and goals (Public Schools of North Carolina, 2000) were used.

For example, some of the national goals referred to included:

For Language Arts

Goal 2

Students read a wide range of literature from many periods in many genres to build an understanding of the varied dimensions (e.g., philosophical, ethical, aesthetic) of human experience.

Goal 7

Students conduct research on issues and interests by generating ideas and questions, and by posing problems. They gather, evaluate, and synthesize data from a variety of sources (e.g., print and non-print texts, artifacts, people) to communicate their discoveries in ways that suit their purpose and audience.

Goal 8

Students use a variety of technological and information resources (e.g., libraries, databases, computer networks, video) to gather and synthesize information and to create and communicate knowledge.

Goal 11

Students participate as knowledgeable, reflective, creative, and critical members of a variety of literacy communities.

At the state level, some of the objectives in Social Studies include:

Analyze the strengths and weaknesses of the government framed by the new Constitution of the United States, noting the extent to which liberties were granted to various groups.

Describe the history and status of minorities and women in the antebellum period.

Identify and assess the impact of major Civil War campaigns and battles on life in North Carolina.

Social Studies Skills

Skill 11: The learner will use information for problem-solving, decision making and planning.

Skill 111: The learner will develop skills in constructive interpersonal relations and social participation.

Bragaw and Michael (1995) also point to the need to practice inquiry learning and problem solving in the classroom:

> Our present technological ability to generate data—raw information—and to manipulate it in manifold ways, forces everyone concerned with education to realize that the learning process must be based on inquiry, problem solving, and decision making. The sheer volume of data can no longer be committed to memory; only the ability to conceptualize enables students to separate and efficiently use all the information available to them.

One of the goals that this unit aims at achieving will be that of encouraging students to problem solve and construct meaning for themselves based on readings and research.

BACKGROUND TO THE UNIT

This unit began in January and ran for nine weeks. Historically, in January there is the Martin Luther King holiday and February is Black History month. My students often request that I do a unit related to these important events, and that is how this unit was born. Since I taught both Language Arts and Social Studies during this school year, the process of curriculum integration was made easier for the students and me. Students were encouraged to explore some essential questions during the unit (see Figure 7.1):

1. What does freedom mean to you? What freedom do you cherish the most and why?
2. How do nations, people obtain freedom? How do nations and individuals maintain their freedom?
3. Explore the contributions of individuals like George Washington, Abraham Lincoln, Frederick Douglas, John Kennedy and Martin Luther King to our freedoms. (You may add to the list as you desire).
4. How does the Constitution of the United States guarantee the freedoms we enjoy today?
5. Why was the Civil Rights movement of the 1960s necessary and what are the present concerns of citizens in the U.S. regarding freedom and justice?

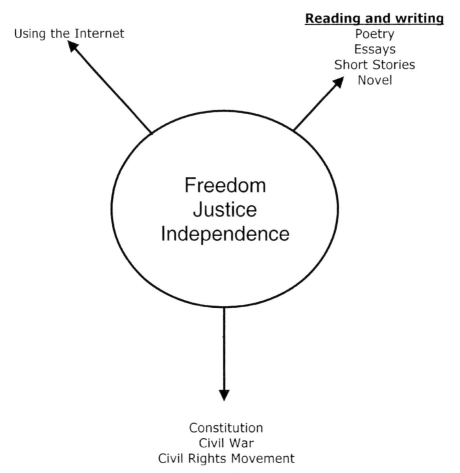

Using the Internet

<u>Reading and writing</u>
Poetry
Essays
Short Stories
Novel

Freedom
Justice
Independence

Constitution
Civil War
Civil Rights Movement

Figure 7.1.   Integrated unit on freedom and justice.

IMPLEMENTATION

I began with getting the students to enjoy poetry since according to Chance (2001), most middle school students do not enjoy this genre. Students heard a recording of some poems and listened to music with the lyrics all written out. We talked briefly about their enjoyment of music and how that is related to poetry-rhyme, rhythm, repetition, sound, verse and theme, etc. This was followed with a brief pretest that sought to find out when they last read a poem, when they last wrote a poem, what poetic elements they knew and if they enjoyed poetry at all. Results from this short pretest were used in designing some parts of the lessons.

We read and discussed several poems, most of them centered on the areas of national freedom, personal freedom, justice and independence. In reading Longfellow's Paul Revere's Ride," students refreshed their memories on the events leading to the war of independence, the beginnings of national freedom from British rule. When we read Langston Hughes' "I, too, sing America," we talked about both the disappointments and hopes/dreams of the persona. In reading Alice Walkers "Sit-ins" we talked about non-violence as a means of getting one's point across. In reading Gwendolyn Brooks' "We Real Cool" and "Sadie," we talked about education as an important ingredient for personal freedom. A poem like Hughes' "Mother to Son" was used to illustrate the idea that responsibility, hard work and never giving up has to be part of personal freedom while in Hayden's "Frederick Douglas," we saw the strengths of Douglas and why he is a hero. Other poems studied are listed in Appendix.

During the study of poetry, students were to keep a log of poems they read and to share some of these daily with the class. Many of the students participated by writing and reading their poems. Students were also to complete a project. The project topics are given towards the end of this paper.

During this time, we discussed the rights enshrined in the American Constitution in the Social Studies classes. We discussed the Bill of Rights and students were asked for their reflection on these rights. Students also were given a writing prompt:

Think of all the freedoms (religion, association, press, etc) that you have in this society. Which do you cherish (love) the most and why? OR

What freedom would you not want taken away from you and why?

During the study of the Amendments to the Constitution, students were put in groups and asked to discuss the topics, "What are the responsibilities of a nation to the individual?" and "What are the responsibilities of a good citizen?"

After the study of poetry, we began studying essays and writings related to freedom. We began with writings related to the abolitionist movement—Ann Petry's "Harriet Tubman: Conductor on the Underground Railroad." In Language Arts, students had the opportunity to discuss how persistence and caring for others can lead to personal freedom for those under bondage. In Social Studies, we used this text to talk about the Fugitive Slave Law and the treatment of Blacks during the period. The text also afforded us the opportunity to talk in groups about basic ideas like: Why was there slavery? What was the Underground Railroad? Why was the Underground Railroad necessary? Do you think Harriet Tubman was a hero? Would you take a personal risk, even to your life, to help others? Are there benefits in taking a stand like Harriet Tubman did?

From these discussions, we went on to study the Civil War in Social Studies
—causes,. important characters, important events, how it ended and what
were the benefits for Blacks. Students read the "Gettysburg Address" and discussed what the speech meant to them.

The next major study was Ernest Gaines' "The Autobiography of Miss Jane
Pittman." This text chronicles the life of Jane Pittman from the period of the
Civil War to the Civil Rights Movement. When we read the chapter titled
"Freedom," students were asked to write on the prompt, "What does freedom
mean to you?" When we read the chapters that Jane insisted she was going to
Ohio, students discussed the topic, "What are the character traits of a successful individual?" When we read the chapters on Ned Douglas, students
used a compare/contrast graphic organizer to write down the similarities/
differences between Ned and Frederick Douglas. We read the chapter "Assassination" and compared this event with the assassinations of the Kennedys
(John and Robert) and Martin Luther King Jr.

The Autobiography of Miss Jane Pittman also provided us the opportunity to integrate Social Studies skills. First of all, in the chapter "Freedom," we discussed the Emancipation Proclamation of 1863. Section 4
provided us the opportunity to talk about Reverend Martin Luther King Jr.
and the freedom marches in Alabama, Mississippi and Georgia. We also
discussed the work of Rosa Parks and her contributions to the Civil Rights
Movement. The rights of being an American citizen were also discussed—
e.g., the right to vote. As we read, students were given a map of the U.S
(see Figure 7.2 at end of chapter) and the assignment was: The following
states and cities have been mentioned in *the Autobiography of Miss Jane
Pittman*. On the map provided, write down each state and city mentioned:
Ohio, New York, Kansas, Maine, Texas, Louisiana, Cincinnati and New
Orleans.

Choose two of the states and write down one important event that happened and what each is associated with. For example, Kansas is a State where
Ned worked and got an education. Another map was given for them to label
the rivers mentioned in the "War Years" section. (See Activity 1 and Figure
7.2 at end of chapter). In implementing this unit, projects, movies, field trips
and student performances were also used.

1. Projects

Students were to complete several projects as part of the unit. These projects were aimed at improving student writing skills, computer and research
skills, problem solving and reflective abilities. The project titles are given
below:

Poetry—Prepare a poetry log of poems you have read)

Instructions

In preparing your log at home, you may want to use the following sites:
http://www.nku.edu/~diesmanj/poetryindex.html
http://www.poets.org/
http://search.yahoo.com/bin/search?p=LANGSTON HUGHES
http://www.poetry.com

Using these sites and others you may want to, select 20 poems. Record these poems in your Reading Log. Choose any three poems from the list and write a two page report. As much as possible, the poems selected should be related to freedom, independence and justice. Your report and reflection may also include drawings.

If that is not possible, you may write 2–5 poems and present some to the class, or, you may choose a poet, do a chronological sketch of his or her life and of his/ her works.

The Underground Railroad

On the map of the U.S., draw and label the route that Harriet Tubman took to get slaves up north. Using the internet, write a 2–3 page report on the life of Harriet Tubman. In your opinion, was she a hero?

The Autobiography of Miss Jane Pittman

Write a speech to be delivered at the funeral ceremonies of Professor Douglas.

Write a letter to a friend explaining how you felt after reading the chapter "Assassination."

"Sometimes there is a price to be paid for obtaining personal freedom and freedom for others." Argue for/against this statement.

Three themes in *The Autobiography of Miss Jane Pittman*

Three reasons why Ned is likeable/interesting character

Life for Blacks then (1860s–1890s) and now.

Other Areas of Research

Write a paper on any of the major civil rights leaders: Martin Luther King Jr., Ralph Abernathy, Rosa Parks, Frederick Douglas and/or Benjamin Banneker.

Write on these symbols of liberty: Liberty Bell, Statute of Liberty and Mount Rushmore. Which is your favorite and why? (If you have visited one of these, write about the experience).

2. Movies

Several movies were shown to the students: *Forms of Literature, George Washington: The Making of a Rebel, Harriet Tubman: The Underground Railroad, The Autobiography of Miss Jane Pittman and Eyes on the Prize.*

At the end of each movie, students were given the opportunity to discuss the movie, reflect on each and give some lessons learned.

Community Resources

We undertook two trips in the community to help strengthen the teaching and understanding of the unit. The first was to Historic Stagville. This is a museum that shows the living condition of Blacks on plantations. During the visit, students were shown the slave quarters, the home of the master and informed about the working conditions for Blacks during this period. The second visit was to Bennett Place State Historic Site. This is where some of the Confederate soldiers surrendered to the Union soldiers in 1865.

Student Performances

Every February in our middle school, there are student performances celebrating Black History Month. Often there is a motivational speaker that comes in to talk to students. All students are encouraged to attend these celebrations and to actively participate in poetry reading, miming, dancing, dramatization, etc.

TAKING CARE OF MULTIPLE INTELLIGENCES

The concept of multiple intelligences provides different strategies to individual learning. Howard Gardner in discussing intelligences (1995, 1996), talks about these types: verbal/linguistic, mathematical/logical, bodily/kinesthetic, musical, spatial, interpersonal, intrapersonal and naturalist. In looking at the school system, he sees a major problem being that schools and tests emphasize the first two: linguistic and mathematical/logical. This unit had activities to cover more than the first two. The activities included Visual: students saw movies, talked about these and were encouraged to sketch their poems. They were presented with maps, graphic organizers, etc. and asked to complete exercises using these maps.

Music: students were encouraged to sing music that reminded them of some aspect of freedom and justice. Some of the movies had songs and students sang to the tunes.

Interpersonal: Group tasks and discussions were encouraged.

Intrapersonal: students were to keep a log of poems read and to write reflective journals.

Body/Kinesthetic: students engaged in dance and skits during Black History month celebration and participated in field trips.

Notable Accomplishments

1. Reading and reflecting on several poems, essays and a major novel on freedom and justice
2. Keeping a reading log

3. Students writing poems and expressing themselves
4. Learning using different sources: movies, guest speaker, field trips
5. Reflecting on the concepts of freedom and justice and independence and responsibilities that go with these: getting an education, voting and helping others.

CONCLUSION

In carrying out this unit, the aim was to teach an integrative unit that allowed students to explore the concept of freedom, justice and independence. The unit was to enable students to develop these skills: communication, problem solving, research and personal construction of meaning. Most of the students kept a reading log of poems read, shared with their peers some of the poems they read at home or those who wrote talked about what freedom and justice meant to them. Each completed at least one of the writing/research topics. At all points, students were engaged in groups and participated in the successful implementation of the unit.

BIBLIOGRAPHY

Beane, James. *Middle School Curriculum: From Rhetoric to Reality*. Columbus, OH: National Middle School Association, 1993

———. "Inntegrated Curriculum in the Middle Schools." *Educational Leadership*. 1991 http://ericps.crc.uiuc.edu/eece/pubs/digests/1992/beane92.html (June 7, 2003)

Bragaw, Donald and H. Michael Hartoonian. "Social Studies: The Study of People in Society" in *Content of the Curriculum* 2nd ed. Ed. Allan A. Glatthorn. Washington, D.C.: ASCD, 1995. http://www.ascd.org/readingroom/books/glatthorn95book.html (June 7, 2003).

Chance, Rosemary. "Beyond Silverstein: Poetry for Middle Schoolers" *Voices from the Middle*. 9.2 (2001): 88–90. http://www.ncte.org/pdfs/subscribers-only/vm/0092 dec01/VM0092Beyond.pdf. (October 17, 2003).

Gaines, Ernest. *The Autobiography of Miss Jane Pittman*, Columbus, OH: Glencoe/McGraw Hill, 2000.

Gardner, Howard. "Reflections on Multiple Intelligences: Myths and Messages" *Phi Delta Kappan* 77 No. 3 (Nov.1995) :200–9.

———. "Probing More Deeply into the Theory of Multiple Intelligences" *The National Association of Secondary School Principals Bulletin* 80. No. 583 (November 1996): 1–7.

Jacobs, Heidi. *Integrating the Curriculum: Video 1* Salt Lake City, UT: Video Journal of Education, 1994.

Kellough, Richard D. and Noreen Kellough, *Teaching Young Adolescents: A Guide To Methods and Resources*. Columbus, OH: Merrill Prentice Hall, 2003.

Mason, Lorna et al. *America's Past and Promise*. Boston: McDougal Littell, 1998.

National Council of Teachers of English. "Standards for the English Language Arts" http://www.ncte.org/standards/standards.shtml#1. (January 8, 2003).

Public Schools of North Carolina, *Reference Guide for Integrating Curriculum 2000–2001. Grade 8* Raleigh, NC: Department of Public Instruction, 2000.

Tchudi, Stephen and Stephen Lafer, " Interdisciplinary English and the Contributions of English to an Interdisciplinary Curriculum" *English* Journal 88, No. 7 (1997): 25.

Viadeio, Debra. " Middle School Gains over 25 years Chronicled" *Education Digest*. May 1996 http://www.edweek.org/ew/ewstory.cfm?slug=36middle.h15 (October 23, 2003).

Willis, Scott. "Interdisciplinary Learning: Movement to Link the Disciplines Gains Momentum" *Curriculum Update*, 1992.

APPENDIX

Angelou, Maya, "Still I Rise," "Phenomenal Woman,"

Brooks, Gwendolyn, "We Real Cool"

Dickinson, Emily, "I'm Nobody, Who are You"

Hayden, Robert, "Frederick Douglas"

Hughes, Langston, "The Negro Speaks of Rivers," "I Too, Sing America," "Cross," "Mulatto," "Mother To Son," "Let America Be America Again"

Johnson, James W., "Lift Every Voice and Sing"

Longfellow, Henry W., "Paul Revere's Ride"

McKay, Claude, "If We Must Die"

Whitman, Walt, "O Captain, My Captain"

Language Arts: Activity 1

Etim Name _____ Period ____

Ernest Gaines, *The Autobiography of Miss Jane Pittman*

Answer all the questions (based on pp. 1–110) of the story.

1. The following cities and states are mentioned in "The Autobiography of Miss Jane Pittman." Label each on the map provided:
   a. Louisiana (Luzana) (p. 80)
   b. New Orleans (p. 94)
   c. Kansas
   d. Ohio (p. 17)
   e. Texas
   f. New York (p. 33)
   g. Iowa (p. 47)

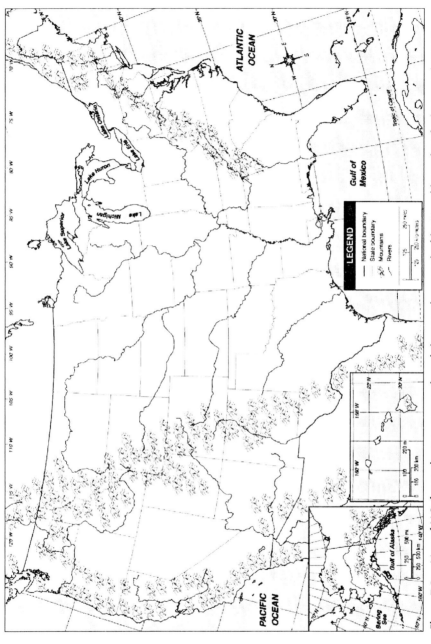

Figure 7.2. Map of U.S. for students to name selected rivers and towns cited in *"Autobiography of Miss Jane Pittman."*

2. Choose any three places mentioned in #1 above and write one important thing/event that happened or was supposed to happen in each place. For example—Kansas—Ned moved here to escape being killed. He sent some money to Jane. This money was useful to Jane especially when they wanted to go away from Col. Dye.

   a. _____

   _____

   b. _____

   _____

   c. _____

   _____

3. The following rivers are mentioned on p. 49. Label each on the map:
   a. River Mississippi
   b. River Arkansas
   c. River Missouri
4. What is the direction for each of the following?
   a. From Louisiana to Texas   _____
   b. From Louisiana to Ohio   _____
   c. From Louisiana to Kansas   _____

Chapter Eight

Integrative Studies: A Teaching Model To Promote Connective Thinking

MaryAnn Davies

The integrative studies model addresses the complexities of today by identifying universal patterns that cut across time and space. Rather than isolating specific bits of information and hoping that patterns of meaning will emerge, this model helps students recognize the interrelationships that shape their world. These patterns (themes) provide a context for understanding content and linking it relevantly to today. Thus, content is remembered because students perceive it as meaningful and useful.

INTEGRATIVE STUDIES MODEL

The integrative model combines the chronological focus of traditional disciplines with the thematic orientation of an interdisciplinary approach. A theme or pattern acts as the vehicle for organization. Data and artifacts from the different modes of perception encourage pattern detection in a rich multi-sensory context. The integrative paradigm highlights the development over time of interrelationships between data.

The figure (Figure 8.1) below illustrates the integrative model. The cube represents the theme or concept in a unit. It encompasses each of the different modes of perception, represented by the four cylinders. The central core symbolizes the development of the theme over time.

Each mode of perception offers different insights into understanding the theme. Mathematics and the natural sciences offer literal, precise representations of content where logical consistency gives meaning (Eisner, 1992). Social scientists study content using a sequential, analytical approach. Language arts provide a forum for communicating ideas. The fine arts use emotive,

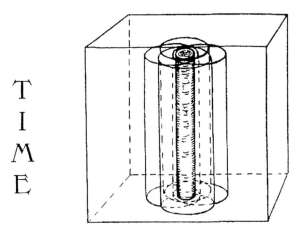

T
I
M
E

Figure 8.1.

visual-spatial imagery and provide insights that enrich humanity and touch our inner selves (Fowler, 1989; Godfrey, 1992). All combined modes of perception enrich understanding, allow for exploring complex interrelationships, and more closely resemble life. The model requires that teachers become connection experts not just subject experts.

Students discover interrelationships through time by examining data from the different perceptual and expressive modes. This varied information might include excerpts from speeches or diaries, photographs, maps, music, poems, literature, works of art or archeological artifacts. In structuring the unit, the challenge is to locate varied resources representing different ways of examining the theme. Access to web-based resources makes the task of locating materials easier.

Theme selected and materials assembled, the teacher uses a four-tier questioning strategy to assist students in identifying interconnections.

1. *Understand the artifact.* These questions assure that the specific artifact is understood. The questions focus on knowledge and comprehension. For example, what does the poem mean?
2. *Explore the inter-relatedness of artifacts.* Ask questions that examine the inter-relatedness of artifacts and connect the data to students' prior experiences. Analysis forms the crux of this level of questioning. For example, have you ever experienced feelings similar to those expressed in the poem? or How are the events in the poem similar/different to those identified in the timeline?
3. *Explore how data might be expressed through other perceptual modes.* Guide students in expressing data through a different mode of perception.

This requires mental flexibility, a key component of creative production. For example, translate the events of the timeline into a poem.

4. *Examine the relationship of chronology to the various artifacts.* Could such a poem have been written fifty years ago? Why or why not? This stage incorporates critical and analytical thinking.

A continual reinforcement of interrelationships as they develop over time comprises the integrative model. This approach acknowledges that the different modes of perception each contribute to the whole pattern. "Every experience actually contains within it the seeds of many, and possibly all disciplines" (Caine & Caine, 1991, p. 119).

A tree analogy illustrates the potential of this model to promote connective thinking. The tree, like the learner, starts out with a single taproot. It gives the tree a basis for growth. The learner's prior knowledge shapes the taproot and creates a scaffold for connecting new knowledge. The tree expands its roots. These roots spread widely and gradually interconnect creating a complex web. Each perspective for viewing information is like a new root. The more one studies a theme using multiple lenses, the more blurred the boundaries between disciplines become. A strong root system enables the tree to grow strong, develop many branches, and live long. Multiple perspectives extend understanding, create neural connections and promote long-term retention.

THE MODEL APPLIED

Sample lessons from a unit entitled Quests for Freedom demonstrate the model. This unit examines the theme of quests for freedom by focusing on two historical individuals, Harriet Tubman and Chief Joseph. The universal theme enables teachers to readily expand the unit by studying additional individuals from other times as well as places. In order to demonstrate the four-tier questioning strategy, the Harriet Tubman lessons label levels of questions.
Quests For Freedom—Harriet Tubman
Goals:

1. Compare similarities and differences in the ways individuals and cultures meet the human need for freedom.
2. Explore causes, consequences, and possible solutions to persistent issues, such as quests for freedom.
3. Critically analyze print and non-print information for interrelationships over time.
4. Express individual perspectives in response to personal, social, cultural, and historical issues.

Procedures:

1. Discuss: What does abolitionist mean? Did all abolitionists advocate the same approaches? Distribute the "Quests for Freedom" decision making handout. Students individually rank the approaches to seeking freedom in terms of perceived effectiveness and then re-rank them in groups using consensus strategies. (*Understand the artifact*).

    a. Discuss: The abolitionists were all on quests for freedom. What is a quest? Can you think of any quests for freedom today? How are they similar or different to the abolitionists' quests? (*Explore the relationship of chronology to this artifact*).

    b. Have you ever been on a quest? What did it require of you? How is/was your quest similar or different to the abolitionists' quests? (*Explore the inter-relatedness of artifacts*).

Quests For Freedom

Descriptions of approaches used by different abolitionists to rid our country of slavery follow. Which strategy do you think was most effective? Place a "1" alongside the most effective, a number "2" alongside the next most effective, and so on. After ranking the effectiveness of these strategies individually, complete the same process in groups.

Ranking

Self   Group

_____ _____   Sojourner Truth. Born into slavery, Isabella Baumfree ran away from her owners in New York. The following year, 1828, New York outlawed slavery. After a religious experience, she changed her name to Sojourner Truth and became a wandering preacher. She walked and talked along the East coast encouraging the abolition of slavery.

_____ _____   Henry Highland Garnet. Garnet studied religion in New York and became a minister. He wrote and spoke against slavery calling for bold action. In 1843, he spoke at the National Negro Convention in Buffalo, New York. Here is part of what he said: "Brothers, arise, arise! Strike for your lives and your liberty. Now is the hour. Let every slave rise up. Then slavery will end. Your lives cannot be any worse than they are now. It is better to die free than to live as slaves. You have been too patient. You have given in too easily. Awake, awake. Let our word be resistance. No one has ever become free without fighting. Trust in God. Work for the peace of all people. And remember that there are FOUR MILLION Blacks."

_____ _____ Frederick Douglass. Douglass was born a slave in Maryland but escaped to Massachusetts when he was twenty-one. He was a gifted speaker and became recognized as a spokesperson for the abolitionists. In 1847, he started an antislavery newspaper, The North Star: "The object of the North Star will be to attack slavery in all its forms and aspects . . . and to hasten the day of freedom to our three million enslaved fellow countrymen."

_____ _____ Harriet Tubman. Born a slave in Maryland, she was determined to be free. "I had a right to liberty or death. If I could not have the one, I would have the other." After escaping North, she returned nineteen times into slave territory and guided more than 300 men, women and children to freedom. As an Underground Railroad "conductor," she bragged "I never lost a passenger." A $40,000 reward was offered for her capture but no one ever caught Harriet Tubman.

_____ _____ Martin Delaney. Delaney believed Blacks would never be treated fairly in the United States. He went on an expedition to Africa to find a location for a colony for African Americans. Later he proposed to Abraham Lincoln that a black army be created.

Assume that you are a/an (abolitionist) (plantation owner) (social scientist today). Write a letter to one of these abolitionists explaining your views on slavery.

2. Listen to the song "Harriet Tubman" (Spring Hill Music, Robbie Gass/On Wings of Song) and watch an accompanying slide presentation depicting paintings of slavery.

Harriet Tubman

By W. Robinson

> At night I dreamed I was in slavery
> About 1850 was the time
> So rose the only sign
> Nothing around to ease my mind
> Out of the night appeared a lady
> Leading a distant pilgrim band
> First mate she yelled pointing her hand
> Take 'em aboard for distant port

Refrain

> Singing come on up—I got a lifeline
> Come on up to this train of mine (Repeat)
> Her name was Harriet Tubman and she

Drove for the Underground Railroad, Railroad
Hundreds of miles we traveled onward
Gathering slaves from town to town
Seeking every lost and found
Setting them free that once were bound
Somehow my heart was growing weaker
Fell by the wayside, sinking sand
Firmly did this lady stand
She lifted me up and took my hand singing

Refrain

Who are these children dressed in red?
They must be the ones that Moses lead (Repeat twice)
Singing come on up—I got a lifeline
Come on up to this train of mine (Repeat six times)
Come on up, come on up to this train of mine
I got a life line

Understand the artifact. What are possible limitations of relying solely on songs for information? Discuss how songs create and convey feelings. How does this song make you feel? What does this tell you about the songwriter's view of Harriet Tubman? Do you think he saw her as courageous? Support your view. In what ways was Harriet like Moses? How were the fugitive slaves like pilgrims? What images of Harriet are portrayed in the slides?

Explore the inter-relatedness of artifacts. Would the songwriter agree with these slide portrayals?

Explore how data might be expressed through other perceptual modes. What kinds of music would you select to portray the other abolitionists studied? to illustrate a quest today? your quest?

3. *Understand the artifact.* Discuss the Compromise of 1850 and the historical context for Congress passing a stricter Fugitive Slave Law. Direct students to read Section 7 of Public Law 31 (Fugitive Slave Law). According to Section 7, what actions were punishable? What were the punishment options?

Explore the inter-relatedness of artifacts. How do you think the abolitionists reacted to the Fugitive Slave Law? Do you think it affected their quests for freedom? If so, in what ways? As an escaped slave herself, Harriet Tubman made nineteen trips into slave territory, assisting many to freedom. She bragged, "I never lost a passenger." What risks did Harriet face as she helped slaves escape on the Underground Railroad? How do you think she reacted to the Fugitive Slave Law?

Explore how data might be expressed through other perceptual modes. What lyrics might the songwriter create about this law? Write a letter to your Congressman expressing your views on this law from the point of view of a former slave, an abolitionist or a plantation owner.

Explore the relationship of chronology to this artifact. Do you think it is ever acceptable to break the law? Explain your position. Can you think of any contemporary examples where individuals chose to break the law because it violated their beliefs? Were they on quests? The original Fugitive Slave Law was passed in 1793. How do you think people reacted to the law then? What factors might account for differences in reactions between the original and the amended (and supplemented) law? Could such a law pass today? Why or why not?

4. Direct students to read the poem "Runagate, Runagate" by Robert Hayden.

Understand the artifact. What does the term "runagate" mean? Explain what the poet meant by "caves of the wish." Why would the poet describe the Midnight Special as being on a "saber track?" Who were Garrison, Alcott, Emerson, Garret, Douglas, Thoreau and John Brown? Interpret the line "means to be free." How does the author feel about Harriet Tubman?

Relate to other artifacts. Do you think the poet views Harriet as courageous? How does the poem make you feel? Compare this to feelings evoked by the song. What might account for these differences? Would the songwriter agree with the poet's description of traveling on the Underground Railroad? Do you think other abolitionists would have agreed with Harriet's use of a pistol to keep the fugitive slaves going? If the poet were in Congress debating passage of the Fugitive Slave Law, how do you think he would have voted? What might he have said to Congress while debating passage of Public Law 31?

Relationship to chronology. What would you change in the poem to make it reflect a current quest for freedom?

Change the mode of expression. Create a timeline depicting major events/individuals mentioned in the poem. Make a map illustrating the Underground Railroad routes.

5. Read the poem "Refugee in America" by Langston Hughes.

> There are words like Freedom
> Sweet and wonderful to say.
> On my heart-strings freedom sings
> All day everyday.
> There are words like Liberty
> That almost make me cry.
> If you had known what I knew
> You would know why (Hughes, 1966, p. 290).

Understand the artifact. Why does the word "Liberty" almost make the author cry? Who are the "refugees" referred to in the poem's title? Why did Langston Hughes label them refugees?

Relate to other artifacts. Would Harriet Tubman agree with this description? The songwriter? Hayden? Other abolitionists? The Congressmen passing the Fugitive Slave Law?

Change the mode of expression. Create a timeline depicting events in U.S. history that blocked freedom for African Americans.

Relationship to chronology. The poem refers to what time period in U.S. history? Could this poem have been written prior to the Civil War?

6. Examine copies of the General Affidavit filed by Harriet Tubman (See Figure 8.2) in 1898 and the response of the Fifty-fifth Congress.

Understand the artifact. Describe the nature of Harriet's claim. How much time elapsed since the services were rendered? What happened to her original request for compensation? How did Congress respond to her 1898 request? Do you think Harriet was satisfied with this settlement? Explain.

Relate to other artifacts. Do you think she felt like a refugee in America? Do you think this action by Harriet required more or less courage than her work on the Underground Railroad? Had Harriet successfully completed her quest for freedom? Explain your position.

Change the mode of expression. Write a poem/song/play or draw a picture expressing Harriet's feelings about filing the affidavit and the Congressional response.

Relate to chronology. Are there current individuals/groups seeking compensation from the government for services rendered? How are these similar/different to Harriet Tubman's affidavit?

Quests for Freedom – Chief Joseph
Materials

1. Chief Joseph's quotations
2. Song, "Earth is Our Mother," *Humanity*, Spring Hill Music
3. Chronology of Chief Joseph
4. Quotations by Jefferson, Sherman and Sealth
5. Map of retreat of Nez Perce in the War of 1877
6. Surrender of Chief Joseph, 1877
7. Excerpt from Chief Joseph's 1879 publication

Procedures

Read Chief Joseph's quotations. What did they reveal about Nez Perce beliefs? How did these beliefs differ from those of white settlers? Was conflict inevitable between the white settlers and the Nez Perce? Explain.

Chief Joseph's Quotations

The earth is the mother of all people, and all people should have equal rights upon it.

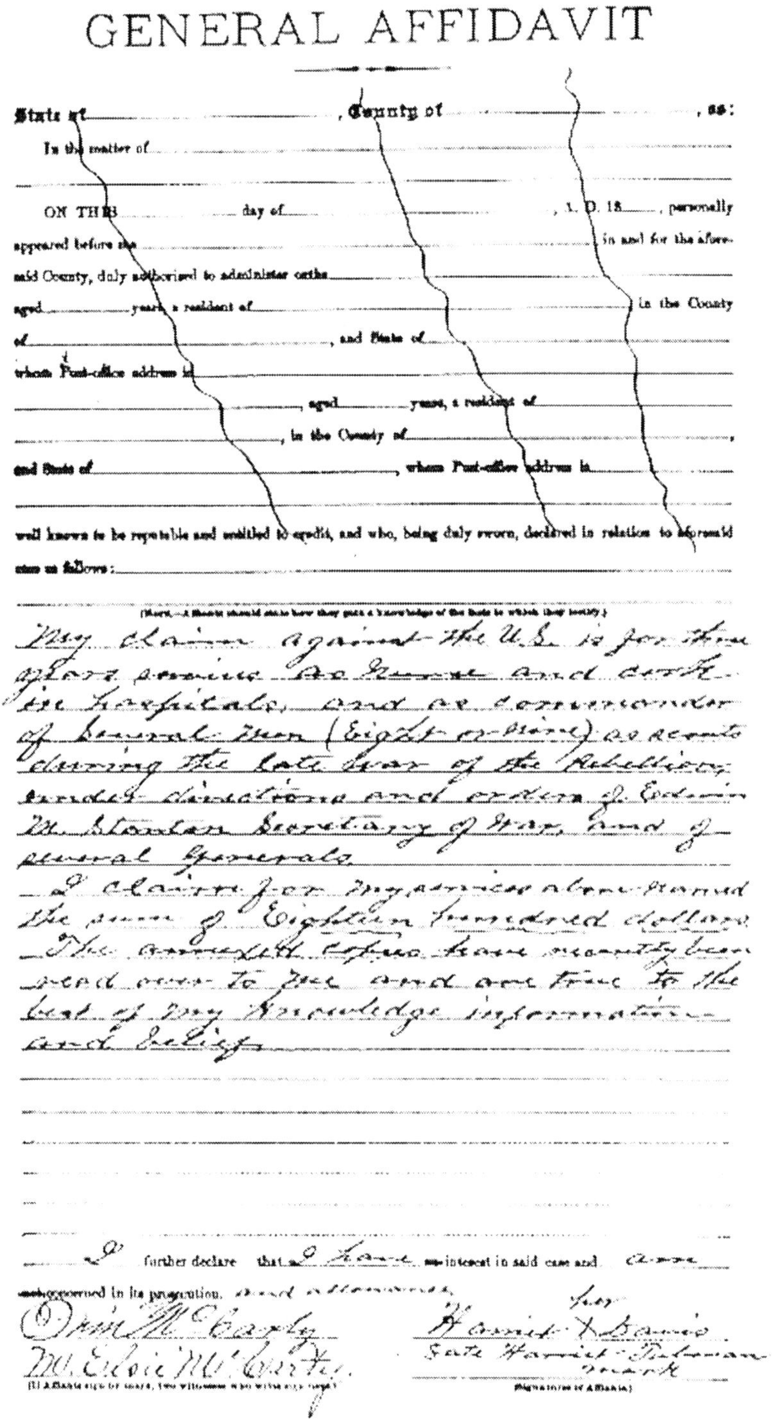

GENERAL AFFIDAVIT

My claim against the U.S. is for three
years service as Nurse and cook
in hospitals, and as commander
of several men (Eight or nine) as scouts
during the late War of the Rebellion,
under directions and orders of Edwin
M. Stanton Secretary of War and of
several Generals

I claim for my services above named
the sum of Eighteen hundred dollars.
The annexed copies have recently been
read over to me and are true to the
best of my knowledge information
and belief

Dan'l M. Carty
M. Elsie M. Carty

Harriet × Davis
late Harriet Tubman
mark

Figure 8.2. Harriet Tubman's Affidavit.

STATE OF _New York_ , County of _Cayuga_ , ss :

Sworn to and subscribed before me this day by the above named affiant , and I certify that I read said

affidavit to said affiant , including the words

erased, and the words

added, and acquainted _her_

with its contents before _she_ executed the same. I further certify that I am in nowise inter-

ested in said case, nor am I concerned in its prosecution; and that said affiant _is_ personally

known to me and that _she is a_ credible person

Wm McCarty
(Official Signature)

Notary Public
(Official Character)

[L. S.]

I, , Clerk of the County Court in and for afore-

said County and State, do certify that

Esq., who has signed his name to the foregoing declaration and affidavit, was, at the time of so doing

in and for said County and State, duly commissioned and sworn;

that all his official acts are entitled to full faith and credit, and that his signature thereunto is genuine.

Witness my hand and seal of office, this day of , 18

[L. S.]

Clerk of the

☞ To be executed before a Court of Record or some officer thereof having custody of its seal, a Notary Public, or Justice of the Peace, whose official signature shall be verified by his official seal, and in case he has none, his signature and official character shall be certified by a Clerk of a Court of Record, or a City or County Clerk.

Figure 8.2.   (Continued)

Fifty-fifth Congress of the United States of America;

At the Third Session,

Begun and held at the City of Washington on Monday, the fifth day of December, one thousand eight hundred and ninety-eight.

AN ACT

Granting an increase of pension to Harriet Tubman Davis.

Be it enacted by the Senate and House of Representatives of the United States of America in Congress assembled, That the Secretary of the Interior be, and he is hereby, authorized and directed to place on the pension roll, subject to the provisions and limitations of the pension laws, the name of Harriet Tubman Davis, widow of Nelson Davis, late a private in Company G, Eighth Regiment United States Colored Infantry, and pay her a pension at the rate of twenty dollars per month in lieu of that she is now receiving.

Thomas B. Reed

Speaker of the House of Representatives.

Garret A. Hobart

Vice-President of the United States and President of the Senate.

Approved
February 28, 1899
William McKinley

Figure 8.2. (*Continued*)

The earth and myself are of one mind. The measure of the land and the measure of our bodies are the same. . . . I never said the land was mine to do with as I chose. The one who has the right to dispose of it is the one who has created it. I claim the right to live on my land and accord you the privilege to live on yours (Gidley, 1981).

1. Play the song, Earth is Our Mother (Gass, 1986) or another selection of native American music. Direct students to rhythmically walk to the music. What does the song reveal about the Indians' relationship to the earth? Would Chief Joseph agree with the song's lyrics? Using the content of the song and the quotations, write a speech that Chief Joseph delivers to white settlers expressing his people's beliefs about the land. Does this song reflect the beliefs of American Indians today?

2. Distribute a chronology of Chief Joseph (see listed web site). Direct students to identify all examples of culture contact between whites and the Nez Perce. For each cntact, discuss if it was a positive, negative or neutral experience from the perspectives of the whites and the Indians. How might the world views expressed in the song and Chief Joseph's quotations help account for these interactions? Describe the changing nature of these interactions over time. What factors account for this? Write a song or poem that reflects these changing interactions from the perspective of a Nez Perce or a white settler. Create a timeline that shows these events and those influencing Harriet Tubman's life (pre-Civil War through the turn of the century). Chief Joseph and Harriet Tubman were contemporaries. Were they influenced by the same events? Why or why not? How were their experiences similar? Different?

3. Read the quotations by Jefferson, Sherman and Sealth. Briefly summarize the view of each individual toward native Americans. What historical/cultural factors might account for the differences between Jefferson and Sherman's views? How might Jefferson have reacted to the decision in 1877 to move the Nez Perce from their homelands to a reservation? Sherman's reaction? For each view, discuss if it still exists today. Would Chief Sealth agree with Chief Joseph's beliefs as reflected in activity 1? What did he mean when he said "the White Man will never be alone?"

Thomas Jefferson: To the Miamis, Powtewataminies and Weeauki
Made by the same Great Spirit, and living in the same land with our brothers, the red men, we consider ourselves as the same family; we wish to live with them as one people, and to cherish their interests as our own.

William Tecumseh Sherman

The more we can kill this year, the less will have to be killed the next war, for the more I see of these Indians, the more convinced I am that they will all have to be killed or be maintained as a species of paupers.

Chief Sealth Of The Duwamish

When the last Red Man shall have perished, and the memory of my tribe shall have become a myth among the white men, these shores will swarm with the invisible dead of my tribe, and when your children's children think themselves alone in the field, the store, the shop, upon the highway, or in the silence of the pathless woods, they will not be alone. . . . At night when the streets of your cities are silent and you think them deserted, they will throng with the returning hosts that one filled them and still love this beautiful land. The White Man will never be alone (Warren, R.P., 1983).

Examine a map of the Nez Perce retreat in 1877 (see web site). Calculate the number of miles traveled. Examine a topographical map and describe the journey. How did the topography aid/hinder their journey and protect/expose them to their pursuers? Why did the Nez Perce decide to leave their homeland? What was their quest? What events prior to their retreat help explain this action? Both General Howard and Chief Joseph wanted to avoid war but ended up fighting against each other. Should one fight for his/her beliefs? How would different abolitionists respond to this question? Based on the song and Chief Joseph's quotations, what do you think was the attitude of the Nez Perce toward the land they retreated over? The attitude of General Howard's men? How does this journey compare to that of the fugitive slaves traveling the Underground Railroad? How were these journeys similar? Different? Can you think of any flights to freedom occurring today? How are they similar or different to the journey of the Nez Perce? Fugitive slaves? What personal qualities are required to make such a journey?

4. Read Chief Joseph's surrender speech (see web site). Why did Chief Joseph decide to surrender? What did he mean by "from where the sun now stands?" Do you think Young Joseph was giving up his quest for freedom? Reexamine the map. Note how close Joseph was to Canada when he surrendered. Chief Joseph believed he was safe in Canada before the final attack by Colonel Miles' army. Do you think this influenced his decision to surrender? Prior to surrendering, Chief Joseph was informed that if he surrendered he and his people could return to the Northwest in peace. Should any previous events have alerted Chief Joseph to doubt these

surrender terms? How might Jefferson react to Chief Joseph's surrender? Sherman? Sealth? Harriet Tubman? Locate music that conveys how Chief Joseph might have felt when he surrendered. What would you have done in Chief Joseph's place?

5. Read Chief Joseph's argument for being allowed to return to Wallowa. What beliefs explain his strong desire to return to Wallowa? How are these related to the beliefs expressed in the song and the quotations? What actions did Chief Joseph take to try and get his people back to their homeland? Why do you think they weren't successful? What perceptions/ misperceptions do you think Joseph was forming of white men, and vice versa? How had prior events shaped these perceptions? What request for freedom did Chief Joseph make? Had his quest for freedom changed? Would Jefferson agree with Young Joseph's concept of freedom? Sherman? Sealth? Harriet Tubman? Other abolitionists? Could a group's request for equal rights be denied by our government today?

April 1879

Joseph publishes his argument in "An Indian's View of Indian Affairs" in *The North American Review,* saying, in part:

> I want the white people to understand my people. Some of you think an Indian is like a wild animal. This is a great mistake. I will tell you about our people, and then you can judge whether an Indian is a man or not. I believe much trouble and blood would be saved if we opened our hearts more. . . .
>
> [On his deathbed my father said:] "My son, never forget my dying words. This country holds your father's body. Never sell the bones of your father and your mother." I pressed my father's hand and told him that I would protect his grave with my life. My father smiled and passed away to the spirit land.
>
> I buried him in that beautiful valley of winding waters. I love that land more than all the rest of the world. A man who would not love his father's grave is worse than a wild animal. . . .
>
> In the treaty councils the commissioners have claimed that our country had been sold to the Government. Suppose a white man should come to me and say, "Joseph, I like your horses, and I want to buy them." I say to him, "No, my horses suit me, I will not sell them." Then he goes to my neighbor, and says to him: "Joseph has some good horses. I want to buy them, but he refuses to sell." My neighbor answers, "Pay me the money, and I will sell you Joseph's horses." The white man returns to me and says, "Joseph, I have bought your horses, and you must let me have them." If we sold our lands to the Government, this is the way they were bought. . . .
>
> I have carried a heavy load on my back ever since I was a boy. I learned then that we were but few, while the white men were many, and that we could not hold our own with them. We were like deer. They were like grizzly bears. We

had a small country. Their country was large. We were contented to let things remain as the Great Spirit Chief made them. They were not; and would change the rivers and mountains if they did not suit them. . . .

[For the coming of war] I blame my young men, and I blame the white men. I blame General Howard for not giving my people time to get their stock away from Wallowa. I do not acknowledge that he had the right to order me to leave Wallowa at any time. I deny that either my father or myself ever sold that land. It is still our land. It may never again be our home, but my father sleeps there, and I love it as I love my mother. I left there, hoping to avoid bloodshed.

[Since the war I have been pleading to be allowed to return to the Northwest.] At last I was granted permission to come to Washington and bring my friend Yellow Bull and our interpreter with me. I am glad we came. I have shaken hands with a great many friends, but there are some things I want to know which no one seems able to explain. I cannot understand how the Government sends a man out to fight us, as it did General Miles, and then breaks his word. Such a Government has something wrong about it. I cannot understand why so many chiefs are allowed to talk so many different ways, and promise so many different things. I have seen the Great Father Chief (the President); the next Great Chief (Secretary of the Interior); the Commissioner Chief (Hayt); the Law Chief (General Butler), and many other law chiefs (Congressmen), and they all say they are my friends, and that I shall have justice, but while their mouths all talk right I do not understand why nothing is done for my people. I have heard talk and talk, but nothing is done. Good words do not last long until they amount to something. Words do not pay for my dead people. They do not pay for my country, now overrun by white men. They do not protect my father's grave. They do not pay for my horses and cattle. Good words will not make good the promise of your War Chief, General Miles. Good words will not give my people good health and stop them from dying. Good words will not give my people a home where they can live in peace and take care of themselves. I am tired of talk that comes to nothing. It makes my heart sick when I remember all the good words and all the broken promises. There has been too much talking by men who had no right to talk. Too many misrepresentations have been made, too many misunderstandings have come up between the white men about the Indians. If the white man wants to live in peace with the Indian he can live in peace. There need be no trouble. Treat all men alike. Give them all the same law. Give them all an even chance to live and grow. All men were made by the Great Spirit Chief. They are all brothers. The earth is the mother of all people, and all people should have equal rights upon it. You might as well expect the rivers to run backward as that any man who was born a free man should be contented penned up and denied liberty to go where he pleases. If you tie a horse to a stake, do you expect he will grow fat? If you pen an Indian up on a small spot of earth, and compel him to stay there, he will not be contented nor will he grow and prosper. I have asked some of the great white chiefs where they get their authority to say to the Indian that he shall stay in one place, while he sees white men going where they please. They cannot tell me.

I only ask of the Government to be treated as all other men are treated. If I cannot go to my own home, let me have a home in some country where my people will not die so fast. I would like to go to Bitter Root Valley. There my people would be healthy; where they are now they are dying. Three have died since I left my camp to come to Washington.

When I think of our condition my heart is heavy. I see men of my race treated as outlaws and driven from country to country, or shot down like animals.

I know that my race must change. We cannot hold our own with the white men as we are. We only ask an even chance to live as other men live. We ask to be recognized as men. We ask that the same law shall work alike on all men. If the Indian breaks the law, punish him by the law. If the white man breaks the law, punish him also.

Let me be a free man—free to travel, free to stop, free to work, free to trade where I choose, free to choose my own teachers, free to follow the religion of my fathers, free to think and talk and act for myself—and I will obey every law, or submit to the penalty.

Whenever the white man treats the Indian as they treat each other, then we shall have no more wars. We shall all be alike—brothers of one father and one mother, with one sky above us and one country around us, and one government for all. Then the Great Spirit Chief who rules above will smile upon this land, and send rain to wash out the bloody spots made by brothers' hands upon the face of the earth. For this time the Indian race are waiting and praying. I hope that no more groans of wounded men and women will ever go to the ear of the Great Spirit Chief above, and that all people may be one people.
In-mut-too-yah-lat-lat has spoken for his people.

Young Joseph (Gidley, 1981, pp. 32–34).

These sample lessons demonstrate the integrative studies model. The ongoing study of varied resources related to the theme enables students to recognize patterns and connections between individuals as well as times. Students become connective thinkers.

CONCLUSION

Our increasingly complex world requires teaching strategies that better prepare students to discover interrelationships and detect patterns. The integrative studies model uses different modes of perception to study a theme across time thus, developing connective thinking. This approach optimizes learning and assists students in coping with the cognitive demands of the 21st century.

Discovering the inter-relatedness of all life is truly the challenge and reward of learning. Like the roots of a tree, we seek connections to better understand and sustain life.

To the young mind everything is individual, stands by itself. By and by, it finds how to join two things and see in them one nature, then three, then three thousand . . . discovering roots running underground whereby contrary and remote things cohere and flower out from one stem. . . .

—Emerson

BIBLIOGRAPHY

Caine, R. N. & Caine, G. *Making Connections: Teaching and the Human Brain.* Alexandria, Virginia: Association for Supervision and Curriculum Development, 1991.

Eisner, E. W. "The Misunderstood Role of the Arts in Human Development." *Phi Delta Kappan* 73 (April 1992): 591–595.

Fowler, C. "The Arts Are Essential to Education." *Educational Leadership* 47 (November 1989): 60–63.

Gidley, M. *Kopet, a documentary narrative of Chief Joseph's last years.* Seattle, Washington: University of Washington Press, 1981.

Godfrey, R. "Civilization, Education, and the Visual Arts: A Personal Manifesto." *Phi Delta Kappan* 73 (April 1992): 596–600.

Hughes, L. *Selected poems of Langston Hughes.* New York, New York: Alfred A. Knopf, 1966.

McCloskey, M.L. "Resource pages on Chief Joseph of the Nez Perce." http://www.gsu.edu/~eslmlm/chiefjoseph.html (16 January 2004).

Warren, R.P. *Chief Joseph of the Nez Perce, a poem.* New York: Random House, 1983.

Chapter Nine

Integrating The Curriculum: An Example Using "Flowers For Algernon"

James S. Etim, Patricia King and Jamal Woods

The National Middle School Association (1995) believes that developmentally responsive middle level schools are characterized by:

a shared vision
educators committed to young adolescents
a positive school climate
an adult advocate for every student
family and community partnerships
high expectations for all

Therefore, they provide:
a curriculum that is challenging, integrative and exploratory
varied teaching/learning approaches
assessment and evaluation that promote learning
flexible organizational structures
programs and policies that foster health, safety and wellness
comprehensive guidance and support services

Several terms are often used to discuss the concept of integration of the school curriculum. These include integrated curriculum, thematic teaching and interdisciplinary teaching among others. According to Humphreys et al, (1981:11) "An integrated study is one in which children broadly explore knowledge in various subjects related to certain aspects of their environment." In discussing the integrative curriculum, Dressel (1958) points out that this planned learning experience not only provides the learner "with a unified view of commonly held knowledge . . . but also motivate and develop learners' power to perceive new relationships and thus to create new models, systems and structures." Shoemaker writes that integrative curriculum cuts across subject-matter lines, bringing together various aspects of the curriculum into meaningful association to focus upon broad areas of study." Since students are removed from the limitations of subject boundaries and immersed in rich environments that reflect life situations, they are able to remember connections and solve problems (Kovalik and Olsen, 1994).

According to Dean Walker (1996), ". . . through integrative education, educators seek to improve students' basic skills in language arts and mathematics while also teaching thinking skills, physical and sensing skills and social skills." While Lawton (1994) points out that integration of curriculum is fundamental to adolescent intellectual development and personal growth, Cummings (1994) contends that problems and issues that confront young adolescents require that schools use an integrated approach in curriculum planning and implementation. However, no matter how educators and scholars define curriculum integration and how they view it, Kathy Lake (1994) points out that most people see it as

a. A combination of subjects
b. An emphasis on projects
c. Sources that go beyond textbooks
d. Relationship among concepts
e. Thematic units as organizing principles
f. Flexible scheduling
g. Flexible student grouping.

BACKGROUND INFORMATION

Several factors have contributed to the ongoing interest in integrative curriculum. The knowledge explosion, fragmented teaching schedules, concerns over curriculum irrelevancies, lack of connections among school subjects, global interdependence and the need for workers to solve complex problems that have interconnected roots are all factors that have contributed to the current interest in integrated curriculum (Lake, 1994; Benjamin, 1989 and Jacobs, 1989). Biondo, Raphael, and Gavelek (1999) opined that in their investigations, they found minimal research that discussed such areas as "what integrated language arts or interdisciplinary curricula look like in the classrooms" and how such learning environments affect students across grades.

They also point out that there are several strategies in the implementation of curriculum integration. They continued:

> For some researchers working in the area of curriculum integration, the reference point is the curriculum (i.e., the "what"), while for others, it is the process that supports integration (i.e., the "how"). In the former, the teachers present the curriculum that has been integrated so that subjects areas is not distinct, in the later, they teach processes that are integrated across subjects.

In the middle school we teach, teachers are expected to have one interdisciplinary unit a quarter. Each team is to decide on what to teach and when to teach the unit. The only proviso is that the unit should be related to the North Carolina Standard Course of Study. We report on the implementation of an integrated undertaken during the 2001–2002 school year.

PLANNING THE STUDY

In planning our study, we took note of Fogarty's ten levels of curriculum integration (as in Lake, 1994). Lake discusses these ten levels and lists the advantages and disadvantages of each. For this study, we chose the Shared Approach involving team planning using several disciplines that focuses on shared concepts, skills and attitudes.

The theme that formed the focal point of the unit was "Intelligence, Self Concept and Identity." We planned that as a team, we will incorporate aspects of Language Arts, Mathematics, Social Studies and Science in the implementation of this theme. We all agreed that we will use technology to enhance instruction. To further carry out the unit, we all agreed to use "Flowers for Algernon" by Daniel Keyes as the text in Language Arts and that teachers in the team will build some skills using the text. (See Figure 9.1).

Flowers for Algernon is a science fiction story. At the beginning of the story, we are introduced to Charlie Gordon, a mentally challenged 37-year-old student. He cannot read, write or spell very well given the fact that his I.Q. is 68. He needs an operation to try to improve his intelligence. The need for this operation has increased given the fact that Algernon, a mouse, has recently been operated upon and its intelligence has grown three-fold. After the operation, Charlie is able to read, write and spell correctly. His I.Q. improves three-fold, and he is able to beat Algernon in the maze exercises. His intelligence leads others to be jealous and uncomfortable with him. He is eventually dismissed at the factory where he works. Dark clouds are introduced — Algernon's intelligence recedes and he dies. Charlie's intelligence slowly

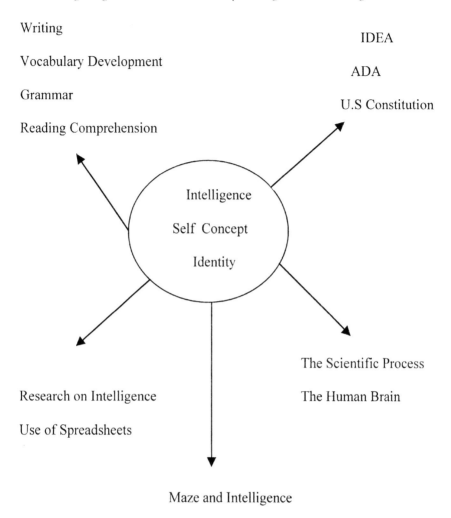

Writing

Vocabulary Development

Grammar

Reading Comprehension

IDEA

ADA

U.S Constitution

Intelligence

Self Concept

Identity

Research on Intelligence

Use of Spreadsheets

The Scientific Process

The Human Brain

Maze and Intelligence

Graphing Intelligence

Figure 9.1. Curriculum Integrative unit using "Flowers for Algernon"

recedes. He cannot read as fast as he used to, his memory begins to fade, etc. Surely, we see the end coming slowly for Charlie.

We began with daily meetings on the text. These meetings lasted between 20 minutes to 40 minutes. The teachers in the team went over the previous days work, planned on how to meet student needs during the day and how to deal with some of the problems we confronted in implementing the curriculum.

The unit lasted five weeks. During the first week, the Language Arts teacher introduced the text to the students. Students read Progress Reports

1–6 and answered comprehension questions, wrote in their journals on such areas as their attitude towards Charlie, what they would do if they found their intelligence greatly improved and how science has been useful to mankind. We discussed the concept of intelligence, school performance, what students can do to improve school performance and self-concept. Students also watched a video that was an introductory piece on the text.

During week two, we introduced the unit to the students in the team (there were four teachers and 68 eighth grade students in this team). The unit included a submission of a project in each area by each student. Each teacher (Language Arts, Mathematics, Social Studies and Resource teacher) introduced an aspect of the project associated with the unit. The presentation on Science was a joint one since each teacher in the team taught the area. In discussing the unit with the students, we shared with them the objectives, how long the unit would last, our expectations, when work was due and grading practice.

This is the age of accountability, of the standards movement, high stakes state mandated testing and rewards for schools and teachers in high performing schools. Vars and Beane (2000) points out that one way to solve the issue of curriculum integration in the age of the standards movement is that teachers "may deal with standards before, during or after engaging students in planning learning experiences . . . by identifying and labeling the standards and competencies included in the unit." This will not only provide evidence that standards are being addressed but will also help the teacher determine what competencies merit further attention in the units that follow. In this unit, we used some of the objectives from the North Carolina Standard Course of Study as applicable for each subject area. Each objective was clearly stated during the implementation and listed on the project instruction handout. The project topics for each subject area was given to each student. Basically, the objectives of the unit were:

1. Integrating the curriculum in Language Arts (reading, writing, grammar and vocabulary), Mathematics, Science, Social Studies and technology around themes that reflect some concerns of middle school students- identity, self concept, acceptance, intelligence, school achievement/performance and testing.
2. Engaging students in projects requiring knowledge and skills in various school subjects, e.g. research skills, writing skills, analysis, synthesis, evaluation, etc.
3. Making use of other sources apart from text-newspaper, magazines, internet to enhance learning.
4. Reflecting on real life problems and writing a learning log.

5. Teaching based on a state standard course of study.

During weeks two to four, each teacher taught according to the agreed upon objectives/activities. For example, we agreed as a team that in Science, each teacher would review the scientific method and go over with students the scientific process as presented in the text. We also agreed that students would be introduced to the brain and brief discussions would be held on the parts of the brain and functions of the brain. This was to form the foundation of our discussion on intelligence that was part of the unit.

To integrate technology into these discussions, students were given ample opportunity to use the internet to find the kinds of information they needed to complete their project. For example, students were given several sites to read in the area of Language Arts and Social Studies. In Language Arts, they included:

1. http://www.scifi.com/sfw/issue76/classic.html
2. http://www.pinkmonkey.com/booknotes/monkeynotes/pmAlgernon02.asp
3. http://www.ced.appstate.edu/whs/flowers.htm
4. http://www.bookrags.com/notes/alg/PART1.htm
5. http://www.branson.k12.mo.us/langarts/cmflower.htm

In Social Studies:
www.spiritofada.org
www.abanat.org/disability
www.cds.hawaii.edu
www.disabilityworld.org
www.nichy.org

Characteristics of Students

Of the 68 eighth grade students who participated in the study, about 70 percent were on grade level in terms of reading achievement as measured by the North Carolina End of Grade Examination. Many were receiving help through tutorials, after school programs and Saturday academies in Language Arts and Mathematics.

These students were part of a middle school with more than 700 students (in grades 6–8). During the last three years (1999–2002), several curriculum innovations have been introduced as a means of improving curricular offerings and enhancing student achievement. These have included Balanced Literacy, Interdisciplinary Studies/Curriculum integration and Working on the Work.

IMPLEMENTATION

The unit began in the Language Arts class. During the five weeks of the unit, students had opportunities to answer comprehension questions, discuss the story, write a daily learning log and study vocabulary and grammar using the text. Apart from writing learning logs, students had other writing assignments in class. For example during the first week, they wrote on the prompt:

You woke up this morning and were told that you have a superior intelligence. Your I.Q. moved from average (about 100) to superior (135–155). What would you do with this new found ability?

NOTE. As you write your paper, think of these questions: a) How would your school work be affected, b) How would your graduation from high school, college be affected and what would your friends think of you; and d) How would your career goals be affected?

After you read about his so-called friends making fun of him and given the fact that peers and peer group pressure is an important part of middle school, we asked students to write on the topic "Friendships." We asked students to consider who their friends were, why they were their friends, the role of friends in character building, etc. Other writing topics included "Application for Employment" letter after reading about Charlie's dismissal from his factory job and a prompt *"Have you ever felt mistreated or misunderstood? Write about it, describing the situation and what you did to ensure that you made your feelings point of view known to those involved."* Another prompt was *"How do you feel about tests?* Describe your feelings in 200 words."

The last topic was an important one to them. Given that most have been tested on standardized tests since they were in third grade, we wanted to find out how they felt about tests and how we can use some of their ideas to help prepare them better for the end of year tests which they will be taking.

In Social Studies, students used the Internet to search for information, analyze information and write their report (see some cites given in Appendix 3). Students were introduced to IDEA and ADA. Discussions centered on the disabled, how they are treated in society and the need to treat others with respect and dignity. We discussed how his teacher treated him with more dignity than those in the factory. Students discussed how families and significant others help give each individual an identity. Globally, we discussed the Bill of Rights and how that helps give citizens an identity as an American citizen.

In Mathematics, students created mazes and produced bar graphs based on the information from the text. In Science, students produced poster boards on the scientific process and showed how each part of the scientific process was reflected in the text. For example, students were asked to identify the scientific problem in the text. Some were asked to use the data provided on Algernon and Charlie to write a conclusion about science's ability to improve intelligence. Many used the internet to find information on the brain.

Students worked in groups (of 2–3 students). Scheduling was flexible especially during the writing of the project. This allowed students to spend a longer time with any teacher or in the internet lab to gather information or prepare and edit their projects.

The projects and the specific areas are as follows:

Directions: Investigate, research, and answer one question per subject area. Report findings in a well-thought out, typed (12 point font) paper.

Language Arts (Standard Course of Study objectives: 1.02, 1.03, 1.04, 6.01).

1. Choose one of the Progress Reports. Correct it in Standard English
2. Write daily Reading or Learning Logs. Present it to class
3. What lessons of life have you learned as a result of reading "Flowers for Algernon?" Write your response in four to five paragraphs

Mathematics (Standard Course of Study Objectives 3.03, 2.11, 2.12).

4. Create a spreadsheet of Algernon's Intelligence quotient based on the journal entries. Create a graph based on the spreadsheet. Write a paragraph describing the meaning of the chart. (You may use data provided to you in class)
5. Construct a maze

Science

6. Review the scientific method and use that to write a standard laboratory report after reading "Flowers for Algernon"
7. Discuss the problems of using human subjects in experimental research
8. Create a storyboard of the brain describing the functions of each part

Technology (Standard Course of Study Objectives: 4.01 and 8.05).

9. Using the internet, write down five sites related to "Flowers for Algernon." Read each cite and write down two important ideas about each cite. What did you learn about life and human character?
10. Go to http://www.branson.k12.mo.us/langarts/cmflower/study.htm and answer three questions between 7–12. E-mail your responses to the Language Arts teacher.
11. Using the internet, write down three to five sites related to the brain or intelligence. Summarize any one and print it out.

Social Studies (Standard Course of Study Objective 11.4, Skill levels 2, 3, 4).

12. How are we different? How do differences in intelligence cause differences in treatment by society? How are those less intelligent discriminated against?
13. Review three weeks of the newspaper (two papers a week). Look at WANT ADS. Choose any ten jobs (the ten jobs should be divided into three categories: professional and skilled class, semi-professional and unskilled class). For each category, write down the qualifications necessary to obtain the job. What does this tell you about education, job type and intelligence?

During the last two days of the project, students presented their project to the team. They were assessed based on the rubrics presented earlier to students.

ANECDOTAL EVIDENCE

In terms of the project, Table 9.1 below shows the completion rate and topic areas covered.

Table 9.1. Completion Rate and Topic Area

Area	Completion Rate %	Topic Area
Science	92.6	Brain
Language Arts	94.1	Rewriting
Mathematics	94.1	Maze
Social Studies	36.7	Jobs Using Newspaper

At the end of the unit, all 68 students were asked to answer four questions:

1. Did you like the unit?
2. In the implementation of the unit, what did you like? (mention one idea)
3. Do you think we need to have more of these kinds of units?
4. What do we need to do in the future to improve the implementation of the unit?

To question 1, 88.2% said they liked the unit. Responses to question 2 are given in Table 9.2.

Table 9. 2.   Parts of the Unit I Liked the Most

Item	n	%
Working in groups	16	23.5
Using the computer for information	25	36.8
Completing a project	18	26.5
Writing learning logs	9	13.2

Table 9.2 above shows that many students enjoyed using the computer during the project to find information, analyze the information and apply it as necessary.

In terms of question 3, 87% indicated that there should be other interdisciplinary units during the year, while to question 4, 58.9% of students felt they needed more time for the project.

For teachers, two things stand out in terms of the success of the project:

1. Planning together to ensure the smooth implementation of the unit
2. More than 90% of the students completed at least three parts of the project.

As teachers in the team, we planned together and this resulted in the success of the unit. Teachers in the team were willing to listen to others and negotiate their views so that both subject goals and unit goals could be achieved. According to Kain (1996), such willingness to collaborate resulted in teachers developing their own meaning of curricular integration and allowed teachers to confront and deal with a number of constraints.

Secondly, as a team, we all took credit for student completion of their work and for their enthusiasm in the classroom.

SUMMARY OF FINDINGS

According to Lake (1994), there was "no detrimental effect in learning when students are involved in an integrated curriculum." (See also Vars and Beane, 2000). Our study did not go that far since we did not have a control group. However, we report that at least 90% of the students completed three sections of the project on time, at least 88% indicated that the unit was interesting, and at least 87% felt there should be other interdisciplinary units. Students used the computer for information gathering and analysis or for word processing. Students enjoyed working in groups and presenting their projects to the class. Some of these findings support Jacobs (1989) who pointed out that an integrated curriculum is "associated with better students self-direction, higher attendance, higher levels of homework completion and better attitudes towards school."

There is however need for further studies in the area of student achievement —for example whether students who go through several integrated units perform better in state mandated end of grade tests than those who do not. There is also need for a more standardized rubric to assess student achievement during oral presentations of projects.

RECOMMENDATIONS

Based on this study, the following recommendations are made for the successful implementation of an interdisciplinary unit:

1. Team planning must be encouraged and maintained. Several meetings should be held weekly.
2. There should be flexibility in scheduling. This will allow students to spend more time in the areas and with teachers when they require more help.
3. Resources should be available for each student. For this unit, the computer with internet capability, newspapers and text were the necessary resources.
4. In an age of standards and accountability, efforts should be made to align the objectives of the interdisciplinary unit to state goals and objectives or national goals.

BIBLIOGRAPHY

Benjamin, S. "An Ideascape for Education: What Futurists Recommend" *Educational Leadership* 47.1 (1989):8–16.
Biondo, Sandra, Taffy E. Raphael and James Gavelek. "Mapping the Possibilities of Integrated Literary Education" *Reading Online,* March 1999. http://www:eadingonline.org/research/biondo/biondo.html (October 5, 2003).
Cumming, James. "Catering for the needs of all young adolescents: Towards an Integrated Approach" *Unicorn* 20 (1994): 12–20.
Dressel, P. "The Meaning and Significance of Integration" *The Integration of Educational Experience*. 57th Yearbook of the National Society for the Study of Education. Nelson B. Henry ed. Chicago: U. of Chicago P, 1958.
Grisham, D. "Exploring Integrated Curriculum" *Reading Psychology* 6 (1995): 269–279.
Humphreys, A., T. Post, and A. Ellis *Interdisciplinary Methods: A Thematic Approach*. Santa Monica, CA: Goodyear Pub. Co, 1981.

Jacobs, H.H. *Interdisciplinary Curriculum: Design and Implementation.* Alexandria, VA: ASCD, 1989.

Kain, D. "Recipes or Dialogue? A Middle School team conceptualizes Curricular Integration" *Journal of Curriculum and Supervision* 11 (1996): 163–187.

Kovalik, Susan and Karen Olsen. *ITI: The Model Integrated Thematic Instruction.* 3rd ed. Kent, Washington: Books for Educators, 1994 ED 379 894.

Lake, Kathy. "Integrated Curriculum-Close Up # 16" School Improvement Research Series. 1994. http://www.nwrel.org/scpd/sirs/8/c016.html (August 20, 2002).

Lawton, E. "Integrating Curriculum: A Slow but Positive Process" *Schools in the Middle*, Nov. 27–30, 1994.

National Middle School Administration. *This We Believe. Developmentally Responsive Middle Level Schools.* Columbus, OH.: National Middle School Association, 1995.

Shoemaker, Betty. "Integrative Education: A Curriculum for the Twenty-First Century" *OSSC Bulletin* 33.2 (October 1989): Eugene, Oregon: Oregon School Study Council. ED 311 602.

Vars, Gordon and James Beane. "Integrative Curriculum in a Standards Based World" ED0-PS-00-6 June 2000. http://ericeece.org/pubs/digests/2000/vars00.html (August 20, 2003).

Walker, Dean. "Integrative Education" *Eric Digest* Number 101. ED 390 112, 1996. http://www.ed.gov/databases/ERIC_Digests/ed390112.html (Dec. 5, 2002).

Chapter 10

Integrating Throughout The Curricula Social Studies Themes Related To Environmental And Social Responsibility And Civic Engagement

Debra Rowe

ABSTRACT

Developing graduates who can and are willing to help solve societal problems is an important goal for our educational system. Humans are living beyond the carrying capacity of the planet and changes in individual and collective behaviors are required to create a sustainable future. Students need knowledge, analysis and change agent skills to successfully express their civic, environmental and social responsibility. Educators have a crucial role in preparing students to be positive agents in these arenas. Research results support that these same skills are necessary for success in family relationships and careers as well. Yet educational curricula often do not adequately address this need to teach the skills and knowledge required for environmental and social problem analysis, environmental and social responsibility and change agent skills.

Many students, graduates and teachers feel overwhelmed by society's economic, environmental and social problems. They feel that the world's problems are so large and complex they cannot do anything about them. Some decide to let apathy and cynicism become their dominant attitudes, often giving up on making the world a better place and just taking care of themselves. Knowledge should be empowering our students to contribute to society instead of making them passive and apathetic. How do we turn this around while teaching our required curricula? This paper explores how to graduate engaged citizens while meeting our state educational standards. Interdisciplinary resources and approaches, successful models and outstanding teaching materials are emphasized.

INTRODUCTION

According to the World Commission on Environment and Development (WCED), sustainable development is defined as "meeting the needs of the present without compromising the ability of future generations to meet their own needs."[1] Many definitions exist, but all definitions of a sustainable future include a positive vision and commitment for society composed of three components: economic viability, social equity and environmental health. We live in a unique time in history. In the past, we had the resources but not the technology to give a high standard of living to everyone on the planet. In the future, if we continue to deplete our natural resources at the present rate, we may have the technology but not the resources to give a decent standard of living to all. This is the first generation where human beings are consuming natural resources at a rate that is exceeding the carrying capacity of the planet. Twenty percent of the world's population occupies around 70 percent of the global ecological footprint.[2] Ecological footprint is the total ecological productive area on Earth divided by the number of inhabitants, including the seas. "Because the total global footprint is, according to a conservative estimate, 37 percent larger than all the ecologically productive areas combined, the wealthiest 20 percent alone occupy a footprint as big as the planet's total carrying capacity . . ."[3] Global problems of poverty, vast inequities in resource consumption, political conflict and environmental degradation weigh upon us.

Yet, in the present, we seem to have both the resources and the technology to have a decent standard of living for all[4]. Education for a sustainable future builds a bridge of skills, knowledge and attitudes that will help us solve these global problems and come closer to our potential of reducing human suffering and environmental degradation and creating a decent standard of living for all. Education for a sustainable future "enables people to develop the knowledge, values and skills to participate in decisions about the way we do things individually and collectively, both locally and globally, that will improve the quality of life now without damaging the planet for the future."[5]

In comparison to the age of the planet and many other species, our species is not very old. The human species is not very sophisticated or mature in terms of creating peaceful, fruitful societies. Some say greed is the problem and greed is human nature. Others say we have not learned from the models available to us from some indigenous cultures and that the Western culture of "rugged" individualism promotes greed and harmful levels of consumption, waste and environmental degradation. Others say we are in the youth of our history as a species, demonstrating the same selfishness and self-absorption of unrestricted adolescents and that the potential to mature is before us. (In support of this last perspective, interpersonal and emotional intelligences are fairly new research fields in Psychology and Business, and teachers have barely begun to include the important basics of conflict resolution, anger management, resilience, self-concept sculpting and other essential skills in school curricula.) A class discussion on the essence of human nature and the viability of a sustainable future is a relevant and fruitful activity in all social science courses. David Smith, from Lamphere High School, recommends asking the following three questions of students: "What does human nature look like now in our society? What did/does human nature look like in other cultures (either indigenous or more environmentally advanced and socially compassionate such as Holland)? What might human nature be like in the future?"[6] Providing information to students on peaceful and environmentally healthier societies provides an important contrast to include in our students' repertoire, helping them to envision a more positive view of human nature. Good examples exist in places like Curitiba, Brazil, where private car use has decreased, hunger has decreased and green areas have increased due to an attractive and efficient and less polluting bus service and waste for food program.[7]

Providing students with positive examples and role models of caring, active communities helps to meet educational standards. One of the main goals of social science education is to produce active citizens who care about and help solve societal problems. State Social Studies Standards often require this as a curricular focus. (In Michigan, for example, state standards include coverage of human/environmental interactions, global issues and events within the Geographic Perspective, American government and world affairs within the Civic Perspective, the consequences of individual and household choices and a discussion of environmental externalities within the Economic Perspective, conducting investigations within Inquiry, identifying and analyzing issues within Public Discourse and Decision Making and responsible personal conduct within Citizen Involvement.)[8]

By choosing curricula that motivate students to become civically engaged as positive change agents, we can help students be more than "armchair pontificators." Armchair pontificators are graduates who have acquired critical thinking skills and can critique but do not have the motivation or skills to help solve societal problems. In contrast, positive change agents can:

1. cope effectively with change,
2. care about societal problems and solutions,
3. envision and are willing to help create a more positive societal future,
4. experience a strengthened political efficacy, and
5. know how to effectively implement change.[9]

Imagine the U.S. population with reduced cynicism and more skilled and educated engagement in solving local, national and even global problems. For a few specific examples, imagine planning officials throughout the country applying the latest information about watershed management and smart zoning regulations, thereby preventing environmental degradation while strengthening communities and local economies. Imagine businesses reducing their consumption of polluting fossil fuels by applying already cost-effective energy efficient and renewable energy technologies, thereby increasing business profits while reducing pollution, decreasing dependence on foreign sources of energy, and building local and national economies. Imagine communities with cost effective health care and social service prevention programs, maintained in part by extensive community involvement and long-term revenue bonds financing for prevention programs, producing decreased incarceration and increased social health. Imagine students applying integrated social studies, math and science knowledge to help solve societal problems, building their skill and knowledge base as well as their self-concepts as active citizens who can make positive contributions to society. How do we move towards these scenarios? Specifically, how do we graduate skilled students who are engaged in making the world a better place for all and still teach our required curricula?

Essential Sustainability Information And Social Science Themes

In order to be literate in the issues of sustainability, a basic set of facts and certain analyses and perspectives must be acquired. In terms of perspectives, students need to understand that the economy is a subsystem of the ecosystem and not the other way around. They need to understand that natural resources are not unlimited and that we are dependent on a living ecosystem for our basic survival.

Students also need an understanding of:

1. the carrying capacity of the earth, a capacity we are presently exceeding;
2. the present distribution of wealth worldwide, where 1% of the population has as much wealth as the bottom 50%;[10]
3. the present rates of depletion of natural resources (e.g., water, energy, minerals, topsoil, fish, forests);
4. major global threats to sustainability, such as climate change, destruction of the ozone layer and fresh water depletion;
5. human population growth, which has doubled since 1960 and is projected to reach 10 billion by 2050[11];
6. food availability and distribution, including that 80% of the world's hungry live in countries that are net exporters of food[12] and that, while there

is enough food produced on the planet to feed everyone more than adequately, "three-quarters of the agricultural land worldwide has poor soil
fertility and about two-thirds of agricultural land has been degraded in the
past 50 years;"[13] and

7. both environmental and financial life cycle analyses.

This knowledge and other relevant facts too numerous to mention here is
not inherent within any middle or high school discipline curriculum, although
most of the environmental facts fit into science courses and the knowledge
about the distribution of wealth is often covered in social science courses. A
good source for up to date information on the carrying capacity of the earth
is available from the Worldwatch Institute at www.worldwatch.org. For information about both social equity and environmental protection, teachers
can visit www.ABetterFuture.org. The United Nations Environment Program
has a section for children and a free online introductory video at http://www
.bigpicturesmallworld.com/unmovie3.htm.

Teaching the facts alone are not enough. Environmental life cycle analysis looks at the overall impact of the production, packaging, transportation,
consumption and disposal of a product. Financial analysis looks at the
costs over the life of the product. What is sometimes not highly cost-
effective (e.g., a 22-year payback on the solar electric array at Oberlin College) can be highly effective in terms of environmental impact (a 2½ year
payback for carbon pollution on the same solar electric array), and vice
versa. Students need to be aware of these trade-offs so they can understand
which behaviors support a sustainable future. Even if students can't compute some of the more advanced math calculations, they can learn the conceptual framework and then use published sources of life cycle analyses to
apply this knowledge to their daily lives in their choices as consumers and
as citizens.

Students also have to understand how to help change the institutions,
regulations and social customs that are not sustainable. One example of an
unsustainable regulation is the government subsidies for fossil fuels that
make some renewable energies less cost effective in comparison. Values
traditionally held by our society and sometimes taught in social sciences
courses as fact instead of choices need to be discussed within classrooms
and analyzed within the context and necessity of sustainability. These values include: private property and the belief that we have a right to do whatever we want with our property as long as it breaks no laws, even if it hurts
the viability of sustainability; freedom to consume whatever we want as
long as it is legal and the belief that the invisible hand of capitalism will
make this the most efficient way to meet human needs, without any con-

cern for the environmental and human negative effects that might be created; the economic assumption of scarcity and competition that is taught in many first grade curricula instead of simultaneously exploring the potentials for cooperation and economic abundance; the belief that economic indicators such as GDP (gross domestic product) measure quality of life when it really only measures economic activity and negative impacts on quality of life increase the GDP because they generate economic activity (e.g., increased health care costs due to environmental pollution); and the mistake often made that capitalism and democracy are synonymous when capitalism is an economic system and democracy is a political system. These are just a few examples of the concepts sometimes taught in our present curricula that must be questioned to incorporate the necessity of sustainability. Capitalism has both strengths and weaknesses that require adaptation, regulation and change to produce a sustainable future. [14] To not include these discussions is to not prepare our students for what they need to be educated consumers and citizens.

What curricular projects include sustainability knowledge and positive change agent skills in a context of civic engagement and fit social studies, math, science and/or language arts state standards? What projects are easily integrated into existing curricula and can be enjoyably utilized by teachers who have not previously taught this knowledge and skills?

Compartmentalization barriers

Science standards include the coverage of environmental problems, yet this knowledge is rarely coupled with the citizenship skills and social problems analyses included in social studies. Math standards include teaching algebra and the difference between arithmetic and geometric progressions. These skills are essential to understanding the geometric growth of human population as well as the patterns of species extinction, yet math textbooks rarely make this connection. Language Arts standards include critical thinking and essential communication skills such as persuasive writing and speaking, skills essential to be an effective change agent, yet these skills are also often taught in isolation. All of the above must be integrated and practiced together to create graduates capable of building a sustainable future. Unfortunately, these different skills and knowledge are often compartmentalized into separate courses. Interdisciplinary projects can help students integrate skills and knowledge learned in separate courses and disciplines. Yet any interdisciplinary project must be easy to implement and fit into existing requirements. The following sections review teacher resources for all disciplines as well as interdisciplinary models.

Successful Models and Resources

What projects are easily integrated into existing curricula and can be enjoy-ably utilized by teachers who have not previously taught environmental and social analysis, responsibility and change agent skills? The following projects are available to teachers throughout the country and are applicable in single discipline courses as well as interdisciplinary projects.

A Global View of Sustainability

A healthy future for the United States requires citizens educated and engaged in global, not just local problems. Luckily, the United States has recently re-joined the United Nations' UNESCO program and the United Nations has de-clared 2005 to 2015 the Decade of Education for Sustainable Development. The United Nations has an outstanding curriculum about environmental and social sustainability education available at http://www.unesco.org/education/tlsf/index.htm. This site shows how teachers can simply integrate sustainabil-ity issues into their existing curricula. Learning activities with all the specifics are included as well as more generalized descriptions that teachers can easily use.

The Center for a Sustainable Future has free, downloadable, learning ac-tivities about sustainability, including ecological footprint activities and some energy curricula, at http://csf.concord.org. Eighteen strategies for confronting the major systemic problems confronting humanity is wonderful material for teaching and discussion at http://www.osearth.com/resources/wwwproject/index.shtml. The Sustainability Education Center has teaching materials at http://www.sustainabilityed.org/. Other resources include the World Wildlife Fund at http://www.worldwildlife.org, the Izaak Walton League of America Sustainability Education Project at http://www.iwla.org/sep, and the World Resources Institute's Earth Trends Environmental Information Portal at http://earthtrends.wri.org.

The Center for a New American Dream created a website for people who want to take simple actions to make the world a better place. The effects of those who sign up to take actions are tabulated and reported on the site at www.turnthetide.org. Students can join others who sign up to take action and see their joint impact on the environment in tons of reduced pollutants.

Mathematical Calculators and Consumption Impacts

Students are more positive toward learning math when they understand the usefulness of the skills they are learning. Basic math and algebra are used in the following calculators that can easily be integrated into any math class as well as any project about environmental and social responsibility. Using these calculators, students can compare the impacts of their choices as consumers. People in the United States comprise approximately 5% of the world's population and consume approximately 25% of the world's resources. For a sustainable future, the U.S. population has to become educated about the waste and pollution in our consumption choices.

For a valuable tool useful in all types of courses, visit an Ecological Footprint Quiz, available at http://www.earthday.net/footprint/index.asp. The quiz calculates how many planets would be needed if everyone consumed resources at the same rate as the person taking the quiz. This site also allows input for potential lifestyle changes and calculates the change in one's ecological footprint.

The Environmental Protection Agency offers a calculator for greenhouse gas contributions at http://www.epa.gov/cleanenergy/powerprofiler.htm. The site also helps students understand how to improve energy efficiency in their homes. Students can learn about car pollution and take the clean car pledge at http://www.environmentaldefense.org/tool.cfm?tool=tailpipe. For information about the food chain, students can access information at http://library.thinkquest.org/11353/food.htm and can take a food chain quiz at http://www.enn.com/features/2000/05/05092000/feature_story_12596.asp.

The Giraffe Project and Efficacy

Research has shown support for inclusion of the following in curricula to produce more active and effective citizenship:

1. optimism skills to reduce cynicism and apathy (Seligman 1998),[15]
2. efficacy skills (via stories of "average" people making a difference),
3. futuring skills (via sculpting self-concepts and envisioning societal scenarios),[16]
4. implementation skills (change agent skills).[17]

The efficacy skills are effectively taught via the Giraffe Project (http://www.giraffe.org/). The project is presently used in forty-seven states to help students construct a self-concept that includes engagement in solving community or societal problems. Part of this non profit Giraffe Project, funded by such diverse groups as private businesses, the Kellogg Foundation and the Navy, is the Heroes Program. This program follows a three step process: hear the story; tell the story; and become the story. Students hear stories from the Giraffe storybank, which holds profiles of over 800 real heroes, people whose courage and compassion touch the heart and inspire action. People like Abdullah Turner and Nero Graham, who led their neighbors in driving out drug dealers, and the Earth Defenders, a group of at-risk kids who take to their neighborhood's crime-filled streets to do clean-ups and recycling; . . .

After students meet people like these, in print and in the public television video that's part of the curriculum, and sometimes in class appearances by actual Giraffes, they're ready to *find their own heroes*, searching their studies, the news, books, movies, television, their communities and their families and reporting back to the class with their "Giraffe sightings."

(After writing stories about local heroes, students then "become the story" by using their new knowledge to contribute to solving societal problems.)

Students look around themselves, decide what they want to change for the better, then design and carry out service projects to make it happen. The Giraffe Heroes Program leads them through a seven-step process that takes them from deciding to succeeding.

Making their own observations and creating a response—rather than just signing up with an existing service program—is critical to their sense of taking responsibility for something beyond their own lives.

When they hear stories of heroes, tell their own heroes' stories, and exercise their own heroic qualities, the success elements of character (*attitudes and skills to become positive change agents*) emerge . . .[18] (italics are author's)

POSITIVE FUTURE SCENARIOS FOR SOCIETY
AND A POSITIVE FUTURES FAIR

This citizenship-building project is fun, inexpensive and easily implemented in any course or as an interdisciplinary project. It was developed at Oakland Community College and has been used at the middle school, high school and college levels. A formal research study designed by this author and Michael Ponder from Oakland University tested the effectiveness of this project. Results support that students who created the scenarios and the fair developed:

1. an increased willingness to participate in solving societal problems,
2. an increased optimism about the future of society,
3. an increased belief that they can make a difference,
4. a self-concept which includes a stronger commitment to social and civic responsibility and participation.[19]

If used as an interdisciplinary project, students from English, Science, Social Studies (e.g., Psychology, Political Science, Sociology and/or Economics) and/or other disciplines are combined and meet as small interdisciplinary groups for 45 minutes each week. These small groups are given the task to envision a positive scenario for the future of society using two themes, creating a more humane society and creating an environmentally sustainable society. Students then use concepts from class to create a story describing how society changed from today to their positive future scenario. The groups present their positive scenarios and their stories in front of the combined classes toward the end of the semester. (In some settings, half the groups work on a more humane future and the other half on a sustainable society. When the students present their scenarios to each other near the end of the semester, they are often surprised to see that, regardless of the given themes, all of the scenarios are often similar in a number of ways.)

As examples, psychology students described how Gardner's expanded definitions of intelligence[20] changed future K–12 school curricula to include a greater emphasis on conflict resolution, trust building, and interpersonal and intrapersonal intelligence. This led to improved employee/employer relations, healthier personal and community relationships and better parenting in society. Economics students used expanded pollution reduction tax credits to create less polluting industries in their portion of the scenario. During the week when groups presented their positive future scenarios, all students were required to hand in individual papers, comparing the stories presented by the groups, writing about their personally preferred scenario, and describing their willingness to help create this positive society in real life.

Early in the project, students are taught the following skills: the four Ps of futuring (brainstorming and positive scenario building skills), the four Ds of doing (implementation skills including teamwork skills), the ABCs of preventing burnout, and Critical Thinking to Critical Action Skills (analysis to action skills).[21] Supplemental materials available in a special section of the library include writings of futurists, books about sustainability and success stories about "average" people helping to improve society. *What the World Wants* (described below) is used to help students understand that the solutions to many global problems are affordable.

After the students create scenarios, they learn how to create a Positive Futures Fair. They acquire valuable skills and the fair is an inspiring school event. Students research which local organizations are creating a more humane and environmentally sustainable future for society and invite these organizations to participate. Students help write a press release and distribute fliers at local schools and places of business. (The Positive Futures Fair can also be a community event.) Each organization has a display table in the exhibits area and gives a short speech in the auditorium about their organization, describing career and volunteer opportunities. Student enthusiasm for the fair is very high. Most students have little previous exposure to how organizations are creating a more humane and environmentally sound society. Many students volunteer after the Fair.

A detailed description of the interdisciplinary project, including both the scenario building, grading, the Positive Futures Fair, and how the teachers can easily implement the assignment is available at http://eduref.org/cgi-bin/printlessons.cgi/Virtual/Lessons/Interdisciplinary/INT0201.html .

What the World Wants

Many people in the United States are not educated about the relative size and costs of global problems and solutions. Often students don't know that ample resources exist to simultaneously solve problems of overpopulation, starvation and malnutrition, polluted drinking water, deforestation, greenhouse gas excesses and ozone depletion, developing nations' debt, and illiteracy.[22] While the web site, entitled "What the World Wants" http://www.osearth .com/resources/wwwproject/index.shtml compares the costs to solve global problems to the annual military budgets, this data does not need to be used to advocate a reduction in military expenditures. It is a very useful tool to educate students about the relative costs of the different challenges we face to create a better future. Personally, it is one of the few handouts I have used in class where I have seen students eagerly read the footnotes for more information. This site also includes eighteen strategies for confronting the major systemic problems facing humanity, which is wonderful material for discussion. While some of the data is a bit dated, the concept of putting in perspective the affordability of solutions to global problems still holds.

Online Sustainability Education Handbook

Teachers can get information on how to teach change agent skills, take action to help keep the planet healthy and habitable while reducing human suffering, and meet curricular standards via "The Sustainability and Energy Education Project". The site includes questions to be integrated into any curriculum that will expand the learning to include sustainability. Quotes and descriptions of what is sustainability, a list of sustainability topics, free learning activities and downloadable curricula for use in social studies, language arts, science, and math courses are available at www.urbanoptions.org/SustainEdHandbook.

The State of Michigan funded this project via the state's Energy Center Network, a consortium of Energy and Environmental Education Centers and teachers. Most of the included learning activities are correlated with state of Michigan standards and benchmarks in Social Studies, Language Arts, Science and Math for quick and easy reporting. Teachers and organizations from other states are encouraged to make their own versions of correlation to state standards and benchmarks, and the webmaster will create links from the handbook.

A Special Word about Climate Change

Climate change is here.[23] Except for a handful of detractors, many of whom are funded by members of the fossil fuel industry, the scientific consensus is that climate change exists and a substantiated culprit is fossil fuels. This information cannot be relegated to science class. Discussions of the implications of climate change and possible actions to mitigate damage and reduce the trend should be included in all courses. CO_2 from the combustion of fossil fuels is contributing to a CO_2 level in the atmosphere that is higher than anytime in 400,000 years. In 1995, the Intergovernmental Panel on Climate Change (IPCC), composed of more than 2,000 scientists from 100 countries, reported to the United Nations that Earth has already entered a new period of climatic instability likely to cause widespread economic, social and environmental dislocations, including sea level rise of up to four feet, increases in floods and droughts, increasingly severe storms and temperature extremes.[24]

In 1995, the IPCC reported to the United Nations that it had discovered the scientific "fingerprint" of fossil fuel emissions, which are contributing to the warming of the planet. That "fingerprint" is graphically and distinctively different from the natural variability of the climate.[25] That same year, a team at the National Climatic Data Center verified an increase in extreme precipitation events, altered rainfall and drought patterns and temperature extremes during the past several decades. The events they identified are precisely what the current generation of climate computer models project as the early manifestations of climate change.[26] The science tells us that to restore our atmosphere to a hospitable state requires us to cut emissions by 60 to 70 percent.[27]

Carbon dioxide stays in the atmosphere 100 years. If we could magically stop all our fossil fuel burning, we would still be subject to a long spell of costly and traumatic weather extremes. Moreover, new research indicates that prehistoric climate changes have happened as abrupt shifts rather than gradual transitions, and that small changes have triggered catastrophic outcomes.[28]

Both public and academic interest has recently increased in the disadvantages of fossil fuel consumption. These disadvantages include not only climate change, but also recent price spikes in natural gas costs, respiratory illnesses related to air pollution, and trade deficits and political instability due to imported oil. Even with this recent increased interest, the U.S. population is fairly illiterate about pressing environmental problems such as climate change. While polls show that the majority of the public is concerned about the health of the environment, only a small minority understands the basic facts of the most urgent environmental problems and how their actions can either exacerbate or mitigate these problems. For the past twenty years, fossil fuels companies have funded media campaigns that discredit the potentials for efficiency and renewable energies, confusing the public. Unfortunately, very few students have had the opportunity to hear about the Union of Concerned Scientists studies that show that the bulk of government tax benefits and subsidies are given to fossil fuels instead of renewable energies, creating a skewed marketplace. Studies also show we could meet all of our energy needs in this country with efficiency and renewables within our lifetime (http://www.ucsusa.org/).

Luckily, many of the solutions to climate change and these other problems are already technologically available and cost effective in the form of renewable energies and energy efficiency technologies. Given the above environmental concerns, the implementation of renewable energy and energy efficiency technologies has become more crucial. Educators have a unique opportunity to educate tomorrow's citizens about climate change. Climate change is inherently interdisciplinary and to educate our students about the decisions they will have to make as citizens, climate change must be taught from the perspective of multiple disciplines. The solutions to climate change are behavioral and political, and require an understanding of applied sociological and psychological principles.

Quality information resources are available for both consumers and educators about climate change, renewable energy and efficiency technologies. Simple applications of these information resources by students have been shown to reduce utility bills, reduce pollution, reduce the release of greenhouse gases into the atmosphere, reduce health problems and reduce our dependence on foreign oil. Use of these information resources by educators can help them meet education standards as well as produce environmentally literate graduates who can use the principles they learn in social science to make positive differences. A review of these resources will hopefully encourage teachers to help students become more environmentally responsible in their utilization of energy and be part of the solution to the above problems. Teachers and students can learn about these issues together. The teacher doesn't have to be the expert. For information about climate change and other pressing societal problems, visit the WorldWatch Institute at http://www.worldwatch.org and the Pew Center on Global Climate Change at http://www.pewclimate.org/projects/index_environment.cfm.

Renewable Energies across the Curriculum

Renewable energies (e.g., solar energy, wind power, biomass) often spark the interest of middle school students. Baking brownies or cooking eggs or lentils in a solar oven or producing drinkable water out of dirty water from a simple-to-make solar "cookit" (www.solarcooking.org) helps to raise the enthusiasm of students. Students can build solar energy space heating/air collectors from low cost materials. Students can either give these collectors to other schools as a teaching tool, or can install these working collectors at community centers, on the school or at non-profit organizations to reduce utility bills, reduce pollution and as a demonstration project. Plans are available at http://www.urbanoptions.org/SustainEdHandbook/BuildYourOwnSolarAirCollector.htm. Comparing the use of relatively non-polluting renewable energies to the pollution caused from fossil fuels, and discussing how renewables can decrease our dependence on foreign oil shows students how they can help create energy and climate change solutions through energy conservation and the use of renewables. This topic can be easily applied to social studies, science and language arts. Teachers can help students overcome their dismay about environmental degradation through the use of a free downloadable handbook about climate change, acid rain, pollution and conservation and renewable energy solutions, available at http://www.urbanoptions.org/RenewableEnergy/index.htm. "The Next Big Wave" is a CD that is available for free from Focus on Energy, the state energy program in Wisconsin (www.focusonenergy.com.) The CD is an overview of all renewable energies and is available by calling 1-800-762-7077.

At the Alliance to Save Energy (www.ase.org), educators will find multi-disciplinary, hands-on educational opportunities, offering free energy-related lesson plans for elementary, middle school, and high school students online. The Energy Smart Schools site (www.eren.doe.gov/energysmartschools/) is designed primarily to help teachers and students locate resources for teaching and learning about energy, acting as a clearinghouse of information so that you can easily get and apply what is most useful. A CD called Get Smart About Energy with 250 learning activities is available for free from the U.S. Department of Energy. Email rebuildorders@rebuild.org or visit their website at www.rebuild.org and click on the solutions center for other free downloadable lesson plans. Learning activities are available for K–12, including a whole series of activities specifically geared to the environment. All activities come complete with materials that can be printed off the CD, lesson plans and a relation to national education standards, making it easy to integrate into any curriculum. For example, "The Awful 8: The Play" activity helps students become aware of different air pollutants and their cause and effects. An entertaining play script, a related fact sheet and a worksheet for the audience are included. This activity relates to social studies and science standards.

In another activity, entitled Pollution Prevention in Schools, the teacher is given materials to share with students about how pollution is caused with in schools. Students then prepare and conduct a survey to find out where wastes and pollutants are created at the school. The students brainstorm ways to prevent the pollution. The expected outcome is that students understand how to reduce waste and pollution and act on this knowledge. In a third activity appropriate to math classes, students learn how to calculate and graph the effects of certain pollutants on climate change.

Green Teacher Magazine (http://www.greenteacher.com/) has a history of quality articles specifically geared to teachers who want to bring ecological awareness into their classroom. Independent reviews have rated the quality of the publication very high. Working with the students and the above materials to create a greener school and community is a great example of how to connect social studies knowledge with place based and problem based learning to help students gain the change agent skills, knowledge and values they will need to become socially and environmentally responsible adults.

Environmental Education As The Integrating Context For Learning In All Areas (EIC)

EIC is an extensive research project in forty schools that looked at the impact of using the environment as the integrating theme in math, science, social studies and language arts. The results of 640 interviews showed that using the environment to tie together learning in different courses produced higher standardized test scores in reading, writing, math, science and social studies as well as less classroom management problems. Students showed a greater enthusiasm and engagement in learning as well as greater pride in their accomplishments. The State Education and Environment Roundtable that supported this research is made up of educational agencies from twelve states. The Council of Chief State School Officers administers project funding and the Pew Charitable Trusts provides financial support. For more extensive information, including best practices and teacher resources, visit www.seer.org

Building With Books and Service Learning

Building With Books (www.buildingwithbooks.org/who/index.shtml) is an international organization started by two University of Michigan graduates. The organization has two main components: building schools in unindustrialized countries and creating sister school relationships between those schools and schools in the United States. Students from 39 high schools and four middle schools in the United States have played a part in the construction of 100 schools on four continents and counting. This organization builds on education's growing commitment to service learning. Many schools now require students to spend a certain number of hours on volunteer service to the community in order to graduate. Service learning teaches students they are valuable members of the community and can help solve societal problems. The National Service Learning Clearinghouse (http://www.servicelearning.org/) is an organization for Kindergarten through higher education, specializing in how to integrate service learning into the curriculum.

Resources for Students To Make a Positive Difference

Students' commitment to social and environmental responsibility would be enhanced by learning experiences in school where students see they can apply their knowledge to make a positive contribution to society. The possibilities for student initiated activism are enormous at the middle and high school level. A few examples are: energy audits of the school with recommendations to the school board on how to reduce utility bills and pollution simultaneously, attendance at planning commission meetings to advocate for sustainable development, audits of local social services and suggestions for improvement of services to families and youth, and the building of solar collectors out of recycled materials that are installed at community and senior citizen centers as demonstration projects. It is important that the students analyze the social or environmental issue, assess the inadequacy of present attempts at solutions, design their own solution that they implement, and then evaluate their efforts and make recommendations for the future.

A number of good resources are available to build such a learning activity into any classroom. A student/youth organization about injustices provides online information at http://www.seac.org. The Canadian Sierra Club has a Sierra Youth Coalition website at http://www.sierrayouthcoalition.org. A youth empowerment center based in California is available at http://www.youthec.org/cbeyond/index.htm. Students can learn about the efforts of college students to build the North American Alliance for Green Education at http://www.naage.org.

All students are also consumers, and the choices they make have impacts on other people and on the environment. Teachers can help students understand the consequences of their choices by creating an assignment where students look up information on the following web sites and then write how they are changing and/or explaining their present and future consumption choices based on their understanding of their impacts. Useful websites include the following:

1. Sustainable Development Gateway: http://sdgateway.net/default.htm
2. Consumer and Investor Power for Social Change: http://www.coopamerica.org/

3. Sustainable Living—Oregon State University Extension Service: http://www.cof.orst.edu/cof/extended/sustain/ (click on education)
4. Ecological Footprint Calculator: http://www.earthday.net/footprint/index.asp
5. U.S. Office of Energy Efficiency and Renewable Energy: http://www.eere.energy.gov/consumerinfo/energy_savers/index.html
6. Center for a New American Dream: http://www.newdream.org/turnthetide
7. Smart Consumer's Website: http://ibuydifferent.org
8. Aveda Corporation and their sustainable "protect the planet" program: http://www.aveda.com/protect/we/default.asp
9. Working Assets—Youth Focus Fund: http://www.workingassets.com/yff_splash_2/
10. The Apollo Alliance in support of good jobs and energy independence: http://www.apolloalliance.org/about_the_alliance

GRADUATION PLEDGE

Graduation is a natural time for students to think about their future. Manchester College created a pledge for students to sign onto at graduation time. While the focus of the pledge has been on high school and college, there is no reason why middle school students couldn't make this pledge as well. The following pledge helps students sculpt their self-concept to include social and environmental responsibility. "I pledge to explore and take into account the social and environmental consequences of any job I consider and will try to improve these aspects of any organizations for which I work." More information is available at http://www.graduationpledge.org/.

DIGITAL LIBRARIES

The Digital Library for Earth System Education (http://www.dlese.org/) is a National Science Foundation funded digital library that is focused on environmental learning activities for teachers at all grade levels and in all disciplines as well as consumers and citizens. The Advanced Technology Environmental Education Center (www.ateec.org) specializes in curricula for community and technical colleges and high school about environmental topics. Their web site has job listings as well as a variety of teacher resources and could easily be used in an interesting assignment, directing students to explore environmental issues, topics and possible careers as a way to help solve society's environmental sustainability problems. The National Science Foundation provided funding to ATEEC to produce an electronic Environmental Resources Library geared to teachers but also open to the public, soon to be available at www.eerl.org. The National Council of Science and the Environment also provides environmental sustainability information to scientists and novices at www.ncseonline.org. The Educational Resources Information Center (ERIC) is a database of sixteen educational clearinghouses, housing over one million resources for teachers (http://www.eric.ed.gov) and is another of the National Science Foundation digital library collections.

GreenCOM (http://greencom.aed.org/dbtw-wpd/gcom.htm) contains a collection of over 3,000 different classroom materials, carefully screened for quality. EE-Link (www.eelink.net) is a project of the North American Association for Environmental Education. This site works to use only accurate resources designed to inspire inquiry, critical thinking and engagement.

In addition to using the above digital libraries to quickly find information about sustainability or learning activities to integrate into a teacher's existing curricula, it is important that teachers post the learning activities they develop on these digital libraries to share with others. It is quite simple to make a submission, and the more examples teachers have to choose from, the easier it will be for them to imagine integrating sustainability (i.e. civic engagement, social responsibility and environmental responsibility) into their classrooms.

FUTURE INITIATIVES TO ENHANCE SUSTAINABILITY EDUCATION

An interdisciplinary association within higher education in North America, called the University Leaders for a Sustainable Future (www.ulsf.org) has been formed to share information, best practices and a tool kit to help higher education become models of sustainability for society. ULSF is also the home of the Talloire Declaration, a statement signed by colleges and universities to declare their commitment to move toward sustainability in all their activities, including teaching, research, operations, purchasing and community partnerships. Middle and high school students could create a middle and/or high school adaptation of the Talloire Declaration. Students could then ask their school administrations to sign on. Middle and high school teachers have no such organization as ULSF, but teachers can use existing multi-discipline national education associations to facilitate networking and information sharing. Interested members in the Association for Supervision and Curriculum Development (ASCD) could start an interest group network and listserv in sustainability. They already have a network in Environmental Education, which is part of the sustainability paradigm but doesn't include the social equity and healthy economy components. Teachers can join the network without being members of ASCD as long as at least 50% of the individuals are members. For network information, go to www.ascd.org/aboutascd/cr/networks/aboutnet.html. The National Council of Teachers of Mathematics (www.nctm.org/), the National Council of Social Studies (www.ncss.org), the National Council of Teachers of English (www.ncte.org/) and the National Science Teachers Association (http://www.nsta.org/) might host joint or overlapping conferences or sustainability themes in all of their conferences as well as a joint listserv on sustainability. They could also create linked or joint web pages that would house syllabi, learning activities and interdisciplinary modules. Regardless of the specific mechanism, a multi-disciplinary central clearinghouse for sustainability learning activities as well as comprehensive training activities for K–12 teachers would be very helpful. In terms of professional development, Don Huising from the University of Tennessee, the Center for a Sustainable Future (http://csf.concord.org/esf/) and Jaimie Cloud at the Sustainability Education Center (http://www.sustainabilityed.org/) offer valuable training, but more teachers need access to such training.

SUMMARY

In this chapter, we explored the need for learning about sustainability. Given the facts of population and resource consumption, the old paradigm of "Man Conquers Nature" is obsolete and dangerous. Education at its best is about producing environmentally and socially responsible adults who have the skills they need to be successful in their adult roles of worker, family member, citizen, and community member. Successful models, useful resources and the creation of networks will all support teachers in their efforts to increase the percentage of graduates with the skills to be change agents for sustainability. Many state education standards already relate to the need to support the development of environmentally, socially and civically responsible graduates with the change agent skills to create a sustainable future, although these standards need to be strengthened and the assessment tests need to reflect the necessity of sustainability-based behaviors and analyses. Interdisciplinary projects, service learning, problem based learning, place based learning and the creation of a jointly hosted listserv about sustainability by national discipline associations can all be used to enhance efforts to increase education for sustainability. The bottom line will be individual teacher decisions to include the sustainability paradigm, knowledge and skill building in their classrooms. The future is up to us.

NOTES

1. World Commission for the Environment and Development. *Our Common Future*. England: Oxford University Press, 1987.

2. Rees, William and Mathis Wackernagel. "Sustainability: the facts" *New Internationalist*, no 329, (November, 2000): 19.

3. Jucker, Rolf. *Our Common Illiteracy: Education as if the Earth and People Mattered*. Frankfurt, Germany: Peter Lang, 2002: 20.

4. Gabel, Medard "What The World Wants." 1997. <http://www.osearth.com/resources/wwwproject/index.shtml> (12 Jan. 2002).

5. Sustainable Development Education Panel. "First annual Report 1998" London Department of the Environment, Transport and the Regions: 30.

6. Smith, David. "Human Nature Exercise" World Future Society annual conference presentation Boston, MA: 1987.

7. Hawken, Paul, Amory Lovins, and L.Hunter Lovins. *Natural Capitalism: Creating the Next Industrial Revolution*. Boston, MA: Bay Back Books, 2000, 288–308.

8. Michigan State Board of Education "Social Studies Vision Statement and Content Standards and Benchmarks" Lansing, MI: The Board of Education (1996).

9. Rowe, Debra., Dennis Bartleman, Michael Khirallah. Martha Smydra, George Keith, and Michael Ponder. "Reduce cynicism and apathy and create positive change agents: Essential and missing components of our educational curricula" Long Beach, CA: Chair Academy Conference Proceedings, 1999.

10. Jucker, Rolf. *Our Common Illiteracy: Education as if the Earth and People Mattered*. Frankfurt, Germany: Peter Lang, 2002: 54.

11. United Nations Environment Programme "Global Environment Outlook 2000: Overview" 1999 www.unep.org/geo2000/(18 Aug.2003).

12. Rees, William and Mathis Wackernagel. "Sustainability: the facts" *New Internationalist*, no 329, (November, 2000): 19.

13. Jucker, Rolf. *Our Common Illiteracy: Education as if the Earth and People Mattered*. Frankfurt, Germany: Peter Lang, 2002: 21.

14. Hawken, Paul, Amory Lovins, and L.Hunter Lovins. *Natural Capitalism: Creating the Next Industrial Revolution*. Boston, MA: Bay Back Books, 2000, 288–308.

15. Seligman, Martin. *Learned Optimism*. New York, NY: Simon & Schuster, 1998.

16. Smith, David. "The 4 P's of Futuring" World Future Society annual conference presentation. Boston, MA:1987.

17. Rowe, Debra. "Creating instructional leaders via an interdisciplinary project." San Francisco, CA: Association for Supervision and Curriculum Development annual conference presentation materials, 1999.

18. Giraffe Project. 1992 <www.giraffe.org.> email at office@giraffe.org, phone: 360–221-7989 (5 Jan.1997).

19. Rowe, Debra and Dennis Bartleman. "A learning community project for all disciplines to reduce student apathy and create positive change agents." Chicago, IL: Fourth Learning Communities Conference presentation paper. 1999.

20. Gardner, Howard. *Frames of Mind*. New York, NY: Basic Books, 1983.

21. Rowe, Debra and Bartleman, Dennis. *"Learning communities to teach solutions to societal problems, reduce student apathy and create positive change agents: essential and missing components of our curricula."* SeaTac, WA: Washington Center for Improving the Quality of Undergraduate Education annual conference presentation paper, 1999.

22 Gabel, Medard, "What the World Wants" O.S. World Global Simulations. 1997 <http://www.osearth.com/resources/wwwproject/index.shtml>(12 Jan. 2002).

23. For more information, see Pew Center on Global Climate Change www.pew-climate.org, U.S. Environmental Protection Agency www.epa.gov.

24. IPCC Working Group I. Intergovernmental Panel on Climate Change (IPCC) report*: "Summary for Policymakers: The Science of Climate Change"* New York, NY: United Nations, 1995.

25. Santer, B.D. K. E. Taylor, T. M. L. Wigley, T. C. Johns, P. D. Jones, D. J. Karoly, J. F. B. Mitchell, A. H. Oort, J. E. Penner, V. Ramaswamy, M. D. Schwarzkopf, R. J. Stouffer & S. Tett. *"A search for human influences on the thermal structure of the atmosphere,"* Nature, Vol. 382 (July 1996): 39–46.

26. Karl, Thomas R., Richard W. Knight, David R. Easterling, and Robert G. Quayle. *"Trends in U.S. Climate during the Twentieth Century,"* Consequences, Spring, Vol. 1, No. 1(Spring, 1995).

27. IPCC Working Group I. Intergovernmental Panel on Climate Change (IPCC) report: *"Summary for Policymakers: The Science of Climate Change"* New York, NY: United Nations, 1995.

28. Lehman, Scott and Lloyd Keigwin. *"Sudden Changes in North Atlantic Circulation During the Last Deglaciation,"* Nature, Vol. 356 (April 30, 1992*):75–762.*

Chapter Eleven

Using The Environment As A Context For Integrating The Middle School Curriculum

Catherine E. Matthews & Ann Berry Somers

INTRODUCTION

Middle school students are ready and willing to become activists for the environment. They are waiting, impatiently at times, for guidance about how they might make meaningful changes to improve our world. This chapter focuses on herpetology (the study of reptiles and amphibians) using box turtles as a specific case study of using the environment as a context for integrating the middle school curriculum. Examples of middle school instruction in language arts, mathematics, social studies, and science, the core middle school subjects, as well as visual arts and technology will be given using a study of the box turtle as the thematic core.

David Sobel's (1999) developmental stage of ecological awareness, which he calls *Social Action: Saving the Neighborhood*, explains that middle school students are interested in themselves, their peer group and their connections to society and are eager for social action such as recycling projects, stream clean-ups or debating land use issues. In addition, adolescents are ready for outdoor challenges that involve social groups, as well as solo challenges. Many teens are drawn to eco-challenges that they see on the Discovery Channel. The Box Turtle Project offers a solution to curriculum integration dilemmas as well as meets young adolescent students' needs to save the environment and meets their interests in the challenges of working outdoors.

CASE STUDIES AND INVESTIGATING ISSUES THROUGH SKILL DEVELOPMENT

Many environmental educators argue that our relationship to the natural world occurs in a 'place,' and it must be grounded in information and experience

(Snyder 1990). Many teachers recommend that students document their learning about place by keeping a nature journal.

Leslie and Roth (2000) in *Keeping A Nature Journal* create a delightful, informative book of colorful sketches, powerful quotations and provocative descriptions. One contributor, a teacher and naturalist-artist, writes of her experiences journaling, *"I've become convinced, that if you want to understand and become connected to your environment, keeping a field journal is one of the fastest ways to accomplish this goal. One simple periodical act—that of marking where the sun rises and sets on your horizon each day—provides a sense of your place on this earth and in this solar system. Noting when the rain falls—or doesn't—sets up another rhythmic connection. Making quick sketches of one or two critters you observe on a walk—another connection."* We strongly recommend that middle school students keep a journal to document their involvement with the Box Turtle Project.

Hungerford, Volk and Ramsey (1992) present two models for finding a place for environmental education in the curriculum: 1) Case Studies and 2) Investigating Issues through Skill Development. The first approach, the case study, is an infusion model that is a teacher-directed analysis of a specific environmental issue such as the reintroduction of the red wolf. This approach gives the teacher much flexibility and control as the curriculum designer.

The second approach, the Issue Investigation Skill Format, is an insertion of skill development into the curriculum for investigating issues. The approach includes writing research questions, obtaining information using primary methods of investigation, interpreting data, investigating an issue and developing issue resolution plans. The investigation skill methodology developed by Hungerford, Litherland, Peyton, Ramsey and Volk (1988) is organized into six modules. Teachers should look at both of these approaches with an eye toward connecting students to place. Issues surrounding water quality, solid waste management, green space, inner city restoration, land use, exotic or introduced species, and endangered species speak to the needs of local communities and invite students to become active citizens on their own behalf.

In the Piedmont of North Carolina a noted middle school teacher (Vickers, 2002) chooses questions that surround issues such as:

1. Where can we find landfill space for our waste in Any City, North Carolina?
2. How can we meet the water needs of a growing city that is not located by a river?
3. What are the pros and cons of constructing the new Federal Express (or any other corporation) Hub in Any City?

4. What are the problems associated with the reintroduction of red wolves in Eastern North Carolina or any other species in any other regional area in any other state?
5. What is happening to the spruce and fir trees on the highest mountain peaks in western North Carolina or trees (or other vegetation) in other states?

Students, in groups, use the local news and newspapers to develop a list of local and regional issues to research, investigate and debate. All research involves interviews and visits to sites beyond the school; thus, students are encouraged to find teachers and experiences from the community and region in which they live. Students make posters, create PowerPoint presentations or develop debates around these issues. Guest speakers are asked to participate. Class time is used to find web sites, practice research skills, develop interview questions, and make plans for their investigations. Working in cooperative teams helps students divide their time and energy to facilitate progress. The teacher functions as an encourager, motivator and facilitator. The final evaluation of each presentation is done with selected criteria that are determined by the class and a self-evaluation is also included. Action criteria may include writing letters to city council members, county commissioners, and/or state legislators or writing newspaper editorials. Students may, in fact, affect local and regional change, as well as inform their communities about pressing environmental issues. The Box Turtle Project offers an excellent example of a curriculum endeavor that lends itself to the investigation of issues through a skills development approach.

RATIONALE FOR THE SPECIFIC CASE STUDY OR WHY THIS IS AN IMPORTANT TOPIC (THE ASIAN TURTLE CRISIS HAS BECOME OUR TURTLE CRISIS)

[NOTE: The following information on the Asian Turtle Crisis comes from a web site maintained by the New York Turtle and Tortoise Society at http://nytts.org/asianturtlecrisis.html. Most of the material has been paraphrased for this chapter to provide teachers with the necessary background to understand this environmental issue and concern and be able to share that information with students in their classes.]

The exploitation of Asian turtles has brought many reptilian species to the brink of extinction. Southeast Asia (including Laos, Cambodia, Bangladesh, Vietnam, Malaysia, and Indonesia) is being stripped of its turtles for China's food markets. A billion people in China are wielding newfound economic power and millions of turtles are being wrenched from their habitats to meet the insatiable demand and high prices offered by Chinese markets.

According to the Chelonia Research Foundation, turtles are survivors of countless millennia including the great extinction of the dinosaurs, but turtles now face imminent demise at the hands of humans. We are facing a turtle survival crisis unprecedented in its severity and risk. Without intervention, countless species will be lost over the next few decades.

The decline of turtle and tortoise populations worldwide has caused serious concern among scientists and wildlife conservationists for more than twenty years. But over the past decade the impact of the Chinese market on the already precarious status of Asian turtles has reached disastrous proportions. All the turtles of Southeast Asia, 65 species, a quarter of the world's total, are now in grave danger.

Two excellent articles on the Asian Turtle Crisis have hot links on this web site. Wendy Williams (1999) describes the arrival of transport trucks, the endless numbers of animals for sale (10,000 turtles were sold in markets in two Chinese cities in just one day), and the slaughter of turtles in China (they are slaughtered live in the markets, including Chinese markets in the USA). Ted Williams (1999) personalizes the Asian Turtle Crisis by describing the three red-eared sliders his sisters kept as pets when they were young children. The trouble is, the three red-eared sliders were actually many red eared sliders that his parents replaced as each turtle died, *disposable pets*, Williams called them. Williams' article details the knowledge that around the world, turtles are being sold as pets and spreading disease.

Many of the turtles sold in Chinese food markets are banned from trade by the Convention on International Trade in Endangered Species (CITES), and many of the turtles are American turtles caught in the wild including Florida soft-shells, red-eared sliders, and snapping turtles.

Most Chinese turtle species have become commercially extinct, and many Southeast Asian species very nearly so. No definitive studies indicate the drain on American turtles. Estimates are that 25 million turtles were exported from the USA for the food and pet trade between 1993 and 1997. The word 'crisis' really takes on meaning when according to one herpetologist given the volume of the turtles sacrificed, there are probably more individual endangered animals being killed for food every day than we could conserve in a lifetime.

Mature, wild-caught turtles are prized in Chinese markets because they are thought to confer wisdom, health or longevity when consumed. Turtle meat is a status symbol. We like lobster; in China, it's turtle. People in China pay handsomely for the chance to eat turtle soup or turtle jelly or take folk medicines made from ground-up turtle shells, including virility potions. A turtle is the perfect gift to give an honored relative. A commercially extinct Chinese three-striped box turtle, believed to cure cancer, sold for $10 fifteen years ago but now brings $1,200.

A third of the world's 266 known turtle species are threatened with extinction. A sustainable harvest of wild adult turtles is not possible. One wild adult represents an enormous genetic investment. And yet wild adult turtles are legally and routinely caught and sold in domestic and foreign markets. Now that old-world turtles are in short supply and, in some cases, protected, North American box turtles are in greater demand. Box turtles, which can live for 120 years, are legally caught and peddled in this country.

Populations get decimated suddenly by experienced poachers or over years by incidental collecting. Steve Garber, studied a wood turtle population for twenty years on 2,471 acres controlled by the South Central Connecticut Regional Water Authority. All was fine with his 133 marked subjects until 1983, when the watershed was opened to public recreation. Immediately the turtles began to disappear. Garber was baffled. He checked disease, road mortality, and predation. Finally, he discovered hikers were taking the turtles home one at a time. In 1991 only 14 remained. In 1992 they were gone.

Spotted turtles and map turtles are stressed by the pet trade. Bog turtles, declared federally threatened in 1997, go for about $1,000 each on the black market. We now take it for granted that birds are totally off-limits, but in many cases catching and selling wild turtles is completely legal.

Pet stores still carry red eared sliders, selling them for $10 to $15 each, but the silver-dollar-size ones are no longer available. In 1975 the USA Food and Drug Administration banned domestic sale of turtles less than four inches in length because they were causing an estimated 300,000 cases of salmonella annually. Today about 8 million hatchlings, most of them laden with salmonella, are annually exported to 60 nations.

The pet-turtle business is infecting people and turtles around the world. When the pets get sick or their owners tire of them, they are tossed or flushed into habitat occupied by native turtles. Red-eared sliders are now established in the wild all over the world. In Washington they are competing with the vanishing pacific pond turtle. In the southeastern states they are compromising the genetic integrity of yellow-bellied sliders by breeding with them. Two years ago the 16-member European Union banned the import of red-eared sliders because of the damage they are doing to European pond turtles. Meanwhile, in the Mississippi system, the one place red-eared sliders belong, they are in decline.

Western desert tortoises and southeastern gopher tortoises are getting a fatal respiratory-tract infection that they may have contracted from imported tortoises unleashed in their habitat. Nearly 250,000 desert tortoises are kept as pets in California, Arizona, and Nevada, and wherever the respiratory disease is encountered, feral (domestic animals that have been released or escaped into the wild) tortoises are found nearby. Recently, the malady has shown up in North American box turtles.

Quickening the spread of turtle disease here and abroad is the belief of some individuals that good karma can be had by being kind to captive turtles, i.e., setting them free. In America and around the world you can buy wild-caught specimens for the express purpose of releasing them, except that in many cases they don't belong in the places they are released. In New York City a dealer of Florida soft-shell turtles, a species that lives in warm freshwater habitats, recently sold a load to a Buddhist temple, then watched while the animals were ceremoniously dumped into New York Harbor.

According to the Director of the Turtle Hospital of New England, in Upton, Massachusetts, virtually all turtles from pet stores are desperately sick when purchased. It takes about six months to clean them up, rid them of parasites and fatten them up; some turtles are half the body weight they ought to be. Approximately 95 percent of the wild turtles that enter the pet trade are dead within a year. Pet stores make their money selling the expensive setup that goes with your pet so if your pet dies, it doesn't matter to them, because with that kind of investment, you are going to buy another.

The primary mission of this Turtle Hospital is to someday restock turtles from Southeast Asia. The Hospital works with nine needy Southeast Asian species that are the most practical to obtain and breed. The main problem is that the turtles arrive in frightful condition. Many haven't eaten for six months; some have been packed on ice. Having been kept in filthy water and mixed with turtles of all species, they are loaded with pathogens and parasites.

The Director of the Turtle Hospital does not believe that we can stop the slaughter. Instead, she says, we must establish refugee populations in as many places as we can, wait for the animals to become extinct in the wild and wait for people to value them alive. The Director states, "The only chance turtles have is for people to care passionately about them. But if you grow up without ever having turtles as pets or ever coming close to them in the wild, you become an adult who doesn't care if turtles stay on the planet. People who want a turtle shouldn't go to a pet store, and they shouldn't catch one. They should contact a turtle society and get the name of a reputable breeder. Turtles sold by breeders are expensive, but more likely to be healthy. People need to understand that turtles are long-lived; nobody should buy one without being willing to make a 50-year commitment." (Williams, T., "The Terrible Turtle Trade," *Audubon*. 1999. <http://nytts.org/asia/twilliams.htm> (1 Nov. 2003)). So, The Asian Turtle Crisis has had lasting impacts in the USA and in our state.

THE LOCAL PROBLEM IN NORTH CAROLINA

The number of turtles taken from North Carolina jumped from 460 in the year 2000, to more than 1600 turtles in 2001, to more than 23,000 turtles in 2002, an increase that worried state wildlife officials so much that they sought and secured legal protection for North Carolina turtles. This law enables the N.C. Wildlife Resources Commission to regulate the harvest of certain reptiles and amphibians. This bill (S825) can be found at http://www.ncga.state .nc.us/homePage.pl and is entitled "Protect Certain Reptiles and Amphibians" (enter web site using Bill Look-Up feature).

This law prohibits the commercial taking of certain kinds of turtles, including basking and sliding turtles, until the state can adopt limits. Other states, including Mississippi and Alabama, have stopped the commercial collection of turtles in recent years.

A fact sheet on turtle harvest in North Carolina and previous press releases are available on the Commission's Web site, www.ncwildlife.org (under Search type in "Press releases/What's New"). The commission believes a third of the state's 21 turtle species are in jeopardy from collectors and habitat loss. International market demand has increased the number of turtles taken in North Carolina, which had no regulations on commercial harvesting of freshwater turtles until 2003. Sea turtles are protected because they are listed as threatened or endangered on the Endangered Species List.

Turtle trappers are casting nets primarily for the yellow-bellied slider, a pond turtle often seen basking on logs. Female yellow-bellied sliders bring $5 apiece. Reptile dealers raise the turtles in ponds, incubate their eggs, and then ship the hatchlings overseas to be sold as pets and consumed as food. Last year, one dealer alone (a Louisiana citizen) trapped 17,000 turtles in North Carolina, all for the price of one $5 permit. He also hauled 30,000 live turtles out of South Carolina in a cattle trailer.

CASE STUDY OF NORTH CAROLINA

There is a slogan among environmentalists that says, "Think globally, act locally," which simply means that as teachers we should focus on the big problems that face our societies today and identify ways to make these global issues locally relevant. There are several relevant global issues that can be broached through a study of local herpetology. The study of reptiles and amphibians as bioindicators (using the presence or absence or abundance of specific living organisms to determine abiotic parameters (physical characteristics such as temperature, pH and humidity) of a habitat) and the declining populations of reptiles and amphibians (a new movement has arisen in the herpetological community with the goal of 'keeping common animals common') both offer a global focus but allows local fieldwork, data collection and data analysis.

The purpose of this project, from a scientific standpoint, is to determine the box turtle population in a particular area and to study the movements, activities and threats to this population of box turtles. Eastern box turtles (*Terrapene carolina carolina*) are long-lived reptiles that are late to mature and have few offspring. Habitat loss, road kill, and international pet trade demands are a few of the reasons that concerned scientists are raising questions about viable population numbers and this species' long-term survival. The United States submitted a proposal to regulate box turtle trade to other member nations of the Convention on International Trade in Endangered Species (CITES) in 1994. Due to a lack of national biological data for this species, conclusive evidence of their decline could not be determined. However, it is the belief of many respected scientists that continued pressures on this species will be detrimental to their survival given their particular biological characteristics (Howe, 1996). All box turtles (genus Terrapene) are now listed on Appendix II of CITES (Dodd, 2001).

The following sections of this chapter offer specific suggestions for the middle school curriculum in six different disciplines all geared toward the Box Turtle Project.

LANGUAGE ARTS LESSONS

In North Carolina, the goal of the middle school language arts curriculum is to foster personal, social, and civic literacy. A spiraling program, it is based on strong connections between oral language, written language, and other media technology; the study of expressive, informational, argumentative, critical, and literary communication; and the study of language and the conventions of grammar, which both under gird and permeate the study of language arts.

Language arts is probably the easiest subject area to integrate with any other subject area and often forms the focus for integration. Numerous units in school are designed around a novel, short story, poem or mystery.

The North Carolina Department of Public Instruction (DPI) developed an 8th grade interdisciplinary unit combining language arts and science around a book called The Weird-O (1991). This book by Theodore Taylor is the story of two teenagers and their interests in black bears in the Dismal Swamp. The book details the controversies among bear conservationists and hunters in the

Dismal Swamp. DPI provided class sets of this short novel to every middle school in the state with the idea that 8th grade teachers would teach an integrated unit planned around the book. It is not uncommon to have grade levels at a particular school focus on specific book studies but the integrated nature of this book project, between language arts and science teachers, was unique.

If reading is not a central focus of an integrated project then writing could certainly be a focal point of any interdisciplinary study. Writing persuasive pieces, drafting legislation, penning myths, and writing scientific reports could all be used in the Box Turtle Project.

Following are several specific ideas about ways to integrate the Language Arts in the Box Turtle Project. One of our favorite books is a book of poems (or nonsense verses) called *Flornithology: How to tell the Birds from the Flowers* which is available on the web at http://www.geocities.com/Vienna/2406/cov.html. This book, written in 1907 by physicist Robert Williams Wood can be read online. The book is actually about a lot more than just telling birds from flowers. The most well known image from this book is probably that of a famous woodcut, comparing and contrasting the pansy and the chimpanzee. I think that students could read and translate these poems (the language is 1907 English) into modern day English. Students might also create their own examples (verses, poems) of *Flornithology* such as the following poem that we wrote called *The Box Turtle and the Crepe Myrtle*

> Summer's Season of Fauna and Flora
> Prefer the humid heat of summer's hurdle.
> Beautiful in their own ways,
> Each will enrich your summer days.
> One travels with its house as home
> The other's flowers make a dome.

Author Paul Fleischman has written two books which are collections of poetry to be read aloud by two readers. *I Am Phoenix* (1985), focuses on birds while *Joyful Noise* (1989) focuses on insects. Each poem is factually based as well as beautifully written. *Joyful Noise* won a Newberry Award. Your students could write poems for two voices about a variety of turtles.

A classic work of American literature that you might want to use with your students is John Steinbeck's *The Grapes of Wrath*. We would suggest using excerpts from the book, especially Chapter 3, which focuses on a land turtle. Steinbeck describes the travels and travails of a land turtle as it lumbers across a field, to a roadside embankment and climbs to the road where it is nearly hit by a car. A truck swerves to hit the turtle, but its wheel strikes only the edge of the shell and spins it off the highway. The turtle lies on its back, but finally pulls itself over and moves forward.

Literary critics suggest that the turtle is a metaphor for the migrant farmers whose stories and struggles are recounted in *The Grapes of Wrath*. The turtle, like the migrant farmers, carries its home on its back wherever it travels. The turtle plods along but is consistently confronted with danger and setbacks, specifically those of modernity and business. Steinbeck made it clear through the symbol of the tenacious turtle that the migrants will be successful in establishing a new life in California.

Another well-known writer, Ogden Nash (1902–1971), a poet of numerous short rhymes had this to say about turtles in general:

> The Turtle
> The turtle lives 'twixt plated decks
> Which practically conceal its sex.
> I think it clever of the turtle
> In such a fix to be so fertile.

Students could read more about Nash or write poems about specific turtle species using Nash's rhyming patterns. You can read Nash's verses online at http://www.aenet.org/poems/ognash4.htm.

Using technical reference sources is a desirable language arts skill. The most highly acclaimed book on box turtles is Dodd's (2001) *North American Box Turtles*. It is an easily readable treatise on the animal that forms the focus of study for this chapter. Middle school students can use it as a resource to compare and contrast information they locate about box turtles from other resources in order to judge the value and reliability of the information they find. Distinguishing between valid and invalid sources of information including information online as well as text materials is an important skill for middle school students to develop.

Many cultures celebrate turtles as symbols. Turtles have been used by some American Indian tribes as instruments and decorations. There are many legends about turtles in American Indian literature. Students find it fascinating to determine the source and wisdom of some of these legends. Another popular activity for middle school students we have worked with is having them write and then share children's books about turtles with students in elementary schools. All of these language arts activities have the potential to contribute significantly to the Box Turtle Project.

Mathematics

Numbers have meaning but in many mathematics classes learning about mathematical operations is typically relegated to the skill, drill and kill basics of memorizing facts and rules for operations. Instruction typically involves almost no application. In the Box Turtle Project students learn to use numbers to support their position statements in persuasive writing pieces, to draw conclusions about data sets, and to gain information about habitat and abiotic conditions in box turtle habitat. The following paragraphs relate our Box Turtle Project to the goals and objectives in the North Carolina middle school mathematics course of study, which is based on national standards in mathematics.

Middle grades students in the US are in an interesting transition mathematically speaking. Some students are ready for pre-Algebra and Algebra concepts which require abstract reasoning skills while other middle school students need another year of transitional mathematics with a focus on advanced mathematical concepts such as percentage calculations and ratio and proportion problems. Working with box turtles and box turtle habitat offers multiple opportunities to have students work with real mathematical ideas and science concepts that depend on an understanding of mathematics. For example, students can count rings on scutes and estimate the age of box turtles. Students can follow nests and count eggs laid and eggs hatched and calculate a hatching percentage. Students can compute simple descriptive statistics such as the average home range area of each turtle, the ratio of males to females in the population captured, sexed and marked, and the ratio of home range to age of turtles captured.

Students can graph data from various sources from the box turtle study including time of day activity is observed, date (month and day) of matings observed, date of first movement above ground in the spring, and last movement above ground in the late fall. The middle school students we worked with estimated dates when turtles would first be found moving in the spring and then organized students' guesses graphically to determine the prizewinner for this box turtle project activity. Our students established informational databases by collecting data, inputting it, organizing it and searching and sorting files to use in the Box Turtle Project.

Students mark box turtles by filing a pattern on their outer scutes with a triangular file, which allows subsequent positive identification of each turtle located. Students also take a number of measurements of each box turtle captured (see Figure 11.1).

Mathematics concepts in measurement, geometry, data analysis and probability, and algebra, can be covered in the box turtle project. The study of perimeter, area and surface area and relationships among length, perimeter, area, and volume are included. Students can draw objects to scale and use scale drawings to solve problems. Students study transformations and become proficient at visualizing and recognizing transformed figures in the coordinate plane. Three-dimensional figures are drawn using different views.

Fill out a separate sheet for each turtle. Use pencil or indelible ink pen.

Site Name: Turtle Species: Turtle #

Date:_____   Time:_____ Recapture? *Y or N*

Observer(s): _____

_____

Name and address of collector (if turtle is brought into the lab):

_____

_____Phone:_____

Is this individual willing to return this turtle to the site of capture? *Y or N*

Exact location of capture (county, nearest town, road no. & distance to nearest

intersection, name of landowner, etc.):_____

_____

Gender: *M*   or *F*   Mass (g):_____

Age: _____Confidence Rate: _____ (0=can't age, 3=sure of age)

Measurements: Scute Counts:

_____Plastron Length to Anterior Hinge (mm)   _____Vertebrals

_____Plastron Length to Posterior Edge (mm)   _____Right Costal

_____Straight Carapace Length (mm):   _____Left Costal

_____Overall Width at Hinge (mm):   _____Right Marginals

_____Max Width (mm):   _____Left Marginals

_____Shell Height (mm):

Y   N   Digital photo taken of carapace?

Y   N   Digital photo taken of plastron?

Turtle's Activity/Behavior: _____

Figure 11.1a.   Box Turtle Morphometric Data Sheet Sample

Students investigate problems involving multiple data sets. More sophisticated representations, such as histograms, box plots, and scatter plots, highlight an increased understanding of the spread and grouping of data and the relationships between variables. Students identify basic patterns and trends in tables and charts and use them to make predictions. Students explore extremes in data and the misuse of representations to communicate information.

Experimental results are compared with theoretical probabilities and students learn that the level of agreement between the two often depends on the number of times an experiment is repeated. Students learn to make inferences and predictions based on the outcomes of their experiments.

From tables and graphs students recognize linear and nonlinear relationships and functions. Students solve relevant and authentic problems using appropriate technology and apply these concepts as well as those developed in earlier years.

As graphing is an integral part of the box turtle project, the following goals and objectives are easily met through the project:

1. Collect, organize, analyze, and display data (including box plots and histograms) to solve problems.
2. Calculate, use, and interpret the mean, median, mode, range and frequency distribution for a set of data.

Mathematics is easily integrated into the Box Turtle Project, providing multiple examples of need-to-know mathematics with applications directly related to the study.

Social Studies

In North Carolina middle school students study Europe and South America in the 6th grade, Asia, Africa and Australia in the 7th grade, and the state of North Carolina in the 8th grade. The social studies program, recognizing both the social-emotional needs of middle grades students as well as their intellectual needs, encourages students to investigate and respond thoughtfully to questions about their world today. This curriculum recommends that teachers and students utilize community-related resources such as field trips, use map reading skills, interpret charts and graphs, and describe factors that determine changes in distribution of populations, resources and climates and then evaluate effects on the environment.

In the Box Turtle Project, students describe the environmental impact of events such as fragmentation and loss of habitat on environments and subsequent populations of box turtles. Studying distribution maps of different species of box turtles is an excellent way to include geography in the curriculum. Range Maps offer yet another way of integrating map studies with your local investigations of herps.

U.S. populations of box turtles can be compared with other box turtles around the world. The Asian Turtle Crisis can be explored in great detail and compared with other issues that threaten turtles in other areas of the world.

A study of the legal system, at both the federal and state levels, is easy to incorporate in the Box Turtle Project. A very appropriate investigation would be to determine how bills become laws at both federal and state levels. In North Carolina our state legislature recently approved a bill to protect certain turtle species from exploitation. For more information on this bill use the "Bill Look-Up" feature and enter the number of the bill: S825 (the name of the Bill is *Protect Certain Reptiles and Amphibians* on the N.C. Wildlife Resources Commission's web site at www.ncwildlife.org.

SCIENCE

The North Carolina middle school curriculum encompasses four strands of study 1) *the Nature of Science* (science as a human endeavor, the nature of scientific knowledge, and historical perspectives of science); 2) *Science as Inquiry* (the ability to understand and do scientific inquiry and the ability to perform safe and appropriate manipulation of materials, scientific equipment, and technology); 3) *Science and Technology* (understanding technology and the ability to perform technological design); and, 4) Science in *Personal and Social Perspectives* (personal and community health, population growth, environmental quality, natural and human-induced hazards, science and technology in local, national, and global challenges, and careers in science and technology).

Middle school students are undergoing extensive psychological, physiological, and social changes, which make them curious, energetic, and egocentric. Middle school science provides opportunities to channel their interests and concerns, provided it maximizes their exposure to high interest topics. Middle school learners need to see a direct relationship between science education and daily life. Investigations designed to help students learn about themselves (human biology/health issues) and their world (environmental quality/space exploration/technology) motivate them.

The following science objectives are easily met through the Box Turtle Project: 1) Describe ways in which organisms interact with each other and with non-living parts of the environment including limiting factors, coexistence/cooperation/competition, and symbiosis. 2) Evaluate the consequences of disrupting food webs. 3) Explain how changes in habitat may affect organisms, and 4) Analyze practices that affect the use, availability, and management of natural resources including land use, urban growth and manufacturing.

Additional science lessons (Smith 2001) that can be taught to help middle school students better understand the Box Turtle Project include lessons on soil pH and temperature, ecology, topographic maps, morphological comparisons between box turtles and middle grades students, sexing and aging turtles, habitat type, succession patterns, and turtle conservation. Full lesson plans (Smith 2001) are available at http://www.uncg.edu/cui/courses/matthews/.

Visual Arts Integration

According to the North Carolina Standard Course of Study in the middle grades, students' art making becomes infused with a variety of images and approaches, including those of popular culture and they may want to incorporate elements from this culture into their art. Study of historical and cultural context gives students insight into the role of visual arts as a record of human activity. Students' understanding and appreciation of art becomes stronger and continues to build as they develop their own level of competence and personal style as artists.

"Visual arts are inherent in the lives and learning of all societies and cultures throughout history. The arts bridge knowledge, imagery and aesthetics across the humanities, mathematics and science. As a result of this interconnectedness, visual arts penetrates all areas of study causing synthesis in understanding for the learner." (DPI website)

The visual arts can be used throughout the Box Turtle Project. Students can illustrate the children's books on turtles that they write. They can use art to illustrate their papers and projects and homework. The students we worked with on the Box Turtle Project designed logos and T-shirts for our Turtle Team members. Art projects focus on art as a means of communication and persuasion including interpreting the environment.

TECHNOLOGY INTEGRATION

Many technology objectives can be met by the Box Turtle Project. Students definitely learn to identify uses of technology in the workplace using GIS units to gather data about turtle locations, using radio telemetry to track turtles, using digital scales to weigh turtles, using computers to maintain a database of information collected about turtles and using keyboarding and word

Weather conditions:_____

Approx. Temp.:_____Did you observe this turtle eating? Y N   If yes, what: _____

Anything identifiable in scat?_____

Habitat:_____ (1 = road, 2 = edge of field and forest (w/i 5m of edge),

 3 = field, 4 = pine/hardwood, 5 = stream or stream bank, 6 = open wetland,

7 = forested wetland)

Injuries/Defects/Parasites:_____

_____

Please indicate below where injuries and defects occur:

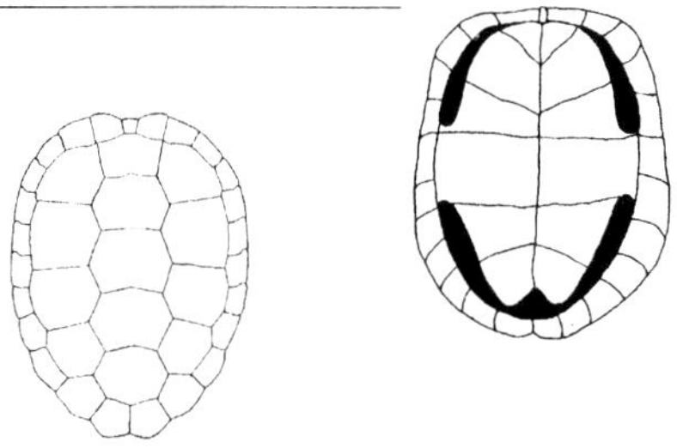

Describe dominant vegetation: _____

Capture Method:_____ (1= signal, 2= visual search, 3= dog, 4 = road capture, 5 = Other)

Date and Time of Release:_____

Was turtle released at point of capture?   *Y N*

If not released at point of capture, please explain:_____

Figure 11.1b.

processing and desk top publishing skills to prepare programs to share their knowledge with others. Students also learn to use simple graphing programs to display data. Technology integration is easy with the Box Turtle Project.

Resources

There are many resources that teachers can use to help them prepare and teach an integrated unit in the middle grades on herpetology. The National Science Teachers Association published a paperback called *Hands-on Herpetology* (2001) that has good information and good lesson ideas, especially in science.

A national organization called PARC (Partners in Amphibian and Reptile Conservation) has a web site at http://www.parcplace.org/. The mission of PARC is to conserve amphibians, reptiles, and their habitats as integral parts of our ecosystem and culture through proactive and coordinated public/ private partnerships. PARC has a number of educational materials on their web site including: wetlands brochures, posters, fact sheets, species accounts, teacher resources and activities.

According the PARC web site, although there are many reasons for the declining populations of reptiles and amphibians including habitat loss, air and water pollution, and disease, the need for conservation action is immediate. Amphibians and reptiles are important parts of our biological diversity and play critical roles as predators and prey in ecosystems. Even more importantly, amphibians and reptiles are sensitive indicators of environmental health and quality. Their declines are clear signals of problems that could ultimately affect human health.

If you live in an area of the country where box turtles are not common, another terrestrial turtle or even an aquatic turtle can serve as your case study. If you happen to live in a place where reptiles are not common, then use an amphibian (frog or salamander) as your case study. Or, if you are more interested in amphibians than reptiles then simply substitute a study of amphibians for reptiles (see Figure 11.2). Whatever your focus, reptile and amphibian populations will benefit from your study as well as your middle school students!

NOTES

1. Distribution of Amphibian and Reptile Species in the USA (from PARC brochure) http://www.parcplace.org/documents/GeneralHerpInfo/learnabout3.htm

BIBLIOGRAPHY

Dodd Jr., C.K. *North American Box Turtles: A Natural History.* Norman: University of Oklahoma Press, 2001.

Fleischman, P. I am Phoenix: poems for two voices. New York: Harper & Row, 1985.
——— . *Joyful Noise: poems for two voices.* New York: Harper & Row, 1988.

Howe, M. *Box Turtle Research and Conservation Newsletter*, 5th ed. Part II. Facts from the USFWS: The Box Turtle, 1996.

Hungerford, H., R. Litherland, R. Peyton, J. Ramsey and T. Volk. *Investigating and evaluating environmental issues and actions: Skill development modules.* Champaign, Ill.: Stipes, 1988.

Hungerford, H., J. Ramsey and T. Volk. "Environmental Education in the K–12 Curriculum: Finding a Niche," *The Journal of Environmental Education* 23, no. 2 (1992): 35-45.

Leslie, C. and C. Roth. *Keeping A Nature Journal: Discover a Whole New Way of Seeing the World Around You*. Pownal, VT: Storey Books, 2000. "A Tribute to the Poet, Ogden Nash (1902-1971)." <http://www.aenet.org/poems/ognash4.htm> (30 Oct. 2003). New York Turtle and Tortoise Society. "The Asian Turtle Crisis." <http://nytts.org/asianturtlecrisis.html> (31 Oct. 2003).

North Carolina Department of Public Instruction (DPI). "North Carolina Standard Course of Study." <http://www.ncpublicschools.org/curriculum/> (30 Oct. 2003).

North Carolina General Assembly. "Bill Look-Up: S825; Protect Certain Reptiles and Amphibians." <http://www.ncga.state.nc.us/homePage.pl> (30 Oct. 2003).

North Carolina Wildlife Resources Commission. <www.ncwildlife.org> (30 Oct. 2003). (under   Search type in "Press releases/What's New").

PARC. "Partners in Amphibian and Reptile Conservation." 1999. <http://www.parcplace.org> (30 Oct. 2003).

Schneider, R., M. Krasny and S. Morreal. Hands-on Herpetology: Exploring Ecology and Conservation. Arlington, VA: NSTA Press, 2001.

Smith, A., *"The Box Turtle Project Lesson Plans,"* University of North Carolina @ Greensboro. 2003. <http://www.uncg.edu/cui/courses/matthews/> (3 Nov. 2003).

Snyder, G. The Practice of the Wild. New York: North Point Press, 1990.

Sobel, D., "Beyond Ecophobia," *YES! A Journal of Positive Futures*, 19-23, 1999.

Somers, A., C. Matthews, K. Bennett, S. Seymour and J. Rucker, "Outdoor Adventures: Tracking Eastern Box Turtles," *Science Scope* 27 no. 3 (2003): 32–37.

Steinbeck, J. *The Grapes of Wrath*. New York: The Viking Press, 1939.

Taylor, T. *The Weird-O*. San Diego: Harcourt Brace Jovanovich, 1991.

Vickers, V. and C. Matthews, "Children and Place: A Natural Connection," *Science Activities*, 39, No. 1 (2002): 16-24.

Williams, T., "The Terrible Turtle Trade," *Audubon*. 1999. <http://nytts.org/asia/twilliams.htm> (1 Nov. 2003).

Williams, W., "The Turtle Tragedy," Scientific American. 1999. <http://nytts.org/asia/wwilliams.htm> (1 Nov. 2003).

Wood, R., *Flornithology: How to tell the Birds from the Flowers*. San Francisco & New York: Paul Elder and Company, 1907. <http://www.geocities.com/Vienna/2406/cov.html> (30 Oct. 2003).

Chapter Twelve

Integration In Teacher Education

Manuel P. Vargas

INTRODUCTION

How do we prepare prospective teachers to value and implement curriculum integration? Is the preparation of prospective teachers due for a complete reform and would an integrative curriculum strategy contribute effectively to such change?

HOW FEASIBLE IS CURRICULUM INTEGRATION IN THE PREPARATION OF PROSPECTIVE TEACHERS?

In this chapter I demonstrate to future classroom teachers and their teacher educators that integrated/thematic instruction should actually begin with the teacher education curriculum they complete in preparation for a teaching career. This approach represents a challenge to the antiquated lecture methods that teacher educator rely on as a common teaching strategy to impart pedagogical knowledge. A lecture approach contrasts sharply with the dynamic nature of K–12 classroom settings where decision-making, problem solving, and inquiries are the order of the day. An integrated approach to learning is not only a challenge for pre-service and teacher educators but it is also a challenge for K–12 in-service teachers who must use creativity and ingenuity to make teaching and learning meaningful experiences.

Consequently, we will present an argument in favor of an integrated approach to teacher education; showcase an integrated thematic unit as an example of what can be done; and offer a word of caution—caveats—regarding integration in teacher education.

HOW IT ALL BEGAN

In the summer of 2001, a group of faculty members at Winston-Salem State University initiated a program to address teaching certification needs of individuals who had been granted temporary K–12 teaching licenses by the state and whose certification requirements needed to be completed. An eight-week summer program was planned, followed by a weekend and evening schedule in the fall semester to complete pedagogical training. Maximizing time was a major objective of this program in addressing pedagogical standards required by the state. Faculty members decided to group required courses in clusters of 9- and 12-hour modules. By clustering these courses into modules, course instructors worked together, deliberately avoided repetition of pedagogical content, and integrated content under the umbrella of thematic units. Although the initial decision of grouping courses into blocks of 9- and 12-credit hours grew out of a practical need, it also provided the idea for developing an integrative curriculum strategy.

Gathering information from this initial attempt and drawing conclusions from lessons learned, we have come to realize the challenges and benefits of integration. We propose here that pedagogical preparation of future teachers be attained through the application of integrative/thematic units that will link major concepts and skills of teacher preparation programs. Such thematic units would be closely related to field experiences that, in turn, may increase the opportunities for integration. Additionally, we anticipate that problem solving, problem-based learning, inquiry methodology, and team-teaching will be strategies more conducive to supporting integration.

In the beginning, one of the questions we needed to answer was that of a curriculum framework that would guide the selection of thematic units. Quite often, teacher education programs become textbook-driven because of the absence of a clearly articulated pedagogical framework. "No single textbook can address the needs of my courses" colleagues often say. For instance, we have standards from state departments of public instruction, content categories from Educational Testing Service (ETS) for those programs that must comply with standardized tests, and standards from professional learned societies. Although there are common threads among these curriculum guidelines, it becomes an unnecessary source of confusion when teacher educators must address multiple curricula at the time of program accreditation.

A review of curriculum samples in teacher preparation led us to select the Interstate New Teacher Assessment and Support Consortium (INTASC[1] 1992) principles as the organizing framework for our themes and modules. The INTASC principles represent a clear consensus of teacher educators, which have also been adopted by teacher education programs in approximately 33 states. Additionally, the INTASC principles represent a framework that aligns itself with a number of curriculum guidelines, including standards emanating from state departments of public instruction; ETS content categories; and subject-area professional organizations. INTASC principles provide the rationale for organizing the knowledge, skills, and dispositions of prospective K–12 teachers. In the example provided we also advocate for a stronger connection between theory and field experiences in order to cast curriculum integration into real-life situations. Initiating problem solving, analysis, and research of K–12 authentic situations will make integration a more compelling case (Susan Kovalik[2] 1984).

A RATIONALE FOR INTEGRATION IN TEACHER EDUCATION

Jean Piaget[3] (1973, 11–12) asserted that discipline-based teachings of standardized curricula might be conducive to learning, but not necessarily to invention. Piaget's assertion clearly highlights the need for the type of curriculum and instruction that promote creativity and invention. By implication, it calls for the evaluation of the way we prepare K–12 teachers. The present state of education calls for more creative ways to prepare our teaching force. Today's pre-service teachers will spend their professional lives in an educational environment vastly different from the one experienced by teachers the last half-century. The ever-changing social structure of today's school communities demand new talent to address increasingly complex educational challenges.[4] (Christine E. Sleeter 1991, 1–23).

Teacher educators, school officials, and the public in general acknowledge the need for highly qualified K–12 teachers[5] (Title I Directors' Conference 2003). Effective teachers must experience the unique challenges of today's communities that, in addition to the traditional knowledge and skills of the recent past, require knowledge, skills, and dispositions to work effectively in culturally and linguistically diverse communities.[6] (James A. Banks and Cherry A. McGee Banks, 1995, 3–24). Consequently, it is imperative for new teachers to go beyond an education that includes a collection of courses that frequently results in a compilation of unconnected pieces. Although the knowledge gained in these courses may be valuable, it may also ignore the realities of K–12 settings that call for a holistic view of educational needs. The call for an integrative view of curriculum requires teachers to broaden the scope of planning, instructional delivery, and interaction in the school community. As two school officials put it: "Teachers must understand that each discipline is part of a larger whole and that few jobs in the real world are as compartmentalized as the traditional academic discipline."[7] (Joseph Peel and C.E. McCary 1997, 4).

It is the holistic nature of real-world experiences, and we must not forget that our public schools are part of the real world, that calls for an integrated view of teaching and learning. The fundamental argument to support curriculum integration is that learning is in itself the making of connections.[8] (Jay Cross 2003). There are connections of concepts, ideas, and meanings; there are connections that bring in the interplay of individual and group relationships in a community of learners; and there are connections all around us that make the world of knowledge and the realities of the classroom setting a complex and challenging undertaking. Connections, however, cannot happen in a vacuum. They take place in an environment where the richness of materials, experiences, and applications provide a natural backdrop for integration. Consequently, classroom instruction and field experiences that enable pre-service teachers to make comparisons, establish associations, explore relationships, evaluate solutions, and draw conclusions are effective processes for the integration of knowledge, skills, and dispositions in teacher education.[9] (Michael Morehead and D. Cropp 1994, 2–8).

When educators and K–12 teachers expose students to real-life situations, the possibility for connections increases. Such experiences, as exploring the diversity of the learning process, the diversity of learners, and other pedagogical themes become ideal topics to bring the holistic dimension of real-life classroom situations. Through the completion of mini-ethnographies, case studies, and authentic research activities, to mention just a few, teacher education candidates are introduced to the richness and complexities of today's school communities. Problem-solving situations compel the learner to address learning in a holistic way. Because a real-life problem is the manifestation of multiple elements of a given situation, the learner who attempts to solve such problems must understand the interconnectedness of all essential and secondary parts.[10] (David Jonassen 1991, 11–12).

SAMPLE THEMATIC UNIT ON DIVERSITY OF LEARNING

Since the "learning process" is perhaps one of the most essential categories of formal education, I selected "The Diversity of the Learning Process" as the title of the first thematic unit. The following INTASC principles provided the basis for our selection:

Principle # 2: The teacher understands how children learn and develop, and can provide learning opportunities that support intellectual, social, and personal development.

Principle # 4: The teacher must understand and use a variety of instructional strategies to encourage student development of critical thinking, problem solving, and performance skills.

Principle # 5: The teacher must be able to use an understanding of individual and group motivation and behavior to create learning environments that encourage positive social interaction, active engagement in learning, and self-motivation.[11] (INTASC 1992).

In the following pages we analyze the learning process from different perspectives and establish connections between and among explanations of learning, instructional methodologies, and assessment. In most teacher education programs, a course in educational psychology incorporates the most essential concepts and skills addressed by pedagogical studies in the preparation of teachers; thus, this course provides an ideal vehicle to initiate thematic units in teacher education. The learning process, the learner, the learning environment, instructional methodologies, and the assessment of learning are essential components implicity or explicitly included in the sample thematic units. Figure 12.1 illustrates the integration of these components.

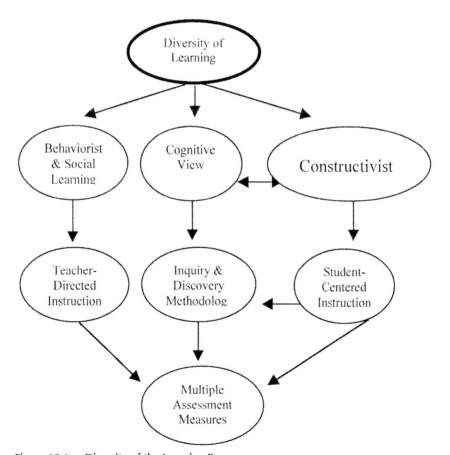

Figure 12.1. Diversity of the Learning Process

OVERVIEW OF THE THEMATIC UNIT

Every semester I begin my Educational Psychology course by describing how *learning* represents the most essential process of formal education. Everything that teachers, parents, and the community expect regarding formal education revolves around learning. Instructional resources, personnel, and methodology converge to make learning a successful experience.

One of the first assignments of this unit includes a brief historical overview of learning process. "Learning about Learning" as a research topic challenges teacher education students to gain knowledge about "learning" through early writings of philosophers and educators, such as Aristotle.[12] (SpaksNotes LLC 2003), Socrates.[13] (Dries Boele 1997, 48–70), Plato (Benjamin Jowett[14] 1998), Rousseau[15] 1979), and non-Western writers. Although it is beyond the scope of this chapter, pre-service teachers are asked to conduct a brief research of pedagogical samples of the following regions: Southeast Asia, Africa, and the Americas. Then we proceed to analyze the learning process through the findings of Edward Thorndike (Anita Woolfolk[16] 2004, 203–204), Ivan Pavlov (Jeanne Ellis Ormrod[17] 2003, 302–305), B.F. Skinner, and Albert Bandura (Robert E. Slavin[18] 2003, 142–163). Pre-service teachers are expected to master central concepts about the learning process from the behaviorist psychologists' perspective. We single out very specific principles in preparation for "focused field experiences." Such principles include mastery of basic terminology such as negative and positive reinforcement; schedules of reinforcement; aversive stimulus, punishment, and shaping; the Premack principle; and social learning. A clear understanding of behaviorist principles of learning coincides with the end of midterm examinations. Pre-arranged field experience sites are assigned to students so they may observe how these principles are being applied in the classroom setting. A "rubric" is provided to guide observers in their fieldwork and complete their field experiences report.

Divergent-, analysis-, and application-type questions guide the research and observation of knowledge about learning, such as the following: What evidence of learning have you identified in the classrooms you have observed? What behaviorist principles of learning do teachers apply? What differences can you identify between Pavlov- and Skinner-type applications of learning? How does the teacher you are observing utilize positive/negative reinforcement? Is there evidence of learning that does not fit the behaviorist view? This last question links our search for other explanations of learning to the next discussion topic: Cognitive view of learning. Referring to the knowledge we acquire, Aristotle (Jeremiah Genest[19] 1978) contended that everything that is on our mind has come through our senses. While we may debate the simplicity of such statement these days, given the complex nature of information-processing principles, the Greek philosopher certainly laid the foundations for the modern explanation of information processing. Not everything we learn begins with a stimulus-response mechanism, as behaviorist psychologists contend, nor does it always relate to overt behavior. Learning, in fact, can be invisible. Cognitive psychologists explore the idea of learning as a covert process. (Mark H. Ashcraft[20] 2002).

By juxtaposing the behaviorist view of learning with cognitive theories, pre-service teachers find themselves in an ideal situation to analyze, inquire, and engage in critical thinking. Teacher-education candidates are expected to compare, contrast, and identify major differences between these two explanations of learning. In order to accomplish this, pre-service teachers must demonstrate command of major components of information-processing models such as sensory register, perception, attention, short- and long-term memory, rehearsal, and schemata. (Mark H. Ashcraft[21] 2002). Questions related to this topic may include, but not limited to, the following: How do we process information? What is short- and long-term memory? What causes people to remember? What causes people to forget? What strategies may we apply to retrieve knowledge stored in long-term memory? What makes what we learn meaningful? How does the awareness of our thinking process—meta-cognition—can help us learn more effectively? How can we become strategic learners? The place where these questions should be investigated, in addition to campus classrooms, Internet, and libraries, ought to be the K–12 classroom settings.

Proponents of constructivist theories (Mary Jo Powell[22] 1995) provide the third explanation of learning. As we have observed above, learning according to behaviorist perspective causes a change in behavior and can be a covert process as evidenced by the processing and retrieval of information. The constructivist view, unlike the explanations of learning previously presented, offers a connection between learning and instructional strategies. A constructivist view of learning places the teacher as a guide of the learning process who, in turn, enables the student to "construct" and develop his or her own knowledge. From this perspective the learner is expected to adopt a more active role in the discovery and "construction" of knowledge. Organized in pairs, students in my Educational Psychology review findings of the main proponents of constructivist thought such as a Jean Piaget[23] (1929), Lev Vygotsky[24] (1978), John Dewey[25] (1958), and Jerome Bruner (1960).

Pre-service teachers are expected to explain the connections that exist between and among constructivist views of learning and information processing, social learning, inquiry methodology, problem-based learning, and perspectives on situated learning. Exploring the constructivist views of the learning process offers an opportunity for students to develop their own explanation of learning; thus living up to the expectations of constructivism.

The following questions serve as a guide for the completion of this exercise: What common threads do you see between constructivist views of learning and information processing? What similarities do you see between constructivist views of learning and Bandura's reciprocal determinism? What examples in your classroom observations can you identify of individual and social construction of knowledge? What instances in the classroom indicate applications of constructivist views of learning? Does the evidence that you have observed support a constructivist or behaviorist approach to learning? What conclusions can you draw between a teacher-led and a student-centered classroom environment? Can you identify what beliefs about learning support the teacher's instructional methodologies?

The above questions cast pre-service teachers into real-life situations where central issues of the learning process must be applied. Future teachers have an opportunity to analyze learning in a more in-depth way. In my Educational Psychology class, the outcome of this exercise has been the initial formulation, on the part of pre-service teachers, of an approach to learning and teaching. Although there is no single approach chosen as the only way to addressing instruction, an eclectic approach is usually selected with specific preferences for one of the above explanations. In reality, this provides the foundation and justification for a preferred approach to instructional strategies. Novice teachers begin to see the advantages and disadvantages of previously proposed instructional strategies. Fundamental beliefs about learning determine teachers' instructional strategies.

A Comparison Matrix is suggested as a strategy to analyze and establish connections. A Venn diagram is recommended to find commonalities between and among different explanations of learning. Pre-service teachers are asked to complete Table 12.1 below or come up with their own graphic organizer that may enable them to develop a holistic view of learning theories. The Type of Learning column is intended to initiate the completion of this table and the rest is left for the pre-service teacher to complete independently or in groups.

Table 12.1.   Perspectives of Learning

	Behaviorist	Cognitive	Constructivist
Type of Learning	Acquire information	Acquire concepts, strategies	Construction/reconstruction of knowledge
Learning Strategies			
Student Role			
Knowledge			
Dimension			
Teacher Role			
Other			

CONNECTING THE LEARNING PROCESS
WITH METHODS COURSES

It is at this point that collaboration begins between the instructor of educational psychology and the instructor responsible for teaching methodology. Logistics not withstanding, educational psychology and methods courses should be taught during the same semester, and in a team-teaching setting. This six-hour module coincides, in our program, with the beginning of a one-day-a-week field experience during which pre-service teachers are assigned for an entire day to the resident teacher who would become the cooperating teacher during the student teaching semester. This long-term collaboration allows pre-service teachers an ideal opportunity to start identifying elements of preferred learning principles and match them up with instructional strategies practices in their resident teacher's classroom.

As it is expected, the approach to teaching will vary depending on those fundamental beliefs about the learning process. Master teacher and apprentice (the student teacher in this case) may or may not agree on a preferred teaching methodology. However, student teaching placements should be sought where creativity and a variety of teaching methodologies are applied. Will the pre-service teacher opt for a student-centered or a teacher-led instructional approach?

In varying degrees, all instruction is teacher-led since it is the teacher's responsibility to initiate planning and implementation of instruction. However, there are degrees of teacher-centered instruction, which allow for a continuum where teacher-directed instruction is at one end of the continuum and student-centered at the other extreme. Mastery and preference of learning principles included above would determine the type of instructional strategies utilized in the classroom setting.

Behaviorist principles, specifically Thorndike's and Skinner's, exerted a considerable influence on the type of instructional designs that dominated the 20th century. The following assignment serves to connect these learning principles to specific instructional applications. We recommend to guide pre-service teachers in researching the following: Contract and mastery learning. (A Hypertext History of Instructional Design 2003),[26] Sidney Pressey's teaching machines. (A Hypertext History of Instructional Design 2003),[27] programmed instruction and task analysis. (A Hypertext History of Instructional Design, 2003),[28] the Instructional Systems Development (A Hypertext History of Instructional Design, 2003),[29] explicit instruction. (David Berliner and Barak Rosenshine 1986, 60–69),[30] and the constructivism of the 1990s (A Hypertext History of Instructional Design, 2003).[31] This last topic should provide a point of connection with the next topic.

Specific examples of behaviorist instruction include drills, games, tutorials, programmed instruction, simulations, graphic organizers/semantic web, and integrated learning systems.

With the exception of constructivism, the above research would yield the type of outcome more fittingly aligned with teacher-led type of instruction. On the other hand, pre-service teachers should explore instructional methodologies associated with student-centered instruction. To this end, the following list should provide a guide to explore student-centered instructional approaches: Piaget's[32] (1954) construction of reality in children; Vygotsky's[33] (1978) constructivism; situated learning; (Barbara Rogoff[34] 1990); Bruner's (1966) spiral curriculum; Dewey's[35] inquiry methodology; (Thomas Matczynski,[36] 2002); Slavin's[37] (1995) cooperative learning and reciprocal teaching; problem-based learning; (Neal A. Glasgow[38] 1997, 169); and critical thinking programs; (Robert J. Marzano and Daisy E. Arredondo[39] 1986).

From this array of choices, pre-service teachers begin to identify potential applications to their teaching experience. Although one particular approach may prove to be insufficient in addressing the different instructional needs, learning to select instructional strategies based information gathered on a daily basis will increase the meaning and learning effectiveness of learning principles. Just as pre-service teachers were asked to compare and contrast behaviorist and cognitive descriptions of the learning process, they now should be able to compare teacher-dominated and student-centered instructional approaches. Table 12.2 provides a starting point for this comparison. Pre-service teachers should identify at least ten more points of contrast.

Table 12.2. Comparison of Teacher-Dominated and Student-Centered Instructional Applications

Teacher-Dominated	Student-Centered
Teacher presents knowledge	Student discovers and constructs knowledge
Students learn meaning	Students create meaning
Students memorize	Students process information
Students learn factual information	Students develop learning strategies Teacher
structures instruction	Social interaction provides instructional scaffolding
Teacher provides resources	Students find resources
Students study individually	Students learn with peers
Teacher manages student learning	Students learn to manage their own learning
Students learn about others' thinking	Students develop and reflect on their own thinking (Patricia Deubel)[40]

ASSESSMENT OF INTEGRATED LEARNING

As a non-traditional approach to teaching and learning, integrated/thematic instruction calls for a non-traditional approach to assessing the effectiveness of the instructional design and student performance. While some of the traditional assessment measures may be replicated within the scope of thematic instruction, the sequence and application must be aligned with the learning expectations appropriate to integrated learning. In traditional applications of instructional evaluation, the teacher initiates, plans, and implements evaluation activities while the students simply become passive recipients of performance assessment measures. In an integrated/thematic approach to learning, students become active participants in the assessment process. For example, students' self-assessments may assist both, the teacher and the student, in modifying elements of the unit as well as in determining student performance. Electronic portfolios, journals, projects, research reports, and written reflections all can be valuable tools for students' performance and teacher's instructional design.

Since an integrated/thematic unit includes other participants besides the student and the teacher, mentors, field personnel, and others working with the students may provide insights into students' performance. Comments, checklist, attendance logs, and other forms of communication may contribute to the final report for the student. Just as there are many participants in the assessment process of the integrated/thematic unit, assessment activities may take place at different times. Consequently, assessment becomes an ongoing process for the teacher, the student, and other professionals involved. In this manner, it can be formative or summative evaluation. It can happen at the close of each activity when students and teacher reflect to determine goal attainment or at the beginning of a learning activity. It can happen during the course of a learning activity when students and teacher re-orient learning activities. It can happen in the field where other professionals may provide feedback to students and teacher in the completion of authentic tasks.

Table 12.3 may be utilized as a checklist to assess general components of a thematic unit, as well as behaviors on the part of the learner. This is actually a sample checklist that I use in my Educational Psychology course. Other rubrics and measurement tools should be tailored to address the goals and objectives of each individual integrated/thematic unit.

CAVEATS OF INTEGRATION IN TEACHER EDUCATION

Although I have come to value integration through experiences in our own teacher education program, I have also learned about potential pitfalls that

Table 12.3.   Thematic Unit Assessment

Name of Student _____ Date _____
Name of the Thematic Unit _____

Student-Teacher Conference

Tell me about the highlight of this unit.
What piece of the research did you find most beneficial? Least? And Why?
What questions were you unable to answer?
Identify at least three areas that need improvement.

Teacher's Ratings of Student Behavior

Scale: 1 = Unsatisfactory; 3 = Satisfactory; 5 = Excellent

Disposition toward the unit	1 2 3 4 5
Conceptual understanding	1 2 3 4 5
Goal achievement	1 2 3 4 5
Independence in task completion	1 2 3 4 5
Research skills	1 2 3 4 5
Use of technology and other resources	1 2 3 4 5
Ability to establish conceptual priorities	1 2 3 4 5
Problem-solving ability	1 2 3 4 5
Collaboration skills	1 2 3 4 5
Participation in large-group discussion	1 2 3 4 5
Quest activities completed	1 2 3 4 5

(Adapted from Victoria Giordano[11] 1996)

such approach may present. In analyzing the pros and cons of this instructional approach, I found an overwhelming support for integration and a few strong arguments against it. What follows intends to provide some reasons for caution.

Most faculty members in higher education and the public in general, through publishers, are a product of a disciplined-based education and for the most part unaware of almost a century of research about how children learn. (Marianne Everett[42] 1992, 57–60). Naturally, proponents of discipline-driven higher education curricula may find threatening any proposed curricular structure that deviate from what has been the norm for years. As Hayes-Jacobs[43] (1998) argued, "validity within the disciplines requires teachers representing each discipline to verify that the concepts identified are not merely related to their subjects but are important to them." (p. 27). While Mark Schug and Beverly Cross[44] (1998) specifically address integration in the social studies area, they actually suggest that integration, if done poorly, may be detrimental: "To attempt to integrate what is not understood will distort, nullify, and simplify content." (p. 6). They further warn, "Meaningful curriculum integration requires a large investment in staff development and planning. [It] requires teachers who are or can become sufficiently expert in understanding their subjects to be able to make meaningful connections across the disciplines." (p. 57).

As a strong advocate of integrated/thematic instruction, James Beane[45] (1995) made a clear distinction between the disciplines of knowledge and school-based subject areas. The first are "a field of inquiry about some aspect of the world" and the second "institutionally based representations of disciplines." (p. 618). Beane described the disciplines of knowledge to be an essential component of integration and the content, which provide power in the process of learning.

CULMINATING ACTIVITY

I recommend that as a culminating activity pre-service teachers participate in the "Research Fair" organized by the School of Education at the end of each academic year. This activity presents an excellent opportunity to demonstrate to the entire group of pre-service teachers what has been accomplished through the completion of integrated/thematic units. Using large print, tri-fold displays, and various forms of technology students prepare summaries of research findings, experiment results, illustrations of learning principles, and other pictorial representations of what they have learned.

Participating students and their instructors will have an opportunity to select the best samples of the thematic units completed during the fall and spring semesters. Being able to showcase their research findings and learning products would benefit the entire group of future teachers.

QUEST ACTIVITY

In the same way in which I have described the "Diversity of Learning," I recommend a thematic unit on the "Diversity of Learners." In collaboration with course instructors in the area of special education, you may apply some of the same strategies suggested above to explore the type of learner that you will be responsible for when you assume full responsibilities of a classroom teacher.

In my Educational Psychology course I make a compelling case about the diversity of learners by explaining that quite often teachers may know all there is to know about the subject matter, instructional design, instructional strategies, and the "learning process" itself. However, if they know little or nothing about the type of learner they will be teaching, the potential for learning becomes limited. Thus, the more reason to make the "Diversity of Learners" the next integrated/thematic unit.

CONCLUSION

Through first-hand experiences I have become convinced of the benefits that an integrated/thematic unit approach has for teacher education programs. As indicated at the beginning of this chapter, it is at the time when we prepare future teachers that we should introduce the concept of integration through concrete examples.

In my own experience, one of the clearest outcomes of this approach has been the involvement of pre-service teachers in authentic learning tasks. Field experiences, problem solving, and cooperative learning, to mention just a few, cast future teachers into meaningful learning situations.

Does it call for more planning on the part of teacher educators? Does it require more resources? Indeed, more time for planning and more resources are needed for this instructional approach. Teacher educators have a great opportunity to advance the cause of pedagogical preparation of future teachers by creating learning environments where creativity may take place. An integrated/thematic unit approach offers this opportunity.

NOTES

1. "Interstate New Teacher Assessment & Support Consortium," *A Program of the Council of Chief State School Officers*. Washington, DC, 1992. http://www.ccsso.org/intascst.html (5 Nov. 2003).

2. Susan Kovalik, "Integrated Curriculum," *Susan Kovalik & Associates 1984*, http://www.kovalik.com/ic.htm (6 Nov. 2003).

3. Jean Piaget, *To Understand Is to Invent: The Future of Education* (New York: Grossman, A Division of Viking Press, 1973), 11–12.

4. Christine E. Sleeter, ed., *Empowerment Through Multicultural Education* (Albany: State University of New York Press, 1991), 3–24.

5. "Highly Qualified Staff," *Title I Directors' Conference*, February 2003. http://www.ed.gov/admins/tchrqual/learn/hqs/edlite-index.html, (6 Nov. 2003).

6. James A. Banks and Cherry A. McGee Banks, eds., *Handbook of Research on Multicultural Education* (New York: Macmillan, 1995), 3–24.

7. Joseph Peel and C.E. McCary, "Visioning the 'Little Red Schoolhouse' for the 21st Century," *Kappan 78*, no. 9 (May 1997): 4.

8. Jay Cross, "Another Look at Learning," *Internet Time Group Research 2003*, http://www.internettime.com/blog/archives/000541.html (24 Dec. 2003).

9. Michael Morehead and D. Cropp, "Enhancing Pre-service Observation Experience with Structured Clinical Experiences," *The Teacher Educator 29*, no. 4 (Spring 1994), 2–8.

10. David Jonassen, "Objectivism v. Constructivism," *Educational Technology Research and Development 39*, no. 3 (September 1991), 11–12.

11. "Interstate New Teacher Assessment & Support Consortium," *A Program of the Council of Chief State School Officers*. Washington, DC, 1992. http://www.ccsso .org/intascst.html (5 Nov. 2003).

12. Aristotle, "Nichomachean Ethics," *SpaksNotes LLC 1999–2003*, http://www .sparknotes.com/philosophy/ethics/context.html (5 Nov. 2003).

13. Dries Boele, "The 'Benefits' of a Socratic Dialogue," *Inquiry: Critical Thinking Across the Disciplines 17*, no. 3 (Spring 1997) 48–70.

14. Benjamin Jowett, "Introduction to the Phaedrus," *Exploring Plato's Dialogues. A Virtual Learning Environment on the World-Wide Web* 1998. http://plato .evansville.edu/public/phaedrus.htm (7 Nov. 2003).

15. Jean Jacques Rousseau, *Emile or On Education*, trans. Allan Bloom, (New York: Basic Books, 1979).

16. Anita Woolfolk, *Educational Psychology, 9th. ed.*, (New York: Pearson, 2004): 203–204.

17. Jeanne Ellis Ormrod, *Educational Psychology: Developing Learners, 4th. ed.* (Columbus, OH: Merrill Prentice Hall, 2003): 302–305.

18. Robert E. Slavin, *Educational Psychology: Theory and Practice, 7th ed.* (New York: Allyn and Bacon, 2003): 142–163.

19. Jeremiah Genest, "Aristotelian Epistemology and Its Arabic Developments," *Ars Magica 1978*, http://www.granta.demon.co.uk/arsm/jg/arist-epist.html (24 Dec. 2003).

20. Mark H. Ashcraft, *Cognition, 3rd. ed.*, Prentice-Hall Distance Learning 2002, http://cwx.prenhall.com/bookbind/pubbooks/ashcraft/ (26 Dec. 2003).

21. Mark H. Ashcraft, *Cognition, 3rd. ed.*, Prentice-Hall Distance Learning, 2002, http://cwx.prenhall.com/bookbind/pubbooks/ashcraft/ (26 Dec. 2003).

22. Mary Jo Powell, "Building and Understanding Constructivism," *SCIMAST*, Southwest Educational Laboratory 1995, http://www.sedl.org/scimath/compass/ v01n03/credits.html (26 Dec. 2003).

23. Jean Piaget, *The Child's Conception of the World* (New York: Harcourt, Brace Jovanovich, 1929).

24. Lev S. Vygotsky, *Mind in Society* (Cambridge, MA: Harvard University Press, 1978).

25. John Dewey, *Experience and Nature* (New York: Dover, 1929; Dover edition first published in 1958).

26. "1920s: Concepts of Objectives", *A Hypertext History of Instructional Design*, http://www.coe.uh.edu/courses/cuin6373/idhistory/1920.html, (Nov. 8, 2003).

27. "1920s: Concepts of Objectives", *A Hypertext History of Instructional Design*, http://www.coe.uh.edu/courses/cuin6373/idhistory/pressey.html (Nov. 8, 2003).

28. "The 1950s: Programmed Instruction and Task Analysis," *A Hypertext History of Instructional Design,* http://www.coe.uh.edu/courses/cuin6373/idhistory/1950.html (Nov. 8, 2003).

29. "The 1960s: Instructional Systems Development," *A Hypertext History of Instructional Design,* http://www.coe.uh.edu/courses/cuin6373/idhistory/1960.html (Nov. 8, 2003).

30. David Berliner and Barak Rosenshine, "Synthesis of Research on Explicit Teaching," *Educational Leadership 43*, no. 7 (April 1986), 60–69.

31. "1990s: Constructivism," *A Hypertext History of Instructional Design,* http://www.coe.uh.edu/courses/cuin6373/idhistory/1990.html (Nov. 8, 2003).

32. Jean Piaget, *The Construction of Reality in the Child*, M. Cook, Trans. (New York: Basic Books, 1954).

33. Lev S. Vygotsky, *Mind in Society: The Development of Higher Mental Process* (Cambridge, MA: Harvard University Press, 1978).

34. Barbara Rogoff, *Apprenticeship in Thinking: Cognitive Development in Social Context* (New York: Oxford University Press, 1990).

35. Jerome Buner, *Toward a Theory of Instruction* (New York: Norton, 1966).

36. Thomas Matczynski, Thomas J. Lashley, II, and James B. Rowley, *Instructional models: Strategies for Teaching in a Diverse Society*, 2nd ed. (Belmont, CA: Wadsworth/Thomson Learning, 2002).

37. Robert E. Slavin, *Cooperative Learning*, 2nd ed. (Boston: Allyn and Bacon, 1995).

38. Neal A. Glasgow, *New Curriculum for New Times: A Guide to Student-Centered, Problem-based Learning.* (Thousand Oaks, CA: Corwin Press, Inc., 1997): 169.

39. Robert J. Marzano & Daisy E. Arredondo, *Tactics for Thinking: Teacher's Manual.* (Aurora, CO: Mid-continent Educational Laboratory, 1986).

40. Patricia Deubel, "An Investigation of Behaviorist and Cognitive Approaches to Instructional Multimedia Design," *Journal of Educational Multimedia and Hypermedia 12*, no.1 (March 2003): 63–90.

41. Victoria Giordano, "Thematic Unit," *FACE Region VI Technology Conference 1996*, http://connect.barry.edu/ect653/thematic/organizational (27 December, 2003).

42. Marianne Everett, "Developmental Interdisciplinary Schools for the 21st Century," *Education Digest 57*, no. 2 (March 1992): 57–60.

43. Heidi Hayes-Jacobs, *Interdisciplinary curriculum: Design and Implementation* (Alexandria, VA: Association for Supervision and Curriculum Development, 1989): 27.

44. Mark C. Schug and Beverly Cross, "The Dark Side of Curriculum Integration in Social Studies," (Special Section: Contrarian Perspectives on Social Studies Education), *The Social Studies 89*, no.2 (October 1998), 54–58.

45. James A. Beane, "Curriculum Integration and the Disciplines of Knowledge," *Phi Delta Kappan 76*, no. 8 (April 1995), 616–622.

BIBLIOGRAPHY

Aristotle, "Nichomachean Ethics," *SpaksNotes LLC 1999–2003*, <http://www.sparknotes.com/philosophy/ethics/context.html> (5 Nov. 2003).

Ashcraft, Mark H. *Cognition, 3rd. ed.*, Prentice-Hall Distance Learning 2002, <http://cwx.prenhall.com/bookbind/pubbooks/ashcraft/> (26 Dec. 2003).

Banks, James A. and Cherry A. McGee Banks, eds. *Handbook of Research on Multicultural Education.* New York: Macmillan, 1995.

Beane, James A. "Curriculum Integration and the Disciplines of Knowledge," *Phi Delta Kappan 76*, No. 8 (April 1995): 616–22.

Berliner, David and Barak Rosenshine, "Synthesis of Research on Explicit Teaching," *Educational Leadership 43*, No. 7 (April 1986): 60–69.

Boele, Dries. "The 'Benefits' of a Socratic Dialogue," *Inquiry: Critical Thinking Across the Disciplines 17*, No. 3 (Spring 1997): 48–70.

Bruner, Jerome *The Process of Education.* Cambridge, MA: Harvard University Press, 1960.

———. *Toward a Theory of Instruction.* New York: Norton, 1966.

Cross, Jay. "Another Look at Learning," *Internet Time Group Research 2003*, <http://www.internettime.com/blog/archives/000541.html (24 Dec. 2003).

Deubel, Patricia "An Investigation of Behaviorist and Cognitive Approaches to Instructional Multimedia Design," *Journal of Educational Multimedia and Hypermedia 12*, No.1 (March 2003): 63–90.

Dewey, John. *Experience and Nature.* New York: Dover, 1929; Dover edition first published in 1958.

Everett, Marianne "Developmental Interdisciplinary Schools for the 21st Century," *Education Digest 57*, No. 2 (March 1992): 57–60.

Genest, Jeremiah. "Aristotelian Epistemology and Its Arabic Developments," *Ars Magica 1978*, http://www.granta.demon.co.uk/arsm/jg/arist-epist.html (24 Dec. 2003).

Giordano, Victoria "Thematic Unit," *FACE Region VI Technology Conference 1996*, http://connect.barry.edu/ect653/thematic/organizational (27 December, 2003).

Glasgow, Neal A. *New Curriculum for New Times: A Guide to Student-Centered, Problem-based Learning.* Thousand Oaks, CA: Corwin Press, Inc., 1997.

Hayes-Jacobs, Heidi *Interdisciplinary curriculum: Design and Implementation.* Alexandria, VA: Association for Supervision and Curriculum Development, 1989.

"Highly Qualified Staff," *Title I Directors' Conference*, February 2003. http://www.ed.gov/admins/tchrqual/learn/hqs/edlite-index.html, (6 Nov. 2003).

"Interstate New Teacher Assessment & Support Consortium," *A Program of the Council of Chief State School Officers.* Washington, DC, 1992.

Jonassen, David. "Objectivism v. Constructivism," *Educational Technology Research and Development 39*, No. 3 (September 1991): 11–12.

Jowett, Benjamin. "Introduction to the Phaedrus," *Exploring Plato's Dialogues. A Virtual Learning Environment on the World-Wide Web* 1998. http://plato.evansville.edu/public/phaedrus.htm (7 Nov. 2003).

Kovalik, Susan. "Integrated Curriculum," *Susan Kovalik & Associates 1984*, http://www.kovalik.com/ic.htm (6 Nov. 2003).

Matczynski, Thomas, Thomas J. Lashley, II, and James B. Rowley, *Instructional Models: Strategies for Teaching in a Diverse Society*, 2nd ed. Belmont, CA: Wadsworth/Thomson Learning, 2002.

Marzano, Robert J. & Daisy E. Arredondo, *Tactics for Thinking: Teacher's Manual.* Aurora, CO: Mid-continent Educational Laboratory, 1986.

Morehead, Michael and D. Cropp, "Enhancing Pre-service Observation Experience with Structured Clinical Experiences," *The Teacher Educator 29,* no. 4 (Spring 1994): 2–8.

Ormrod, Jeanne E. *Educational Psychology: Developing Learners, 4th. ed.* Columbus, OH: Merrill Prentice Hall, 2003.

Peel, Joseph and C.E. McCary, "Visioning the 'Little Red Schoolhouse' for the 21st Century," *Kappan 78,* No. 9 (May 1997): 4.

Piaget, Jean. *The Construction of Reality in the Child,* M. Cook, Trans. New York: Basic Books, 1954.

———. *The Child's Conception of the World.* New York: Harcourt, Brace Jovanovich, 1929.

———. *To Understand Is to Invent: The Future of Education.* New York: Grossman, A Division of Viking Press, 1973.

Powell, Mary J. "Building and Understanding Constructivism," *SCIMAST,* Southwest Educational Laboratory 1995, http://www.sedl.org/scimath/compass/v01n03/credits.html. (26 Dec. 2003).

Rousseau, Jean J. *Emile or On Education,* trans. Allan Bloom. New York: Basic Books, 1979.

Rogoff, Barbara. *Apprenticeship in Thinking: Cognitive Development in Social Context.* New York: Oxford University Press, 1990.

Schug, Mark C. and Beverly Cross, "The Dark Side of Curriculum Integration in Social Studies," (Special Section: Contrarian Perspectives on Social Studies Education), *The Social Studies 89,* No.2 (October 1998), 54–58.

Slavin, Robert E. *Cooperative Learning,* 2nd ed. Boston: Allyn and Bacon, 1995.

Sleeter, Christine E. ed. *Empowerment Through Multicultural Education.* Albany: State University of New York Press, 1991.

"The 1920s: Concepts of Objectives," *A Hypertext History of Instructional Design,* http://www.coe.uh.edu/courses/cuin6373/idhistory/1920.html, (Nov. 8, 2003).

"The 1950s: Programmed Instruction and Task Analysis," *A Hypertext History of Instructional Design,* http://www.coe.uh.edu/courses/cuin6373/idhistory/1950.html. (Nov. 8, 2003).

"The 1960s: Instructional Systems Development," *A Hypertext History of Instructional Design,* http://www.coe.uh.edu/courses/cuin6373/idhistory/1960.html. (Nov. 8, 2003).

"The 1990s: Constructivism," *A Hypertext History of Instructional Design,* http://www.coe.uh.edu/courses/cuin6373/idhistory/1990.html. (Nov. 8, 2003).

Vygotsky, Lev S. *Mind in Society: The Development of Higher Mental Process.* Cambridge, MA: Harvard University Press, 1978.

Woolfolk, Anita. *Educational Psychology, 9th ed.* New York: Pearson, 2004.

Chapter Thirteen

Multiple Intelligences Inserted Into The Lesson Plan

Robert J. Landry, Karen S. Landry
& Holly L. Johnson

INTRODUCTION

Educators have become aware of the issue surrounding traditional I.Q. testing; namely that standardized tests are very reliable, but that their validity, as a measure of intelligence, leaves much to be desired. Traditional I.Q. testing distributes intellect on the bell-shaped curve in which 68.26 % (Slavin, 2000) of the population falls within one standard deviation of the norm. As educators, however, we know that intelligence is expressed in many different ways, and that a number cannot be the sole representative of a student's intelligence. Look around at the number of adults who are successful, not because of verbal and mathematic ability, but because of other skills they possess. The standardized I.Q. test score has come to represent intelligence in two areas, verbal and mathematic ability, yet we know today that intelligence comes in many forms and can be cultivated and expanded.

When you look at students in class, can you tell who is the smartest? If you answer this question based on verbal and mathematic abilities, then you are basing your reasoning on traditional I.Q. testing. However, we intuitively recognize other skills in students that are not identified by the traditional tests. We live in an age of diversity and multiculturalism, the words for differences, which have been more magnified by 9–11 and the recent Iraq War. The connection between multiple intelligences and multiculturalism focuses on the appreciation diverse aspects bring to the understanding of each other. When teachers teach students through the Multiple Intelligences approach, then all are more likely to respect and appreciate the talents of all. The breadth of Multiple Intelligences theory offers opportunities to focus on the child's strengths and boost his or her self-understanding.

WHAT IS MULTIPLE INTELLIGENCES THEORY
AND HOW CAN IT BE UTILIZED IN THE LESSON PLAN?

A problem is created when people are presented with the concept of multiple intelligences because it forces them to think differently about how people process, act, and interact. Once you understand multiple intelligences, you will examine your interaction with others from a different perspective. The strategies surrounding multiple intelligences transcend age, race, and culture. Its concepts are applicable to various settings. Spreading this unique, yet sensible, theory will enhance understanding and acceptance of all peoples. In servicing others, recognizing and encouraging human potentiality is the focus.

The Relationship of Theories

How does the theory of Multiple Intelligences differ from learning styles? Keefe and Monk (1990), writing in the Learning Style Profiles Examiner's Manual, define learning style as follows: "The composite of characteristic cognitive, affective and physiological factors that serve as relatively stable indicators of how a learner perceives, interacts with, and responds to the learning environment." Armstrong (1994) states, "Broadly construed, a person's learning style is the intelligences put to work." Gardner (1999), writing on learning style and intelligence, separates the two concepts: The concept of style designates a general approach that an individual can apply equally to an indefinite range of content. In contrast, intelligence is a capacity, with its component computational processes that is geared to a specific content in the world.

With all the different profiles available and their different interpretations, Gardner (1999) states that the word "style" cannot be assumed the same to all who have used it. He further adds that there is little basis for equating "style" with "intelligence." Keefe (1989) cautions the reader that, in reality, individuals with weak cognitive skills will benefit little from an analysis and matching of style elements. Personality and sensory-channel based profiles have been used successfully for years. We now have access to another profile based on the comfort zones of intelligences for individuals. Below are listed different models and their theoretical basis:

1. Sensory-channel (Auditory/Visual/Kinesthetic)
2. Personality (Myers-Briggs)
3. Cognitive (Multiple Intelligences)

A broader profile of an individual is achieved using the theory of Multiple Intelligences. For example, a person can be simultaneously assessed as "logical," "interpersonal," and "visual." Other theoretical assessments may not profile the wide band of comfort zones. The Multiple Intelligences theory examines how the individual operates on the contents of the world.

With proper information, an educator can more easily advocate for students. How does one consistently define "proper information?" Let us examine your perspectives. As an educator, how do you consistently assess intelligence? What makes up intelligence? Do you pigeonhole yourself into one intelligence? Do you pigeonhole students into one intelligence? Be honest. Do you *provide* and *develop* opportunities for students' intelligences or instead teach to your own? These can be hard, thought-provoking questions, yet answering each of these is essential if you are to truly examine your educational practices. How can *you* best serve the needs of *your* students? This examination begins with an assessment of your students' intelligences.

Salny and Frumke (1986) state that most MENSAs agree that I.Q. tests are fallible instruments, measuring a concept that has yet to be adequately defined. Many are beginning to question the validity of these standardized tests to measure behavior in the real world. The theory of Multiple Intelligences responds to our society's emphasis on standardized testing with lesson plans enriched for all our students.

A description based on Multiple Intelligences yields more information in serving the needs of the student. A more complete picture of the student is obtained and activities can be planned that address the identified intelligences.

In today's society, the word "intelligence" is used loosely and defined with different responses. How do *you* define intelligence? Traditionally, we have narrowly described a person's abilities based on the areas of language and mathematics. Our consistency with this description has not necessarily been due to agreement with the concept, but perhaps because of an unintentional acceptance of the status quo. However, now there is an awakening that people are much more than their ability to use words and manipulate numbers. A focus on the "whole person" allows us to pragmatically describe a person's abilities. This realigned focus allows those in education and management to effectively perceive their clients. This leads to a more efficiently and realistically run organization.

Factors that influence the concept of intelligence are varied and have been well researched and documented. Three notably influential factors are environment, parental socio-economic status and family history. When interviewed, even today's high school students recognize that "being intelligent" is contingent upon, but not confined by, these factors. We should join them in this "revolution of sorts." Finally, Gardner (1983) postulates three crucial propositions concerning the concept of intelligence:

1. it describes something real;
2. it varies from person to person; and
3. it is universal and ancient.

Do you agree with each of these suppositions? It seems reasonable to do so.

Why the Big Deal?

There is a paradigm shift occurring in the psychology and philosophy of intelligence. The norm is not as normal as it used to be. For instance, at one time it was believed that intelligence was a fixed variable at birth. Salny and Lewis (1986) wrote that Sir Cyril Burt, past honorary president of MENSA, was a leading proponent of the thesis that intelligence was primarily a function of genetic inheritance instead of environment. Today it is believed that intelligence is not fixed at birth; in fact, you can increase and expand your intelligences (Garner, 1983; Gould, 1996; Perkins, 1995.)

Past researchers thought that intelligence was found within our skulls, our brains. Today we are starting to believe that intelligence can be found within multiple levels of our brain, mind, and body systems. The universe within our body is vast and not totally known to us. We have believed for so long that intelligence was packaged within a person, and that was it. Wiggins (1993) wrote, "In our so-called culture of testing, 'intelligence' is fixed. As a result, relative ranking matters more than accomplishment." Today we are starting to believe that intelligence can be learned, enhanced, and even taught. All this implies that this paradigm shift gives us the opportunity to increase our intelligence throughout our lifespan.

Now back to this business of "intelligence." Conceptualize for yourself a personal definition of "intelligence;" write it on the lines below.

_____
_____
_____
_____

Hopefully, you have responded in a manner that is pleasing to you. If not, do not give up! You will learn shortly that you are a genius!

There is no *one way* to incorporate multiple intelligences in your classroom; do not try to teach everything in all of the seven ways. Instead, use the intelligences as "hooks" to activate students and give them multiple entry points into the classroom. Rita Dunn (1990) has said, "If a child is not learning in the way you are teaching, then you must teach in the way the child learns." The intent of this chapter is twofold: 1) to present an overview on the theory and its implications and 2) to present a lesson which may assist you in developing your own for your specific students.

Warm-Up Exercise

As a warm-up exercise, look at the picture (Figure 3.1) drawn by Gin Lucas, and locate the perfectly shaped five-pointed star. Relax and enjoy this activity. Found it yet? OK, a few more seconds and you will. Are you using the black and white color combinations? Try looking at the bottom half of the picture. Still looking? Concentrate on the bottom right quadrant and you will see it. What ability is utilized in this activity? Did you say "visual/spatial?" Great; now you are thinking! You are already broadening your concept of "intelligence."

Let us examine a brief history on intelligence. The examination of the intelligence begins with craniometry. Morton and Broca, two Europeans from

Figure 13.1.

the mid-1800s, collected large numbers of skulls and assigned a measurement value to each skull. This field implied that skull size made the difference in intelligence. In 1901, Binet encouraged the utilization of his tests as part of a thoughtful assessment process (Gould, 1981). The Spearman "g", a mathematical co-efficient designed to identify intelligence, was developed in 1904. This theory was founded on the idea that intelligence is inherited through genes and chromosomes and that it can be measured by one's ability to score sufficiently on the Binet I.Q. test and other intelligence tests, which yielded static and relatively stable I.Q. scores (Perkins, 1995).

The Spearman "g" was used by the military as a means to differentiate the masses and to assist in the classification of military duties. The U.S. Army, beginning in the early 1920s, used I.Q. testing as the British did—to differentiate the masses. Do you recollect the type of military combat during this period? It was hand-to-hand, not nearly as sophisticated as modern times. Those who were not "intelligent" were placed on the front lines, whereas those defined as "intelligent," as it were, were given leadership positions. With the end of World War I, the population in the United States became more cosmopolitan. A popular song of the time, "How Ya' Gonna Keep 'Em Down on the Farm After They've Seen Pare" (Victrola Record Company, Victor [18537], Arthur Fields) alerted the aristocracy to the trend toward globalization. There was a need for the masses to be kept in their rightful place by analyzing, categorizing, separating, distinguishing and labeling. Gould (1996) and Perkins (1995) stated, "Some means was necessary to measure individuals' and groups' 'mental energies' to determine who was 'fit' and who was not." In 1924, under the Immigration Restriction Act, the U.S. Immigration Office used this I.Q. concept to decide which people entered the United States.

The 1960s brought about many changes in the U.S. These changes came about due to shifts in public policy. During this time, B.F. Skinner began researching and writing his findings; expounding upon the notion of learned behavior, which could be construed as intelligence. Many of his studies were conducted using mice. Another psychologist, Arthur Jensen, spoke on the variable of heredity and its influence on I.Q. At Harvard University, Howard Gardner began to investigate the concept of intelligence through Project Zero, a project that continues to exist and disseminate research. Gardner developed the theory of Multiple Intelligences, that our intelligence is more than the traditionally accepted version of innate verbal and mathematical abilities. Salny and Frumkes (1986) write that the MENSA organization has acknowledged the concept of the theory of Multiple Intelligences. This theory of Multiple Intelligence will be examined in the remaining parts of this book, and you will perform activities that will accentuate each of the intelligences.

How does Multiple Intelligences operate? Taking a snapshot into the world of neurology, we find that the brain is an amazing organ. The connections found between the brain and the body, how the connections are formed, and what occurs are phenomenal. These connections make us who we are. An individual's work and learning processes derive from this connective pathway.

The Original Internet Highway

The internet highway is a complex structure that the majority of us accepts but does not necessarily understand. Do you know how the structure is composed? Gin Lucas presents two sketches for our next illustration. Look at the pictures above drawn on the left (Figure 13.2) that presents sporadic strings. Do you know what these represent? Look at the picture on the right. (Figure 13.3) It looks like a mess. What is it? They both present a highway that is structured similarly to our modern internet. These are "brain cell internet highways." The one on the left is that of a newborn baby; the one on the right

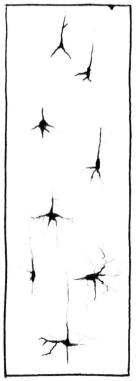
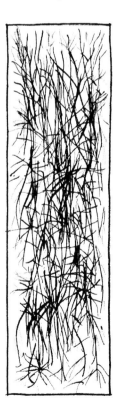

Figure 13.2. and Figure 13.3.

is that of a two-year-old child. Wow, what a difference! Talk about the internet highway-this is the original one! This explains why Gardner can accurately propose that intelligences can be learned and enhanced.

The brain is about internet highways, which means connections. Connections make us intelligent, and the more connections you have, the more effective you are. This is somewhat comparable to the metaphor of electrical connections in your house. If done properly, then all things work well. However, if not connected properly, look out! Sparks and overloads can occur.

Comfort vs. Discomfort

We all experience varying levels of comfort in different degrees in processing information and how one presents what one knows. What about the comfort zones of intelligences of the students you serve? An educator armed with this knowledge is as a surgeon with the information needed to operate effectively and successfully. Moving students towards greater success is a goal for every true professional educator. This allows you to activate both multiple learning and teaching for the student- the teacher. Remember the student and teacher are tied to each other. There is no separation as some on both sides would like to assume. As a great coach knows his athletes and what they can do, so does a great teacher know about his/her students. Do you truly know your students?

Do you, or *will* you, believe that students have rights? Students believe they do, although they often express that they do not get them. Professional educators know better. In addition, they know without a doubt that each student has rights. Consider the following:

Students have the right to be provided with experiences that activate and develop all of their intelligences.

What does this mean to you? It means that students should not be stymied in the educational process. Teachers should enrich the environment with experiences and settings that will invigorate everyone. The activation and development of all the intelligences means that these should be addressed individually and collectively. There is no one right way to incorporate multiple intelligences into your classroom. Instead, you must try various means. Trying to teach to and through each intelligence in every class is not the goal. Rather, use your creative ways to meet the needs of your students.

Students have the responsibility to ask teachers to push them forward.

Succinctly, this statement means that once their intelligences have been appropriately activated, students will naturally hunger for more. They will hound their teachers for more learning. Wouldn't you love to have a room full of eager students?

Reasons Why Multiple Intelligences Theory Makes Sense:

From the findings of the SUMIT (Schools Using Multiple Intelligences Theory) project that includes schools from across the United States, Gardner (1999) reported the following:

1. 78% schools reported positive standardized test outcomes with 63% attributed to Multiple Intelligences practices
2. 78% reported improved performances by students with learning difficulties
3. 80% reported improved parent participation
4. 81% reported improved student discipline, with 67% attributed to the theory of Multiple Intelligences

The above findings may be attributed to three specific reasons that make the theory of Multiple Intelligences so appealing in the field of education:

1. Each child has various intellectual potentials.
2. Multiple Intelligences is child-centered instead of test-centered.
3. Multiple Intelligences appeals to multicultural sensibilities.

The "Testable Age" has so irritated most educators that they are searching for an alternative method for getting improved results in student achievement. Using Multiple Intelligences provides for this by recognizing that students are multi-faceted individuals. Furthermore, it focuses on the child instead of the instrument used to assess the child. Multiple Intelligences is universal in its appeal; the sky is the limit with Multiple Intelligences. Are you ready to soar?

Practical Applications

The Multiple Intelligences theory has unlimited applications. It allows for the assessment of individuals regardless of their classification. It is useful with regular education students as well as those categorized as At-Risk, Exceptional Children, Academically Gifted, and English as a Second Language. The assessment gives insights into learning strategies to accentuate learning opportunities at all grade levels. Group assessments give teachers and administrators a profile on the specific group, which provides for appropriate lesson planning. Schools have used the assessment and analysis as a career development unit. School counselors have used it in developing academic plans, especially at the high school level.

As Multiple Intelligences continues to grow in prominence, other uses will be discovered. We beseech you to find the "Genie-in-you" and in others.

Gould (1999) eloquently writes, "If the misery of our poor be caused not by the laws of nature, but by our institutions, great is our sin." Finally, as Robert Half stated, "There is something much rarer than ability: the ability to recognize ability."

A Lesson Model:

Integrating two or more different courses within a lesson is an excellent model for incorporating the theory of Multiple Intelligences.

Lesson Plan #1 (Middle School) 7th Grade

Language Arts Reading: *The Night of the Twisters* (Ruckman, Ivy)

Integrated Areas: Language Arts and Science

Verbal-Linguistic: Read *Night of the Twisters*. Review the elements of the story (plot, setting, theme, point of view, tone, characters.

Visual-Spatial: Create and present a small collage to describe the literary elements existing in the story.

Logical-Mathematics: Create and review timeline from the reading. Develop an understanding of atmospheric conditions for tornado formation. Complete work-sheet on winds, air masses and projected tornado path.

This middle school lesson plan may be summarized by the following:

Objective: Student will develop an understanding of tornado formation.

Focus and Review: Review timeline created from reading Night of the Twister.

Teacher Input: Assess work sheet completion on winds and air masses. Discuss air currents outside the building using soap bubbles. Does height from affect air movement? What about wind direction?

Guided Practice: Using a map of prevailing wind currents determine directions from which various patterns blow in relation to the specified cities. Direct students to the following site: http://whyfiles.org/013tornado/2.html.

Independent Practice: Look up synonyms for "wind." Describe the different wind patterns from gentle to violent. Direct students to the following site: http://www.tornadoproject.com/fscale/fscale.htm. Write a poem about the "wind" using the synonyms. Group students in 3–4 and identify the literary element that exists in this story. Students create and present a collage detailing the setting of the story addressing at least five elements.

Closure: Review air currents and wind patterns. Relate wind current patterns to tornado prone areas.

Assessment: The student will write a one-page reflection discussing the story and what was learned collectively. Student completions of work-sheets represent understanding of winds and air masses culminating with a tracking project.

Finally:

The connection between multiple intelligences and multiculturalism focuses on the appreciation diverse aspects bring to the understanding of each other. When teachers teach students through the Multiple Intelligences approach, then all are more likely to respect and appreciate the talents of all. The breadth of Multiple Intelligences theory offers opportunities to focus on the child's strengths and boost his or her self-understanding.

BIBLIOGRAPHY

Armstrong, Thomas. *Multiple Intelligences in the Classroom*. Alexandria, VA: ASCD 1994. Fields, Arthur. "How Ya' Gonna Keep 'Em Down on the Farm after They've Seen Pare?",Victor [8537], Victrola Record Company.

Gardner, Howard. *Frames of Multiple Intelligences: The Theory of Multiple Intelligences*. New York: Basic Books, 1983.

Gardner, Howard. *The Unschooled Mind: How Children Think & How Schools Should Teach*. New York: Basic Books, 1991.

Gardner, Howard. *Intelligence Reframed, Multiple Intelligences for the 21st Century*. New York: Basic Books, 1999.

Gould, S.J. *The Mismeasure of Man*. New York: WW Norton, 1996.

Keefe, James W. *Learning Style Profile Handbook*, Reston, VA: National Association of Secondary School Principals, 1989.

Keefe, James W. and Monk, John S. *Learning Style Profile Examiners Manual*, Reston, VA: National Association of Secondary School Principals, 1990.

Lucas, Gin. Drawings: 13.1, 13.2. 13.3 (January 25, 2004).

Perkins, D. N. *Outsmarting IQ*. New York: The Free Press, 1995.

Salny, Abbie F. & Frumkes, Lewis. *MENSA-Think-Intelligent*. New York: Harper & Row, 1986

Slavin, Robert E. *Educational Psychology: Theory and Practice*, 6th. Boston: Allyn & Bacon, 2000.

Wiggins, Grant P. Assessing Student Performance: Exploring the Purpose and Limits of Testing. San Francisco, 1999.

Chapter Fourteen

Integrating Learning and Assessment: The Development Of An Assessment Culture

Judith Allen Brough and Jonelle E. Pool

> *"Good teaching is inseparable from good assessing. The question, therefore, is not whether to evaluate students, but how to measure performance in ways that will enrich learning, rather than restrict it."*[1]

Ernest Boyer's words suggest a culture of assessment that goes beyond mere assignment of grades on a report card or a mark at the top of the first page of a test. This philosophy depicts assessment as a tool essential for learning to occur, one that teachers and learners value rather than dread. In an assessment culture the focus becomes learner centered because assessments are used to determine individual student progress rather than to compare one student's work to that of another student. The purpose of classroom assessment is twofold: 1. to inform the teacher, individual student, and caregivers of the student's progress toward mastery of stated objectives, and 2. to inform the teacher about effectiveness of the curriculum approach and instructional strategies used to present the objectives to the students. Without well-planned effective assessment, educators lack data to make critical decisions about teaching and learning.

In an integrated curriculum approach, assessment assumes the role of gauging students' progress toward and effectiveness in solving real-world problems, thus assuming more widely encompassing techniques than mere paper-pencil tests allow. In order to prepare students to become life-long learners, we must also teach them to become reflective and effective self-evaluators. Because an integrated curriculum delivery assumes meaningful transferable content, student progress is regularly assessed and instruction is structured to assist students on their academic journeys. Assessments, then, ideally show the students where they are in relation to their set goals and allow them to design means to make further progress toward those goals. The setting of goals and their assessment becomes a transparent collaborative process that engages students in their own learning and offers them the opportunity to monitor and assess their personal progress. That is, students and teachers describe their learning outcomes, define how they will be assessed, and determine a means for reaching their goals. The design of assessments always precedes and guides decisions regarding instruction.[2] This philosophy assumes that the construction of assessments must be a thoughtful, deliberate, and collaborative process of planning valid tasks. Effective assessments, therefore, share these common characteristics:

1. Assessments directly align with stated goals and objectives. Teachers, students, and parents understand curriculum goals and what is necessary for achieving them.
2. Assessments are ongoing. They provide multiple snapshots of student progress toward stated goals and objectives. They are formative and summative in design. Objectives are used to determine means of assessment and assessments are used to suggest further objectives.
3. Assessments inform classroom practice. Instruction is guided by students' academic progress and learning needs.
4. Assessments provide descriptive and corrective feedback. Such feedback is concrete and specifically stated.
5. Student and teacher self-assessments are a critical form of learning.
6. Assessments are varied in scope and delivery. Alternative assessments, those other than paper/pencil tests, give students with varied learning styles opportunities to show what they know and are able to do.
7. Teachers and learners use assessments as fodder for meaningful reflection.

In this article we explore the benefits of developing an assessment culture for the delivery of an integrated curriculum, and to examine how the above factors contribute to an increased emphasis on fostering student learning goals.

1. ALIGNMENT OF GOALS, OBJECTIVES, AND ASSESSMENTS

Regardless of the curriculum delivery approach, educators must define the goals and objectives for any unit of study. These academic targets may be established by federal, state, or local curriculum mandates, by teacher knowledge of student academic needs, and by interests articulated by the learners themselves. The most effective integrated units blend all of the above, thus meeting specific standards while addressing the needs and interests of the learners.[3] Goals and objectives must specify content to be learned, skills to be addressed, and habits of the mind to be nurtured. "A thoughtful assessment system does not seek correct answers only, therefore. It seeks evidence of worthy habits of mind; it seeks to expose and root out thoughtlessness — moral as well as intellectual thoughtlessness."[4] Goals are meaningful and relevant to the students' lives and provide them with understandings, abilities, attitudes, and habits that can be transferred to many challenges students may encounter. These goals and objectives are well-known and understood by students and their caregivers. It is essential that the students realize where their academic journey will take them and why it is a worthwhile trip. If students and caregivers have input into the selection of relevant objectives, instruction, and assessment, they will more likely view the unit as a worthy investment of their time and attention. Integrated units, then, are not viewed as academic "fluff," but as a means of learning important "stuff."

Assessments are designed to determine individual student progress toward and mastery of these articulated aims. Instead of being graded on recitation of trivial pieces of information, students are actually observed performing the objectives formulated for the unit, using identified essential knowledge, and applying relevant skills. Students' thoughtful use of the content is carefully monitored and used to show the evolution of students' levels of thinking and working. In this way, assessment becomes authentic and students value the use of their newly acquired abilities.

2. ONGOING ASSESSMENTS

A variety of assessments provide multiple snapshots of student progress toward stated goals and objectives. They are formative and summative in design and include pre-assessments to determine levels of skills and content prior to instruction. Benchmarks that indicate student progress are then defined and teachers and learners use assessments to gauge development throughout the unit of study. Therefore, defined objectives and their pre-assessments are used not only to determine further means of assessment, but also to suggest a sequence of appropriate objectives. Lack of student progress toward the objectives is identified early; assessments indicate areas of difficulty, and objectives and instruction are appropriately adjusted to insure student success. In such a culture, a student may show misunderstanding, but is then redirected prior to any summative evaluation. As such, individual accountability is assured. This kind of assessment culture does not rely on one individual performance as a true measure of student learning. Rather, progress is monitored on a regular basis, not merely by written tests and quizzes, but also through observation of authentic tasks. Assessment, then, becomes part of the culture, thus minimizing students' anxiety. Students learn to value assessment as a learning tool that will aid them in their development. This kind of culture also assumes that if the objectives are important enough to teach, then all students should learn them. Multiple assessments concretely show students their progress, thus motivating them to continue learning. Not all of these assessments will be graded A through F as assessment is a concept different from evaluation. Evaluation involves a judgment of student work, usually stated in terms of a grade. More often, educators should employ assessment practices that are judgment-free and are designed to give students and their teacher data to indicate the direction learning must take. In effective assessment procedures, specific and concrete feedback is given so that students can see what they have learned and understand what they need to do to. Through the use of these assessment data, students come to realize that the important concept is their learning, not the grade achieved on an individual assessment. Arranging for interactive and collaborative assessment formats between the learner and the teacher encourage and motivate students as they begin to acquire new skills by making the environment "safe" enough to try.

3. INFORMED CLASSROOM PRACTICE

Instructional practice must be determined by students' progress and academic successes. Ongoing assessments give teachers data necessary to guide their instruction appropriately. Instead of measuring pedagogical effectiveness on assumed criteria, teachers use data from assessments to determine the extent to which students are "getting it." Many times, teachers will discover that a teaching strategy must be supplemented, or a lesson must be re-taught using a different approach. These data allow teachers to group and regroup the students according to their actual learning needs, to offer mini-lessons, or to change the lesson completely. If many of the students seem not to have mastered the specific content and skills, the fault may lie with the instructional strategies chosen rather than with the students. In such a case, students are not penalized in their grades. Instead, instruction is adjusted and further assessments determine the degree of successful learning. Analysis of results of assessments also can give teachers information regarding students' learning styles. This information can then lead to appropriate groupings of students for further instruction.

In the past, lesson design formats took precedence over identification of assessments. While certainly the lesson design is important, it cannot be prepared effectively without prior identification of the goals to be addressed and the assessment to be used to determine level of student mastery. To put it another way, once we know where we're going and how we'll know if and when we get there, then we can map out our directions for the journey. Carrying this analogy, we must recognize when the trip demands a detour and a whole new route is required. That is why strategically placed assessments are critical. Effective educators do not wait until the end of a unit of study to determine students' success; rather, they assess student progress frequently and change direction when necessary.

The information teachers analyze through these assessments enables them to articulate teaching success in terms of what the students have accomplished rather than in terms of what the teacher him/herself has done. Sometimes it will be useful for teachers to collaborate in assessment analysis in order to get more than one opinion and to increase assessment accuracy. This approach to assessment is a big step in embracing the mindset that student learning is the ultimate goal. The philosophy of assessment culture emphasizes that all students can and should be able to accomplish defined tasks and that it is the teacher's responsibility to analyze assessment data and to design subsequent instruction so that all students will find academic success. When such a philosophy is implemented in the integrated classroom, we alter our emphasis on what teachers are doing in the classroom to what individual students are accomplishing.

4. SELF-ASSESSMENTS, DESCRIPTIVE AND CORRECTIVE FEEDBACK

Feedback is essential for learning to occur—both for the student and the teacher. Students must understand explicitly how to improve and make academic progress and teachers must understand how students are faring. An aim of education is to assist students in becoming independent life-long learners. Students can not progress when they make a mistake, but are uncertain of where they went wrong. Too often, demands on teachers' time result in stunted feedback. Comments like "awkward" or "no," for example, do not give students enough critical information to be able to make adjustments in their thinking. The development of rubrics and specific evaluation criteria help students and teachers to pinpoint areas of learning strengths and weaknesses and to clarify student progress, but even then, teachers must provide further elaborative comments regarding individual progress. Students can and should be involved in the development of these assessment criteria. In this way, students concretely learn what it means to produce quality work on an assignment, and they have a voice in defining what a quality performance means.

It is good practice for teachers to develop a critical analysis of tasks students are expected to perform. Steps necessary in the sequence of learning are concretely articulated so that both teachers and students can determine where student work lies in the learning continuum. Students understand where they are and what they must do in order to be successful in achieving the goals and objectives set with and for them.

5. TEACHER AND STUDENT SELF-ASSESSMENTS

An effective assessment culture places importance on the ability to self-assess accurately. Teachers can model self-assessment practices through the use of think-alouds and examples of good work and best practice. When students learn what good work entails, they can and should practice a reflective review of their own work and learn to critique it thoughtfully. Since our goal is to foster independent learning, students can not rely merely on others' assessments of their work. This is a particularly important criterion for work in integrated curriculum settings because students often are pursuing tasks that are personally meaningful and are solving real-world problems.

Teacher modeling and instruction of self-assessment techniques should also emphasize the fact that most learning involves making mistakes. Students must internalize the idea that mistakes do not always carry a negative connotation or earn negative grades. Teachers must consistently convey this message in their assessment practices, a primary reason why some assessment must not carry judgment with it. Particularly when students' mistakes show that they are beginning to reformulate old ideas or put information together in new ways, an assessment culture acknowledges student efforts to complete challenging work and to take intellectual risks. Too often, students look at the grade they received, but even if the teacher provides specific feedback, either the students don't read it or, if they do, the assignment is completed and the students lack the opportunity to employ the changes suggested by the teacher's feedback. By analyzing their own mistakes, students learn how to correct them and use the newly acquired skills and information in future opportunities, thus truly demonstrating mastery of required goals and objectives. Students also learn to analyze good work, including their own best examples. They gain skills in the articulation of their academic growth and can identify concrete goals for their continued learning. While giving the students opportunities for self assessment is important for developing learning goals, an assessment system that values and appreciates student efforts for demonstrating self-assessment skills also must be encouraged.

6. VARIATION IN SCOPE AND DELIVERY

Alternative assessments, those other than paper/pencil tests, give students with varied learning styles opportunities to show what they know and are able to do. Since an integrated curriculum approach centers learning on solving central questions, authentic assessments become necessary. Teachers observe students in the engagement of real work. The National Middle School Associations position statement, This We Believe, advises that "ways of assessing and evaluating students' growth must address the many other aspects of a student's development including critical thinking, independence, responsibility, and those other desired personal attributes and dispositions that have lifelong influence. This requires a variety of assessment strategies including journals, electronic portfolios, demonstrations, peer feedback, teacher-designed tests, and audio or video evidences of learning."[5] Because the integrated curriculum involves the exploration of real world problems that engage the learner and use the various subject matters, assessment strategies must be just as engaging and varied as the instruction. A teacher's creative design of assessment tasks can motivate learners to give their best efforts. Such a variety of assessments also provides students with multiple ways of showing their growth, thus giving the teacher a truer picture of student learning.

7. MEANINGFUL REFLECTION

Integrated curriculum and assessments encourage a culture where critical thinking and reflection are paramount. Students need time and opportunities to think about their work realistically and mark their progress not only in curriculum content, but also in such important skills as developing a positive work ethic, collaborating effectively, making thoughtful decisions, and demonstrating responsibility. After a pre-assessment is given and analyzed, students should set goals concerning curriculum and habits of mind. They and their teacher(s) can then periodically conference regarding accomplishments, successes, and areas of strength and weakness. Students should get into the habit of analyzing their own work and resetting goals as they progress.

Portfolio presentations are a valuable way to encourage students to summarize their efforts and share their accomplishments with a wider audience. Students need to get into the habit of sharing their work with others besides the teacher. At the conclusion of a unit of study students could be encouraged to reflect on their work and create a way of demonstrating it. Electronic portfolios and video-taping are efficient ways of storing self-assessments for continued reflection about one's growth.

Student-led conferences are an effective forum for students to practice the articulation of their growth and needs. Students should be able to show teachers and caregivers what they have accomplished and what they have planned for future endeavors. Such a format for reporting student growth emphasizes progress and areas of challenge free from judgment, as opposed to a teacher conference focusing on a discussion of an A–F graded report card. In this way, learning takes center stage as opposed to an emphasis on grades, which are an indication of someone else's opinions of one's work. The point is that assessments should help students to be self-reliant and independent learners.

CONCLUSION

Assessment is a powerful learning tool when it is used with an integrated curriculum that emphasizes individual student accomplishment and high-level student reflection. A culture of authentic assessment used with authentic curriculum delivery encourages students to take academic risks, to analyze their own strengths and weaknesses, and to identify a means for optimizing their own learning. In addition, this philosophy of assessment helps teachers to prepare educational opportunities that individual students can value. Successful assessment encourages students to make connections about learning across content areas, contexts, and situations.

With our knowledge base expanding so rapidly, our challenge is to provide students with means for solving real problems, of asking important questions, and appropriately evaluating their own achievements. By keeping student learning at the center of our assessment practices, we can design valid and reliable assessments that motivate students and enrich thinking and reflection. Our reward is that we will prepare a generation of life-long learners.

NOTES

1. Rees, William and Mathis Wackernagel. "Sustainability: the facts" *New Internationalist*, no 329, (November, 2000): 19.

2. Gabel, Medard "What The World Wants." 1997. <http://www.osearth.com/resources/wwwproject/index.shtml> (12 Jan. 2002).

3. Smith, David. "Human Nature Exercise: World Future Society annual conference presenttion. Boston, MA: 1987.

4. Michigan State Board of Education "Social Studies Vision Statement and Content Standards and Benchmarks" Lansing, MI: The Board of Education (1996).

BIBLIOGRAPHY

Boyer, Ernest L. *The Basic School: A Community for Learning.* New York: The Carnegie Foundation for the Advancement of Teaching, 1995.

Brough, Judith A. "Designing Effective and Meaningful Integrated Units." *Middle Ground* 7, No. 1 (August 2003): 27–8.

McTighe, Jay, and Grant Wiggins. *The Understanding by Design Handbook.* Alexandria, Va: Association for Supervision and Curriculum Development, 1999.

National Middle School Association. *This We Believe: Successful Schools for Young Adolescents* Westerville, OH: National Middle School Association, 2003.

Wiggins, Grant P. *Assessing Student Performance: Exploring the Purpose and Limits of Testing.* San Francisco: Jossey-Bass Publishers, 1993.

Subject Index

Author Index